DARWIN
Growth of a City

The 1880s

Derek Pugh OAM

Foreword by The Hon. Austin Asche AC QC
13th Administrator of the Northern Territory

Derek Pugh OAM: Author.
DARWIN: Growth of a City: The 1880s.
Text © Derek Pugh 2021.
Original Photographs © Derek Pugh 2021, unless otherwise attributed.

ISBN: 978-0-6481421-8-8

Design and layout by Michael Pugh: michael.pugh@bigpond.com

Notes: Includes bibliographical references and index.

Subjects:
Palmerston: Darwin, Port Darwin.
Northern Territory: History—British military attempts at settlement.
Australian Aborigines: Larrakia, Woolwonga, Tiwi, Wulna.
Chinese people in North Australia in the 19th Century.
Overland Telegraph Line.
N.T. gold rush.
Pioneers: Northern Territory—social conditions—health.
Palmerston to Pine Creek Railway.
Northern Territory cattle industry and pastoralism.
Northern Territory agriculture (sugar).

Front Cover: The 'government quarters' at Port Darwin. (c. 1886, LANT PRG-280-1-2-238).

Contact: derekpugh1@gmail.com
www.derekpugh.com.au

A catalogue record for this book is available from the National Library of Australia

Acknowledgements

The Honourable Austin Asche is the only person to have lived in both Government House and the 'Mud Hut' other than John Knight, who designed and built the latter in 1883, and died whilst in office in the former, in 1892. No one is better qualified than Austin to put together a foreword for a history of Darwin in the 1880s and I asked him on his 95th birthday. Austin happily agreed but would also have liked a new book on the Overland Telegraph Line. I promised him—that is next.

I thank, once again, Peter Whelan, and Lon Wallis for editing, and Michael Pugh for his excellent book design. Also, thanks to others who were helpful, and generous with their time: Neville Jones, Ian 'B2' Brown, Jared Archibald, the anonymous 'Prospector 1', the staff at the Mitchell Library in Sydney, the State Library of South Australia, and the Northern Territory Archives and Library Service in Darwin.

This project was supported by the Northern Territory Government through the Northern Territory History Grants Program of the Department of Tourism, Sport and Culture.

Larrakia, Wulna, Woolwonga, Tiwi, and other indigenous people need to be aware that this is a history, and therefore inevitably contains images of people who have died. Thank you for your past and continuing welcome to your ancestral lands.

Books by Derek Pugh

History

Darwin: Origin of a City.

Darwin 1869: The Second Northern Territory Expedition.

Darwin 1869: The First Year in Photographs.

Escape Cliffs: The First Northern Territory Expedition, 1864–66.

Fort Dundas: The British in North Australia, 1824–29.

Fort Wellington: The British in North Australia, 1827–29.

Port Essington: The British in North Australia 1838–49.

Memoir

Turn Left at the Devil Tree.

Travel

Tambora: Travels in Sumbawa and the Mountain that Changed the World.

Young Adult

Tammy Damulkurra (2nd edition).

Schoolies.

The Owner's Guide to the Teenage Brain.

www.derekpugh.com.au

Contents

Table of maps

Timeline

Palmerston's second decade: the 1880s

	The Darwin area is home to the Larrakia people for millennia.
5 Feb, 1869	The Second Northern Territory Expedition arrives at Port Darwin on the *Moonta*, under George Goyder. The survey takes 8 months.
Jan 21, 1870	The *Kohinoor* arrives bringing new settlers and some families.
Jan 21, 1870	First police, under Sub-Inspector Paul Foelsche, arrive on the *Kohinoor*.
Jan 21–June 1870	James Stokes Millner is the Acting Government Resident. He has 43 men on the government payroll. Dr Peel returns to Adelaide.
1871	First telegraph office is built in Palmerston. John Little is appointed 1 August as the officer in charge.
Nov, 1871	Undersea telegraph cable is hauled ashore and cable is laid to Banyuwangi, Java.
July 1872	Gold is discovered in post holes at Yam Creek.
22 August 1872	First telegram is sent from Palmerston to Adelaide after the OTL is connected at Frew's Ironstone Ponds.
15 June 1874	First meeting of Palmerston District Council.
July 1876	Edward William Price takes over as Government Resident.

Jan, 1877	First government school opens after schooling becomes compulsory in South Australia. The teacher is John Holt.
March 1877	Manuel Gomez discovers 'Chinaman's Rush' alluvial gold deposit, and 400 Chinese diggers are quickly there.
October 1877	First Coolies are brought in directly from southern China.
June 1878	Maurice Holtze is employed as gardener.
Dry seasons 1878 and 1879	Price organises a relief work system, to avoid mass starvation of Chinese diggers, during the dry seasons of 1878 and 1879.
1879	The first purpose-built school room is built.
June 1879	Springvale and Glencoe Cattle Stations are started.
December 1879	Thomas Wingfield is killed by Wandy Wandy on Croker Island. Wandy Wandy is sentenced to 10 years hard labour.
1880	Constable Ferguson arrested and tried for stealing a gold shipment. He is sentenced to seven years hard labour. He becomes a leader of the prisoners' labour teams—building several government buildings and houses.
1880	About 10% of Chinese miners in the goldfields perish of a fever.
20 June 1880	A large fire burns Chinatown to the ground, causing the loss of $25,000 worth of shop stores.
April 1881	Delissa Pioneer Sugar Company is formed and begins farming sugar can on Cox Peninsula.
14 May 1881	Wandy Wandy is sentenced to 10 years in gaol for murder. He is hanged for subsequent murders on 15 July 1893.
21 February 1882	The South Australian Parliamentary Party, 1882, visit and tour the goldfields and assess agricultural and pastoral opportunities, under Education Minister John Langdon Parsons.
April 1882	Northern Territory Racing Club is started.
10 October 1882	Saint Joseph's Mission is started on the banks of Rapid Creek. It closes in 1891.
1882	William Sowden publishes *The Territory As It Is*, about his observations on the Parliamentary journey.

5 March 1883	Palmerston Town Hall is opened. It is destroyed by Cyclone Tracy in December 1974.
6 March 1883	Edward Price leaves Port Darwin on the *Bowen*.
6 March 1883	Gilbert Rotherdale McMinn stands in as acting-Government Resident for 14 months.
1883	John George Knight uses prison labour to build 'Aspendale', his house. It becomes known as the 'mud-hut', or 'Knight's Folly'. It burns down in 1923.
1 June 1883	*North Australian*, Palmerston's second newspaper begins.
4 July 1883	David Lindsay leaves Katherine to begin an exploration of Arnhem Land.
20 September 1883	Fannie Bay Gaol is opened.
October 1883	The Palmerston Club Hotel is re-opened on the corner of Mitchell Street and Herbert Street by Edward Prosser Hopewell.
1884	Pearl shell is discovered in Darwin harbour and a new industry starts.
21 February 1884	Constable Charlesworth drowns in Peters Creek.
15 March 1884	John Langdon Parsons is appointed government resident.
May 1884	John Langdon Parsons arrives in Palmerston and takes over as government resident. Justice Thomas Kennedy Pater arrives on the same ship.
1884	The new town of Burrundie is established on the goldfields.
15 August 1884	Four miners are murdered at the Daly River Mine. Three revenge/retribution expeditions massacre more than 150 Aborigines.
December 1884	Justice Thomas Kennedy Pater is appointed the 'Judge of the Northern Territory.'
30 December 1884	Delissaville Sugar Plantation company fails and is ended. Much of the equipment is moved to Daly River.
1885	The town of Borroloola is established to service the growing pastoral industry. G.R. McMinn becomes the town's stipendiary magistrate.

February 1885	The foundation stone for Brown's Mart is laid.
March 1885	William Wishart and his team arrive to build the railway jetty and their houses on the railway reserve. It is completed in 1886.
December 1885	Nammy is tried for the murder of Houschildt.
May 1886	Mining magnate, Ping Que, dies.
1886	Father Donald MacKillop starts the Daly River Mission station.
May 1886	The Millar brothers sign a contract for the construction of the railway. Construction starts immediately.
4 December 1886	The *Sandfly*, a steam locomotive arrives in Port Darwin, on board the *Armistice*.
1887	The Commercial Bank is built on the corner of Smith and Bennett Streets. It is known as the 'Stone Bank'.
1887	The Government Gardens are moved to the current Botanic Gardens site, displacing several Chinese market gardeners.
August 1887	First case of smallpox in Palmerston is diagnosed. The victim and his close contacts are taken to quarantine.
October 1887	Saunders and Hingston explore across Melville Island
2 March, 1888	The South Australian Parliamentary Party, 1888, arrive to tour the goldfields and assess agricultural and pastoral opportunities, under Education Minister, Joseph C.F. Johnson.
16 July 1888	The first passenger trains travel between Darwin and Adelaide River.
1888	The 'Chinese Immigration and Restriction Bill' is passed in the South Australian Parliament. There are 6,122 Chinese living in and around Darwin.
1888	A Catholic Church is built on the site of the current cathedral.
27 April 1888	SS *Ellengowan* sinks in Darwin Harbour.
16 July 1888	Railway service to Adelaide River begins.
10 December 1888	Railway service to Burrundie begins.

1889	30 per cent of land held under pastoral leases in the Northern Territory is rescinded as stations collapsed.
30 September 1889	The railway line is completed as far as Pine Creek (145 miles) and the contractors hand it over to the Government (without fanfare).
1891	The Jesuit Mission at Rapid Creek is closed. The missionaries then focus on Daly River Mission.
25 July 1893	Wandy Wandy is the second man legally executed in the N.T. for the murder of some Malay fishermen.
1901	The Immigration Restriction Act of 1901 is enacted. It becomes known as the 'White Australia Policy'.

Maps

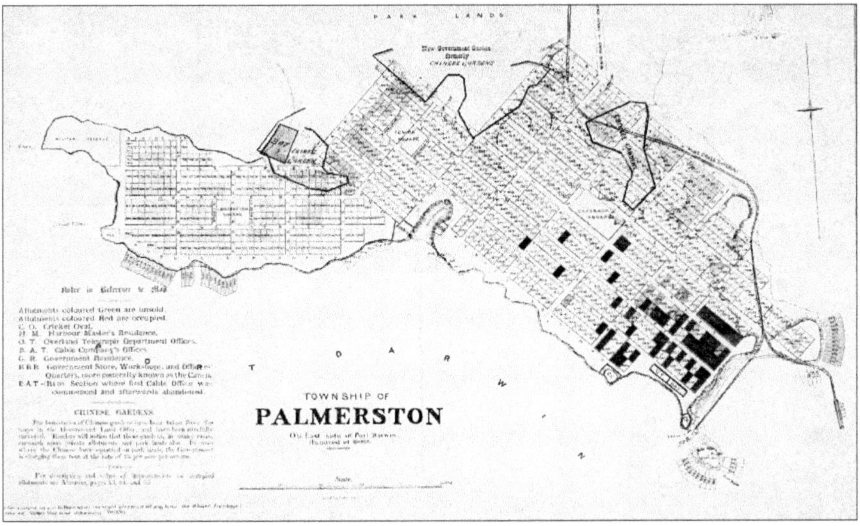

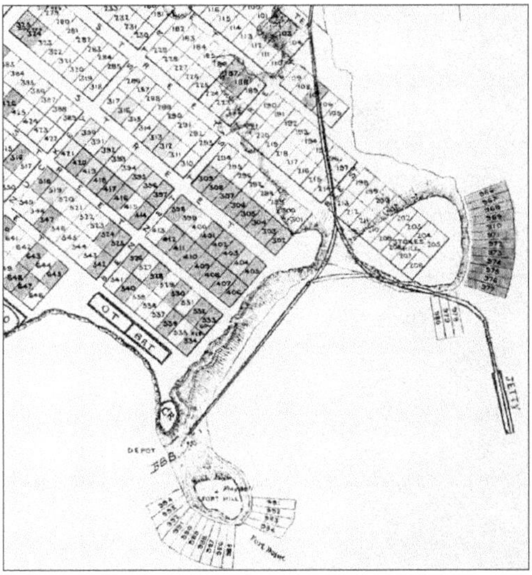

Map 1: Palmerston and Port Darwin (*NTTG*, Solomon, 1887).

Map 2: Palmerston 1887 detail. The unshaded lots were unoccupied. CO: Cricket Oval, OT: Overland Telegraph Office, BAT: British Australian Telegraph, GR: Government Residence, BBB: Government Store, Workshops, and Officers' Quarters ('The Camp') (NTTG, Solomon, 1887).

Map 3: The Top End in 1887 (Daly, 1887).

Map 4: The Northern Territory of South Australia lasted from 1863 until 1911. When the Commonwealth government resumed control, the name was changed, simply, to Northern Territory (Johnson map, 1903).

Foreword

The Honourable Austin Asche, AC QC

Derek has already done us great service. His earlier historical studies have told us of the stuttering commencement of what is now the Northern Territory of Australia. Three isolated 'garrisons', which, as the famous Mr Brown would say, had 'capabilities', abandoned before any serious development in that direction; followed by the disastrous failure of the settlement at Escape Cliffs.

Finally, a modest beginning at the settlement called 'Palmerston', named after a British prime minister whose interest and knowledge of the place could, over-generously be described as 'minimal' (see also 'Gladstone').

This time the planning was professional and the administration competent; but the challenges were great, and development necessarily slow.

This book builds on the foundation we have already been given in the earlier books, tracing development through events generated by the environment, and the gathering together of a strangely varied group of immigrants reacting, not always successfully, with the original inhabitants.

Of course, every city has its local events and local characters, and examples will be enthusiastically cited as proof of its 'difference' from others. The task which Derek has embarked upon is to establish that

Darwin is outside the span of the usual suspects; a superior variety of difference. He succeeds.

For instance, over many years while state governments and, later, the federal government endeavoured earnestly to prevent Asian immigration, the Chinese greatly outnumbered the European population in Darwin, despite efforts to dissuade or deport them. The Territory owes a great deal to their enterprise and this is properly acknowledged in the book. Palmerston (Darwin) could be properly described, in population, as a Chinese town between 1860 and 1940; except that, by the second generation, the children had become distinctively Australian. The goldmines, the railway (so far as it went) and, most importantly, trading and commerce, were thereby substantially developed.

Darwin was the commencing point for the introduction of the Overland Telegraph into Australia, and Derek tells a history here which should be far more widely known to all of us because it was an immensely successful enterprise, completed under harsh and challenging conditions, by workers who knew little of a Central Australia of blazing sun and scarce water. Without the technological advantages of today, they relied, basically, on human and horsepower to connect Darwin to Adelaide within two years. Considering the conditions of the time, it was a feat of which all Australians, and particularly South Australians, should be proud. This chapter in the book should be introduced into all schools as part of our heritage.

Since this book is one of a series which will cover the complete growth-plan of the city, it must be noted that the period specifically dealt with here falls within the time during which the Northern Territory and the town of Palmerston were, for all practical purposes, part of the Colony of South Australia. There is a certain geographical irony in the fact that one of the northernmost parts of Australia was the responsibility of politicians far to the South. It took weeks to travel from a (generally) disordered parliament in the South to a (generally) disordered town in the North. From the accounts given in the book, readers can make their own assessments as to how assiduous the various parliamentary representatives were to the Northern settlement; but it is fair to remember that no other colony indicated any more than a tentative interest, so that whatever development occurred came from the South Australians; and that many of those sent to serve as police, teachers, surveyors, and public servants of various kinds, elected to stay after their period of service.

The Top End has always grown by fits and starts. Drovers from Queensland and South Australia pushed in, and cattle stations appeared. Explorers pushed out, discovering the Territory, and, more importantly, how to live with it. Various crops were tried, some failing, some succeeding, at least in part. The government gardens, under highly competent management, proved an outstanding success for research, local development, and recreation—and remain so today. Population diversified, local industries and businesses developed; and the reader will meet many strange, adventurous, and exotic characters, either formed by the environment, or forming it.

At the time this book concludes, the city was sufficiently sure of itself to be confident it would not fade back into a cluster of abandoned huts and rubbish that had been the fate of the earlier settlements at Fort Dundas, Fort Wellington and Port Essington; or the disaster of Escape Cliffs. The future may be a little cloudy, and much of that future would have been impossible to imagine at the time. Derek will bring us up to date in books to follow; and we look forward to reading them.

Austin Asche,
Patron, Historical Society of the Northern Territory

Darwin: Growth of a City

Preface

Figure 1: Lord Palmerston (1784–1865).

Palmerston, a popular name

This book is about a remote city that was initially named after a British lord. Henry John Temple was the third viscount of an Irish barony named Palmerston. He was a popular career politician who served three times as foreign secretary and twice as prime minister of the United Kingdom. He was prime minister in 1859, at the height of his power, just as the South Australians began thinking of setting up a colony of their own.

'Palmerston' was his inherited title, but when Temple died in 1865, the title died with him because he had no children. His name lives on, however, in several distant towns that were named after him. Palmerston was a popular name in the nineteenth century; it was used in each of New Zealand, Canada, Zimbabwe, the Cook Islands, Ireland, and Queensland, as well as the Northern Territory of Australia. This book is about the last of them, which dropped the name in 1911. It is now the City of Darwin.

Five years before this successful settlement of the north coast, Palmerston was also the name given to South Australia's failed colony at the mouth of the Adelaide River, in the Northern Territory, in 1864. This lasted just two years—1864–66—and consisted of 'North' and 'South' Palmerston. Confusingly, these places also had other names: 'Escape Cliffs' and 'The Narrows', respectively.

The name was thus already recycled when Goyder named the townsite he surveyed on the peninsula that curls south into Darwin Harbour.* Palmerston became the name of the colony built on the peninsula.

Of course, the peninsula was already known. Its original inhabitants, the Larrakia, call it *Garramilla*, as their forebears had for thousands of years.

The new town of Palmerston was usually called 'Port Darwin', or just 'Darwin', by its early inhabitants, which is why, eventually, its name was officially changed. These days, there is a third Palmerston in the Northern Territory†. Established in 1981, it is a satellite city some 20 kilometres south of Darwin.

History is a bowl of spaghetti

History is a bowl of spaghetti. Every strand connects with a thousand others and there is a story at every touch. This book tells stories from Darwin and the Top End's second decade after settlement, the 1880s. They are sourced through records kept by the European settlers and their newspapers, and as a result, is not complete. The voices of Aborigines and Chinese people from the 1880s are harder to hear, and many of their stories are untold. Every history book contains a sample of the events of the past. From them, we learn about the people of the times, the society they lived in, their interactions with others and challenges they faced, but many, if not most of the settlers, and those who passed through, remain anonymous. There are thousands of other stories not told here. For example, have a look at the anonymous man in Figure 27—we know nothing more about him than the story told by the photograph.

To readers who find ancestors who lived in the Territory just three or four generations ago in these pages, I hope their stories

---

* The harbour was named after Charles Darwin when it was discovered and named by Stokes in 1839, although Darwin never visited anywhere near it.

† Temple Terrace is one of the major thoroughfares through today's city of Palmerston, also named after Lord Palmerston.

add to your appreciation of those long gone. Many of the people in this history are remembered in the street names of Darwin and the surrounding areas.

Boom times in a Chinese town

The early 1880s were boom times for many of the new arrivals in the north. Palmerston was a Chinese town, ruled by a handful of white men and governed by a distant colonial parliament. Timothy Jones identified how the Chinese in the early years of the Territory were treated differently from those in the rest of Australia:

> … There is a widespread image people have of the Chinese on the goldfields as being workers who toiled on the periphery of mining and who faced hostility and distrust by the wider European community. By and large, the presence of the Chinese was resented in most of the Colonies, but a very different situation prevailed in the Northern Territory. There, for many years the Chinese formed the major part of the population and were an essential part of the workforce. The two races, European and Chinese, were mutually dependent, racial animosity was minimal and not at all significant. What little agitation there was against the Chinese emanated from a small group of Darwin businesspeople whose profits had suffered from competition by Chinese merchants (Jones, 2003).

The decade began optimistically: gold mining was joined by tin, silver, and copper; cattlemen carved up the country into huge pastoral leases, some bigger than small European countries; the Aborigines, thought by many whites to be a doomed and dying race, were 'controlled'; and farmers planted sugar, tobacco, coffee, and anything else that might take off. Labour was cheap—if you could get enough Asians or press-ganged Aborigines to work. The railwaymen knew this—the Northern Territory Railway was constructed by Chinese workers.

Figure 2: The North Australian Office and J.T. Bull's store (c1886 SLSA, B-10137).

Remarkably well-told stories

Parts of the story of the Top End are remarkably well told by the newspapers of the day. Unlike the modern era, the papers published everything, from full court transcripts to town council minutes and government resident reports. The papers also collected information about the events (including gossip) on the goldfields through a number of unnamed correspondents. Advertisements, which then filled the front pages of the papers, tell us a great deal about hotels and their proprietors, what goods were available, shipping arrivals and departures—including summaries of passenger lists and cargo manifests—and a whole host of interesting facts.

Palmerston's two newspapers of the 1880s were the *Northern Territory Times and Gazette*, and the *North Australian*. The former was edited by Joseph Skelton (1876–84), and Vaiben L. Solomon (1885–90), and the latter by George Mayhew and Charles Kirkland (1883–90). Each had their own voice but they were usually united in their views on the Chinese (which changed as the Chinese population grew) and Aborigines, reflecting the Euro-centric racism of the times.

The *Times* held the contract for publishing the *Government Gazette* until June 1889, when it was transferred to the *North Australian*, which thus became *The North Australian and Northern Territory Government Gazette*.

Palmerston's newspapers in the 1880s rarely published authors' names. Instead, they used expressions such as 'From Our Correspondent', or nothing at all. Of course, the editors wrote much of the copy themselves, which was extremely time consuming, but large sections of the papers were regularly given over to written transcripts of the courts, for example, which was provided to them, so must have saved time. Nevertheless, editorials of 4,000 or 5,000 words were common—clearly, these men worked long hours.

Other sources of information used in this history include government reports, diaries and letters of residents or travellers, reports of explorers, published telegrams, contemporary books, and the excellent research of many who have recorded the Northern Territory's history before me.

The man in charge

The man in charge in the Northern Territory after settlement was the government resident. At the beginning of the 1880s, it was Edward William Price, who held the office from 1876*. Price was an old hand in the Territory—originally arriving in 1873 with his Irish wife, Minna Hamilton, and their five children. Price worked under Government Resident George Scott

Figure 3: Edward William Price (1832–93).

---

* Edward William Price (1832–93) was born in Dublin, Ireland in 1832. As a young man, he spent five years in the Royal Navy and fought in the Crimean War. He was discharged at his own request in 1856. He emigrated to South Australia three years later and became a civil servant, working as a court clerk in Gawler and in the Police Court in Adelaide. He was 41 years old when he first arrived in Port Darwin. Tragically, his wife, Minna, and their five children drowned in the *Gothenburg* disaster in 1875. However, Price returned to serve as the government resident for the Northern Territory in 1876, a position he held until 1883. He died in London in 1893, aged 61.

Figure 4: A picnic 'in the jungle' near Palmerston, 1887. Note the Chinese man at the rear left is probably a servant (Foelsche, LANT, ph1060-0070).

as Stipendiary Magistrate and Justice of the Peace for several years. He had an effective legal mind, and most of the improvements in the legal system in those days can be traced back to him.

In February 1875, Price sent his family home to Adelaide for a holiday. Tragically, they travelled on the ill-fated final trip of the *Gothenburg*, and Price never saw them again[*]. The *Gothenburg* was caught in a cyclone off Bowen, and more than 100 people were drowned, including his entire family. In grief, Price resigned and returned to Adelaide alone.

After George Scott retired as the government resident in 1876, the government needed a new resident with skills in administering the law, and there was no one more experienced in Territory affairs than Price, so he was recruited. On his return in July, he was heartily welcomed by the leaders of the community. David Lindsay told him:

> … as an administrator, he had yet to be tried, but as an old
> friend, they all knew him, and accepted him as such (hear,
> hear). He trusted they would all join in giving him a hearty
> welcome, and when he gave up the reins, he hoped he
> would have the happy consciousness of having succeeded in
> conferring the greatest amount of happiness on the greatest
> number (loud cheers) (*NTTG*, 27 July 1876).

The new government resident then rose to respond to Lindsay's address, to 'loud and continued cheering'. He thanked them for their welcome and said they had to 'take him on trust as Government Resident [but] hoped to carry out all Mr Lindsay had said' (NTTG, 27 July 1876). He then recapped on his activities of the previous eighteen months and spoke in glowing terms of the Territory and its

---

[*] A letter to the *Times* in 1889 called for charity for a white woman 'who looked wretchedly poor, forlorn, and ill'. She was left behind by Mrs Price when she boarded the *Gothenburg* in 1875: 'She is a native of the soil; she came to Palmerston quite a young girl, as a nursemaid in Magistrate Price's family… she did not leave with Mrs Price and family, and so escaped being drowned in the ill-fated S.S. *Gothenburg* … she has fallen low … I believe she is dying from want and privation; it is horrible that this be in a place where people call themselves Christians' (*NTTG*, on 16 February 1889).

future. He envisaged a 'tramway' or railway through the goldfields, which he thought was inevitable. It would help open the pastoral country, which was, as he spoke, being leased in huge amounts as far away as Barrow Creek. He knew that there were people already interested in growing sugar in the Territory and was keen to attend to the necessary public works in Palmerston, such as a jetty and the government gardens (*NTTG*, 27 July 1876).

Price was experienced in Territory affairs after his time as a magistrate, and he was enthusiastic—with cheap labour, good planning, and with adequate funding, he was sure, the Territory would soon be self-supporting. He had a vision for the development of the pastoral, mining, and agricultural industries. These would form a tripod upon which the Northern Territory would rise.

Firstly, he opened up more land: sheep and cows were being droved from Queensland or South Australia, but they were sold on the meat market on arrival. In the 1880s, the pastoral industry, at last, found its feet, and for the first time, meat was produced and sold locally.

Agriculture held a similar opportunity: plantation agriculture with cheap Asian labour looked promising.

The mining industry looked healthy, but it also needed support. In 1877, Price orchestrated a Chinese 'rush' to the goldfields by seeking a 'moderate immigration of the celestials' (*NTTG*, 11 August 1877). In March 1878, the 'moderate immigration' became a flood. On 16 March, 384 Chinese arrived, and from then on, 200–400 more came every week.

Palmerston's businesses had never had it so good, but unfortunately, it was not to last. In the last half of the decade, economic depression followed drought, the world's price of wool and copper plummeted, banks failed, and governments became, understandably, very cautious. Many people left the Territory, but for those who stayed, opportunities were there for the taking.

Darwin: Growth of a City

Chapter 1
Settlement

In 1869, Goyder's survey parties had completed their work by August, but more than half of the expedition needed to wait for the first settlers to arrive on the *Kohinoor*—on 21 January 1870—before they could go home.

However, some of the expeditioners stayed. They became the nucleus of the new colony—especially as several wives joined their husbands, and brought eighteen children with them.

By February 1870, there were 43 employed workers in Palmerston, including six policemen, three carpenters, and three surveyors. Port Darwin was comprised of 29 buildings—mostly huts, stores, and mess rooms in the original camp area. There was a long stable for the government horses, a stockyard, a dynamite magazine, 24 tents, a lime kiln, three wells, and a 'gymnasium' (two swings in a tall frame). The first road climbed up to the Palmerston plateau, but little had been done up there, apart from clearing the scrub and surveying half-acre blocks (Daly, 1869). Work began in earnest. The newcomers were watched closely by the original inhabitants of the land, the Larrakia, and at this stage, they were mostly welcomed.

Palmerston District Council

Four years later, the streets were a stinking mess; dogs and pigs ran rampant, and there was little forethought for the future. The town needed another level of governance. So, in 1874, Palmerston District Council was formed.

The first meeting was on 15 June. Four leading citizens (Joseph Skelton, Judah Moss Solomon, Richard Wells, and Robert Caldwell) were nominated by the government to organise an election, determine who the electors and rate payers would be, and how much their properties were worth (a task carried out by William Whitfield, the teacher).

Elections were held, and on 11 July, Palmerston's first elected councillors took their seats: Joshua Jones was chair, with Robert Caldwell, William Barlow, and Robert Fiveash. They set to work, enthusiastically organising the clearing away of rubbish and weeds, repairing wells, and building fences to manage animals.

The council's members changed several times during the 1870s, but at the beginning of the next decade, it was the town's businessmen who were still leading it. This is unsurprising—Port Darwin was little more than a gathering of businessmen, civil servants, telegraph company workers, and Chinese shopkeepers. Few had any intention of staying on, and everyone knew those who did—they became known as the 'Old Territorians'*. They included Inspector Paul Foelsche of the police, John Knight (civil servant), Vaiben

PHILIP R. ALLEN & CO.,
GENERAL STOREKEEPERS,
Importers and Shipping Agents,
PORT DARWIN.

BRANCHES-
PALMERSTON,
SOUTHPORT,
PORT DARWIN CAMP,

Agents for the New Zealand Fire and Marine Insurance Company.
Agents for Gibb's line of Steamships from China to Australia.
Agents for Brandt's Lager Bier.

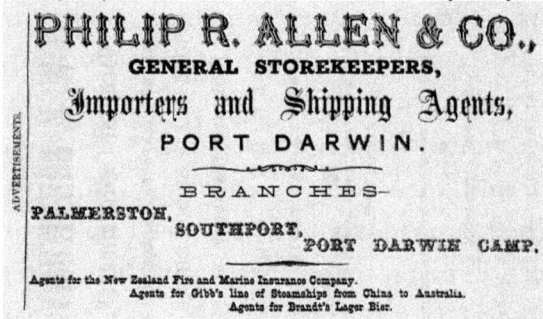

Figure 5: Storekeeper's advertisement 1883 (*NTTG*).

---

* The press promoted the idea of the 'Old Territorians' as a social class and lamented their loss. For example: ... 'The deaths of two old Northern Territorians are recorded as having occurred at Pine Creek during the week. The deceased are Henry Allwright [hotelier] and Walter Abbott, both of whom had lived in the Territory for a great many years and were well known to residents of long-standing. Abbott ... was a single man, but Allwright leaves a widow to mourn his decease. The former had lately been working at the Eveleen Mine and was in good health when he came into Pine Creek; but soon afterwards he contracted dysentery and in five days was dead' (*North Australian*, 31 March 1888). Allwright left a wife and a three-year-old son.

Louis Solomon (businessman, newspaper editor, and future politician), the Adcock brothers (shopkeepers and businessmen), Vincent V. Brown (merchant and shipping agent), Alfred Jolly (merchant and agent), Gilbert McMinn and David Lindsay (surveyors), Philip R. Allen (merchant), Joseph Skelton (merchant and the editor of the *Times*), James Pickford (hotelier and storeman), and tradesmen like Tuckwell and Hayball. Some of these men had families—and sons and daughters who married and bonded the families together (for example, George Adcock married Ellen Pickford at Palmerston on 10 June 1888).

In 1880, the Palmerston Council chairman was Vincent V. Brown, and the councillors were V.L. Solomon, William Endrupp Adcock (merchant), Otto Brandt (baker and confectioner), and James Pickford.

Joseph Skelton became involved in Council in 1882. He was acting chairman when he and the council clerk, John George Kelsey*, met with writer William Sowden in their 'official hall'. The hall was 'about the size of three small piano cases and ventilated in much the same way,' said Sowden. The council had put aside £500 for a 'Town Hall and Institute' but were having trouble finding a piece of land to build it on. This was an ongoing problem for decades: the peninsula had been divided into 1,019 half-acre blocks by Goyder but, by 1882, only 40 of them were occupied.

The rest were owned by absentee landlords from Adelaide and London. These owners thought so much of their purchases (which for many, were thrown in as an enticement to buy 320-acre rural blocks for £60, in 1869) that they now asked £2,500 for a town block—if they had any interest in their remote purchases at all (Sowden, 1882).

Nevertheless, in 1879, enough land had been secured in Woods Street for a school building. The government school from then on

---

* J.G. Kelsey had left the Telegraph Company and was employed as Clerk of the District Council on a salary of £100 p.a. He died in April 1889 in Blackwood, S.A., at the age of 74. He 'was one of the few Territory settlers who succeeded in making a large circle of friends, and few, if any, enemies' (*Times*, 24 April 1889).

featured regularly in the town's newspapers, where proud parents could read about the successes of their children:

> … On Thursday afternoon the children attending the
> Government school assembled to receive the prizes promised
> them by their master, Mr Kitchin*. Three members of the Local
> Board of Advice being absent, only one put in an appearance.
> The children, who presented a cleanly and healthy appearance,
> were examined, and most of them showed that they had
> considerably improved during the past three months. The
> number in the school was twenty-three. Master Tuckwell was
> awarded the first prize of ten shillings, James Glyn, and Ah
> Sing†, five shillings each, and Ellen Kelsey and John Glyn two
> shillings and sixpence each for general improvement. In the
> second class, the largest prizes were taken by Harriet Nelson and
> Master Sing. In the first class, prizes were given to Hilda Kelsey
> who replied very promptly to any questions put to the class.
> At the close of the proceedings, three cheers were given for the
> master, Mr Kitchin, and also for the only member of the Board
> present, after which Mr Skelton improvised a few foot races
> in which nearly all the children took a part, and were suitably
> rewarded (*NTTG*, 1 April 1882).

A town hall

The British Australian Telegraph (B.A.T.) Company 'owned' the best land on the peninsula. Their offices and staff housing, including a lawn tennis court, were spread along the Esplanade, including the

---

*   Francis Patrick Kitchin started teaching in the Port Darwin State School in January 1880. Kitchin was married, and he and his wife had a baby daughter the following November. He was a sharpshooter of note, regularly winning prizes at the Palmerston Rifle Club. Mrs E.C. Kitchin and two children left Port Darwin in September 1888 on the S.S. *Chingtu*, and Kitchin followed soon after, to become Principal of Appila North School in South Australia. He was replaced by Mrs Pett, in January 1889.

†   A cook named Ah Sing was tried for assault in 1882. A reward of £10 was offered for the apprehension of a man named Ah Sing after he escaped custody at Collett's Creek in 1884 (he was to be tried for larceny). Another Ah Sing died at Bridge Creek, in 1883, and in 1889, a cook named Ah Sing died of tetanus, and another died at No. 3 Well on the O.T. Line in 1892. Ah Sing appears to have been a common name, and it may not be possible to unravel the few threads of their histories.

site where Parliament House now stands. Twelve acres of land 'in the heart of the town' were known as the B.A.T. Paddocks. This was the land the council needed access to, and by mid-1882, they finally succeeded in securing some of it for new offices.

The availability of an experienced architect was serendipity. John George Knight (1826–92) was a qualified engineer and architect who had arrived in Melbourne from England, in 1850, aged 24 years. He then worked for over 20 years in the city of Melbourne in his profession, culminating in, with a partner, designing the Victorian Parliament buildings.

When Knight was asked to design the town hall in 1882, he was thrilled that his 'long dormant professional qualifications have at last been called into action on a small scale' (*NTTG*, 19 August 1882). The councillors then called for tenders to build Knight's design, and suddenly everybody seemed to be in a rush.

> … tenders received for the construction of the hall only—a building 80 feet by 35 feet … The tender of Messrs. Hall and Hughes, for £1800, was accepted. Tenders were received from F. Stone, £1836 10s.; Ah Soey, £2,750; Tom Fore, £2,800. It was resolved that Mr J. G. Knight be requested to supervise the erection of the building and to obtain the signatures of the contractors for the work to be done as per specifications. The whole of the outside walling and roofing to be completed within six months, and the whole of the interior work to be finished and handed over to the council before the 1st of March 1883 (*NTTG*, 1 July 1882).

In August, most of the town turned out for the laying of the foundation stone. Government Resident Price was requested to perform the duty, but no one had thought to order the traditional silver trowel from Adelaide, so he used a standard metal one. Someone suggested that was better because people usually did not lay concrete well with ceremonial silver tools. Under the foundation stone was placed a 'memento', which was, in modern words, a 'time capsule' that may still be there (*NTTG*, 19 August 1882). It included a list of councillors of the time:

The foundation stone of this hall was laid by the Government Resident, Edward William Price, Esquire, on the seventeenth day of August 1882, in the 46th year of the reign of our Most Gracious Majesty, Victoria, Queen of Great Britain and Empress of India.

The Governor-in-Chief of the Province being Sir William Francis Drummond Jervois, CB. G.C.M.G. The Architect: John George Knight, Esq., Fellow of the Royal Institute of British Architects. The Contractors: Messrs. Hughes and Hall.

The Council for the present year consists of five members:

CHAIRMAN: Victor Voules Brown, Esq.

COUNCILLORS: Messrs. John Corber Hillson, James Pickford, Joseph Skelton, Vaiben Louis Solomon.

AUDITORS: Messrs. Walter Harrison, Thomas Wilshere Morris

CLERK TO THE COUNCIL: John George Kelsey.

The following are the names of the Councillors elected when the first Council was formed in the year 1874:

CHAIRMAN: Robert Caldwell, Esq.

COUNCILLORS: Moss Judah Solomon, Joshua Jones, William Barlow, Joseph Skelton.

AUDITORS: A. Schmidt, John Rudall.

CLERK: William Whitfield.

A copy of the *Northern Territory Times and Gazette* of 12 August was also enclosed.

Long were the speeches on the evening, one of the most notable of which was the toast for the health of the government resident, Edward Price, by Council Chairman Brown:

> ... We have to thank Mr Price for the manner in which he came forward today and performed the ceremony of laying the foundation stone; I trust we shall see him Government Resident of Port Darwin for many years to come (*NTTG*, 19 August 1882).

But the town hall was Price's swansong—he left Palmerston the day after he opened the hall, on 5 March 1883, congratulating the council for:

> ... having such a fine structure, the equal of which he did not
> think was possessed by any other District Council in any part
> of South Australia... The cheers having been enthusiastically
> given, the door was unlocked, and Mr Price declared the
> Town Hall of Palmerston open to the District Council and the
> citizens forever (*NTTG*, 10 March 1883).

The hall was a solid stone building with arched windows and a corrugated iron roof with two ventilators. It was paid for by the ratepayers and a loan from one of the new banks that had been established in the town. It held the council offices and a room for the Palmerston Institute, and was a venue for 'public entertainments'. The first was put on by the Palmerston Dramatic and Musical Society on 5 April 1883:

> ... The stage and proscenium had been decorated and
> arranged with flowers and ferns very tastefully, and the whole
> of the arrangements for the comfort of the large audience were
> perfect.

Figure 6: The Palmerston Town Hall was built in 1883. Its ruins still stand in central Darwin (Foelsche, 1883, SLSA B-5059).

The performance was opened by the Palmerston Surprise
Party giving a series of songs and choruses, all of which were
so creditably rendered that it would be almost impossible
to select any one of them for special criticism. The jokes
of Messrs. Hingston and Buckland evoked hearty laughter
and frequent applause, and the latter gentleman's local song,
brimful of witty hits, was an unqualified success and secured
for Mr Buckland a round of applause which made the walls
of the Hall ring again—all of the solos and choruses had
to submit to well-deserved encores, they being rendered in
excellent time. The second part of the entertainment opened
with an instrumental quartette [sic] by Mrs Christoe, Messrs.
McMinn, Ward, and Schwartz, which so pleased the audience
that the performers were called upon for a repetition. Mr
Harvey's rendering of the old familiar 'Englishman' resulted
in a similar compliment being paid to him. Mrs Searcy
followed with a song 'When Sparrows Build,' which was
sweetly rendered in a very clear soprano voice, and that
lady had to pay the usual penalty of a recall. Mr Mayhew's
cornet solo and Mr Baines' song 'Angels listen when she
speaks', both of which were recalled, concluded the second
portion of the programme. Many of the audience were
rather disappointed at Mr Baines refusing to respond to his
encore, but the indifferently feeble manner in which the solo
was accompanied on the piano was sufficient excuse for any
singer. A laughable farce entitled 'Snozzle's Holiday' in which
Messrs. Buckland, Whitelaw, Hingston, and Harrison kept
the audience bubbling over with laughter for nearly an hour
concluded one of the best entertainments ever presented to a
Palmerston audience (*NTTG*, 7 April 1883).

A new entertainment venue was necessary because the warehouse
that had long been used had been weakened so much by termites that
it had blown down by the end of 1881.

Termites (white ants) were the enemy of every wooden building.
The Darwin area is home to the giant northern termite (*Mastotermes
darwiniensis*). The 12-millimetre-long workers eat trees or wood from
the inside out, leaving behind hollow shells as thin as paper. Their
effect on the economy of the north cannot be understated—wooden

houses, furniture, clothing, boots, saddles, paper, fence posts, mining tools such as pick handles and cradle rockers, and telegraph poles were all fair game.

The Residency

The Residency (Government House) was not immune to the attacks of termites. It had been rebuilt and renovated continually since it was first constructed on the Esplanade in 1870 by Bloomfield Douglas. By the time Edward Price took over as government resident, it was an 'unsightly shanty, more like a cowshed than a government residence' (Cross J., 2011). After a part of the roof collapsed because the rafters lost all strength, Price complained to the Governor of South Australia. The Residency was so bad, he claimed, no one would stable a horse in it. Price ceased to have the building repaired and demanded funds on the sub-estimates for a second stone-walled room to replace some of the 'fear-inspiring portions of the Residence'. Finally, approval was granted, and the renovation went ahead. It was not grand—just two of the parliamentary party could be accommodated there in 1882 (Sowden, 1882), but its position was the best in the town; the Residency still sits on the cliffs overlooking the harbour. John Knight used prison labour to build extensive terraced gardens, which Sowden predicted would become an 'exceedingly beautiful lasting monument.'

Public baths

Knight, in his role as manager of the gaol, put the prisoners to other good works too. These included the public baths extending out from Fort Hill. The walls were extensive enough to ensure water was available at every tide, and the bathers were safe from sharks and crocodiles.

The baths were near Goyder's original campsite, on the saddle between the plateau and Fort Hill. Here Gilbert McMinn lived in a 'pretentious, cool and comfortable residence next to the 'Modern

Figure 7: Palmerston Archery Club, 1888. Regular winners of the competitions were Miss Mary Jane Foelsche, F.C. Ward, J.C. Hillson, and Miss Edith Little, all of whom are probably in this photograph (Foelsche SLSA B-24245).

Camp' which contained the 'Government bachelor officers'. Also on the saddle were the government workshops and stables, the customs and harbour master's offices, and several small houses for 'minor government officials'. John Knight and McMinn took regular 'constitutional dips' together on the 'bathing ground' on Fort Hill. They were not alone:

> Sea bathing in Port Darwin is now beginning to regain its old popularity, and morning and evening the bathing enclosure is alive with heated humanity, enjoying the luxury of a cooling dip (*NTTG*, 1 October 1887).

Sport

Swimming was an early sport activity in Palmerston, and races are occasionally recorded between community members. Running races were more common:

> ... A Grove Hill correspondent, under date June 7th, sends us the following: 'A most exciting footrace took place today on the Port Darwin Camp racecourse between Cooper of Port Darwin Camp and Hildebrandt, for £5; distance 2 miles. Cooper led at the start and kept ahead for about a mile and a quarter. Then Hildebrandt spurted and got the lead, which he kept till half a mile from home when Cooper passed him again and led to the finish. Mr F. Morck acted as judge. The race was so smart that it took the spectators all their time to keep their horses up with the runners; in fact, some of them on old screws had to cut off most of the corners'. The same authority advises us that another race will shortly be run at Port Darwin Camp, one party giving the other 3 yards start in 100 for £10 (*North Australian*, 11 June 1887).

Barney Lamond described many running races, but 'a great favourite of cattlemen' was called 'fifty yards around the post' and:

> ... a man with a horse and rider are stood on a starting line, as starting for a race. A post is stood up fifty yards in front of them which neither must touch nor knock down. A pistol is fired to start them, and they race round the post and back. The man has the inside running. Where there is a tape held the first one to touch the tape is a winner. Hundreds of pounds are won and lost on these camp horse races (Lamond 1986).

Other sports of the 1880s included horse racing at Fannie Bay, cricket on the dedicated oval on the Esplanade (where the cenotaph is now located), lawn tennis[*], sailing (the Port Darwin Regatta Club first met in May 1884), rifle shooting, and archery. The Palmerston Archery Club held regular matches and was particularly popular with the ladies of Palmerston society, who competed for a trophy presented by the minister's wife, Mrs Johnson. The wives and daughters of the town leaders are often listed among the prize winners, particularly Mary Jane Foelsche and Edith Little.

The city streets

Palmerston town was well laid out, with its main roads running parallel down the peninsula. They had been cleared and formed by gangs of destitute Chinese diggers employed by Government Resident Price to avoid their mass starvation in the dry seasons of 1878 and 1879. John Knight's team of prisoners then ensured the roads drained well, and they were never boggy, even at the height of the wet season.

In 1882, there was room, said Sowden, for a population of 30,000 people. John George Kelsey told him—from his knowledge of Palmerston's houses and their occupants—that the population was around 470, made up of 170 Europeans, and about 300 Chinese[†]. Just two of the original seven public houses were still in business, plus three English stores, and ten Chinese stores.

There were so many empty blocks that weeds were a problem. The introduced horehound[‡] (*Hyptis suaveolens*) grew to two metres and 'completely overran the place'.

---

[*] The Palmerston Tennis Club started in 1883, with a court constructed in 'the corner of the cricket oval'. The members were all male, but members had 'the privilege of introducing ladies to play on the Club's ground' (*NTTG*, 28 April 1883).

[†] In contrast, both New South Wales and Victoria passed the one million people mark about this time.

[‡] Horehound (*Hyptis suaveolens*)was introduced to Palmerston by Christian Schmidt, from Timor in 1870. Used widely for its medicinal qualities, it is a weed that quickly spread across the Top End. In Palmerston, they called it 'Schmidt's folly'.

Council employed a Mr I. Owen and two Aborigines to clear the weeds (the latter for food and tobacco as payment), but, as weed management was discussed at most council meetings in the 1880s, and tenders were repeatedly called to clear them, getting it under control appears to have been difficult. In 1888, the *North Australian* reminded the councillors:

> ... that a good turn can be served the ratepayers by keeping the vacant allotments in the town clear of horehound weed. This useless stuff has now become an annual nuisance, and it will never be eradicated except by being pulled up before it goes to seed—a fact which need hardly have been mentioned, only that we notice many allotments covered with the troublesome weed very close to seeding pitch (31 March 1888).

In 1882, William Sowden was impressed by his first close-up view of Palmerston, after climbing the track on the escarpment (now called Hughes Avenue) with theparliamentary party (see Chapter 4) and standing at the end of Smith Street. He described the row of government offices along the Esplanade as 'architecturally pretty' stone buildings that were 'capitally designed for comfort' in the heat, as they caught every breeze through a 'hundred apertures' and had no ceilings. On his left were the B.A.T. and Overland Telegraph Offices, and on the clifftop, The Residency.

Sowden and the parliamentarians were met by Mr Whitelaw, the Resident's private secretary, David Lindsay, a surveyor, and 'the courteous Police Inspector Foelsche and his courteous family* in their private residence', attached to the public offices.

Moving down Smith Street, which Sowden called a 'terrace', he saw the town gaol (Governor Mr Laurie), courthouse (which was so termite damaged it would do for a 'second rate stable'), doctor's residence, and police quarters.

The only other government buildings in 1882, were the school (taught by Mr Kitchin), the harbour master's residence (Mr Marsh),

---

* Inspector Foelsche was married to Charlotte Georgina Smith (1840–99). They had two daughters: Emma (1860–1940) and Mary Jane (1863–19 May 1932).

the Fannie Bay Gaol (still incomplete), and the 10-bed hospital. The latter was at the other end of town, through scrub patches, past Chinese gardens, and over the hill with 'rich clusters of deep green undergrowth and spiral young trees and wiry long-stretching creepers'.

Termites were so ubiquitous that there was no part of the hospital where they had not turned their destructive talents. As a result when it rained water would pour through the roof onto the beds.

The courthouse walls suffered too—they were full of holes and the veranda was collapsing. It would do for a 'second-rate stable' said Sowden.

A small iron building in that section of Smith Street housed the Palmerston Institute. This was an organisation begun in the late 1870s, run by a committee with an initial budget from fees of £10. It continued for decades, with members paying an annual subscription. By 1882, it had an income of £100 and about a thousand books. What the members paid for was access to these books. The institute was housed, more appropriately, with the council, when the town hall was built*.

The Palmerston Gaol

Next door was the gaol—two tiny stone-walled cells and one smaller, insulated, iron-walled cell, plus a yard surrounded by a 9-foot-high fence. It was so easy to escape, Sowden tells us, that a Chinese prisoner—who was re-arrested in the streets—complained that he was not escaping but had just popped out to post a letter. Incorrigible prisoners were kept in shackles to keep them inside, but there was nowhere for the others to go anyway.

Sowden toured the gaol with John Knight. He 'interviewed' the prisoners and counted 'nine blacks, eight Chinese, three Malays, and two Europeans'. One of the Aborigines was Wandy Wandy, serving 10 years for murder (see Chapter 14). Most of the others were locked

---

* Darwin City Council took over the Institute and its 2,500 books (90% fiction) in 1934 and called it a library.

15

Figure 8: The 'Stone Bank'—Commercial Bank—Lot 387 corner Smith and Bennett Streets—The stone façade still exists (Foelsche 1887, SLSA B19138).

up for theft—including ex-Police Mounted Constable Ferguson (see Chapter 3), who had stolen gold at Southport. He seemed to Sowden to be a 'thoroughly broken man' and suffered 'acutely from some sort of rheumatism'. He still had five years of his seven-year sentence to serve*.

Palmerston banks

In the centre of town there were three banks, all along Smith Street—the Commercial (manager, Mr W. Harrison), the Town and Country (manager, Mr J.C. Hillson), and the English, Scottish and Australian Chartered Bank (manager, Mr N.F. Christoe). The latter was the oldest. It managed the Government accounts and was the largest buyer of gold (without assay). It was now in a new building built solidly of iron sheeting on an iron frame—termites had destroyed

---

* Things might have not been so bad for Ferguson—Knight called him his 'right-hand man' and he was the leader of the prisoner work gang employed in the building of several Palmerston landmarks (Carment et al, 1993).

Figure 9: The rebuilt 'Tin Bank' (English, Scottish and Australia Chartered Bank) in Smith Street (Foelsche 1887, LANT ph0754-0050).

their previous building. It became known as the 'tin bank'* (Wilson, 1994), and the Commercial Bank, for obvious reasons, was called the 'stone bank'.

Palmerston hotels

The main two hotels that were operating in Palmerston in the early 1880s were 'both fairly good for this place, but second rate if placed in comparison with the average public-house in the South' (Sowden, 1882). They were the Family Hotel (James Pickford) and the Exchange Hotel (Mrs Parker). Both were in Smith Street.

In October 1883, the Palmerston Club Hotel was re-opened on the corner of Mitchell Street and Herbert Street by Edward Prosser Hopewell[†] (it had been owned by John George Kelsey in the

* The tin bank building existed until the 1950s, but by then it was the premises for the Northern Territory News production press and offices. The site is new a garden between Browns Mart and the Christchurch Cathedral.

† After 17 years in the Territory, Edward Hopewell died in 1888, aged 46—from

17

Figure 10: Palmerston Club Hotel (SLSA B-10152).

Figure 11: Terminus Hotel, Cavenagh Street, and the 'Tree of Knowledge'
(c. 1905 Ted Ryko, ph0413-0079).

'retrocedent gout' and Bright's disease. He was buried in plot number 47 in the Palmerston cemetery (NTRS 686/6). His widow, Mrs Hopewell, informed 'her numerous patrons and the public generally that she is determined to continue with the Business of her late husband, and hopes by civility and careful attention to the wants of customers to merit a fair share of public support'. The daily tariff at the hotel was then 10 shillings. (*NTTG*, 5 May 1888). According to Andrew King, when the Terminus Hotel was finally demolished in the 1930s, the materials were used in the construction of the gun emplacements at East Point, possibly as formwork for the concrete.

late 1870s—it is now the site of the current Darwin Hotel). He was an experienced 'Old Territorian' who arrived in 1871. A publican, Hopewell had owned several public houses on the goldfields. The *Times* heralded the hotel's opening, saying that the hotel had 'no pretensions to architectural beauty', but would, 'vie in comfort and excellence of internal arrangements with any place of entertainment north of Brisbane' (20 October 1883).

In 1885, the Terminus Hotel opened on Cavenagh Street (Mr Henry Ruthven), with 'very pleasing' linoleum matting on its cement floors (*North Australian*, 13 March 1885). There was another hotel mooted, but it was never given a licence to operate. Samuel Brown's application to open the 'Coffee Palace Hotel' was knocked back by the magistrate in 1887, because, he said, it would have to be a two-storey construction that would cost at least £5,000, and Brown did not have the money (he did manage to open a licenced billiard hall, which he called the 'Coffee Palace').

But then in 1889, Mrs Ellen Ryan, who certainly did have the money, moved to Palmerston from the goldfields. She had joined the gold rush with her husband, William Ryan, and arrived in the Territory from Adelaide in 1873. On the goldfields at Yam Creek, they soon realised there could be more money to be made by selling alcohol and accommodation to the miners than in digging for gold, so they leased the Miners Arms Hotel. When William Ryan began to drink the profits and proved himself to be a violent drunk, Ellen divorced him and took out a protection order against him, 'owing to his threats, cruelty, and drunkenness'. Ryan left Palmerston shortly after, in 1877, stating he had 'had quite enough of the Territory and the people in it'. Ellen kept working, bought land in Palmerston, took on several mining leases, and in 1885, took over the Margaret Crossing Hotel in the Port Darwin Camp.

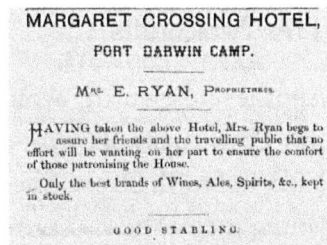

MARGARET CROSSING HOTEL,

PORT DARWIN CAMP.

Mᴿˢ E. RYAN, Pʀᴏᴘʀɪᴇᴛʀᴇss.

HAVING taken the above Hotel, Mrs. Ryan begs to assure her friends and the travelling public that no effort will be wanting on her part to ensure the comfort of those patronising the House.

Only the best brands of Wines, Ales, Spirits, &c., kept in stock.

GOOD STABLING.

Figure 12: Advertisement in the *1886 Almanac* (Solomon, 1885).

Figure 13: The North Australian Hotel / Victoria Hotel, constructed in
1890 by Mrs Ellen Ryan (Foelsche, SLSA B 72713.15).

In 1890, Mrs Ryan opened the first stone two-storey hotel in
Palmerston and named it the North Australian Hotel. It was soon
called the Victoria Hotel, and it still stands on Smith Street. Then,
in 1896, she also took over the Palmerston Club Hotel from Mrs
Hopewell. She was a wealthy woman when she died in Adelaide in
1920 (James, 1990).

The Tuckwells

Another noteworthy woman offering accommodation in Palmerston
was Eliza Tuckwell, with a boarding house she called the 'Resolution
Villa' in Smith Street. She advertised space for 'four steady, respectable
young men'. She also earned an income as a midwife and nurse to the
Palmerston Community. Eliza was one of the first women to arrive
in Port Darwin, on the *Kohinoor*, in January 1870. She and her four

children came to join her husband, Ned*. Eliza wrote about the day she arrived:

> … The morning we arrived in Darwin was very nice, and we
> dressed our children to meet their fathers in the afternoon but
> on coming into the harbour we ran into a sandbank so that
> delayed us for some hours to get us off and when she got off
> the sight was to see the *Gulnare* in the harbour, so you may be
> sure we were pleased. Crowds came aboard. No women were
> expected. There were several log huts built for the men, so they
> turned out and let the women have them. They had to put up
> tents for themselves. Next day our luggage had to be landed.
> There was no jetties, only the beach, so we had to settle down
> in the huts. We had very little room you may guess, there were
> five huts built on the piece of land opposite the doctor's house
> at the camp … We got on alright. We had to make our fires
> under the hill and all the women of the working class took in
> washing from the men who were going away, and we made a
> good bit of money (in James, 1989).

By the 1880s, the Tuckwell's had added two children to their family, Eleanor, and Charles. Ned made a living as a builder and blacksmith in Smith Street: 'All descriptions of Engineering and Mechanical Work done with despatch and Reasonable Terms', he advertised. With Ned Ryan, he built the stone walls that still stand as part of The Residency, now called Government House. Unfortunately, Ned was a serious drinker, and this caused friction in his marriage. Wisely, he appointed Eliza as his attorney and she mostly controlled the family's finances, although she advertised in the *Times* that she was not responsible for her husband's debts. These may have been substantial: he was fined, for example, 40s. and 30s. costs 'for using indecent language within hearing of the Esplanade… (*NTTG*, 8 April 1876).

---

* Ned Tuckwell was a member of both the first (at Escape Cliffs, 1864) and the
second (at Port Darwin, 1869) Northern Territory Expeditions. It was he who saved
the 16 members of McKinlay's expedition by building a punt, named the *Pioneer*,
from bush timber and the hides of the expedition's last 16 horses, on the banks of
the East Alligator River (Pugh, 2018).

The Tuckwell's home at the rear of the Commercial Hotel, meant that Eliza could watch events there closely:

> ... there were several boats arrived ... with passengers and cattle and yes you may be sure that they brought plenty of bottled stuff. They got sales for this as this was a dreadful place at the time. The foolish men drank themselves blind. I have seen them have to walk on crutches. One also went blind and I am sorry to say some of the so-called ladies were as bad as the men (James, 1989).

Ned died in 1882 at the age of 52. He was a popular man and nearly the whole community followed his coffin to the cemetery:

> MR EDWARD TUCKWELL, one of our oldest residents, has passed from amongst us very suddenly at the comparatively early age of fifty-two. Probably no man met with more vicissitudes, more ups and downs, than our deceased friend during his life in the Northern Territory... His remains were followed to the cemetery by nearly the whole of the residents of Port Darwin, the service being read by the Government Resident, Mr E W. Price. In concluding this brief notice, we say by his death the Government have lost a good, honest, and faithful servant, and one whom they will find it difficult to replace. (Obituary, *NTTG*, 29 April 1882).

Four of their children were still young, and Eliza raised them alone. Her second son, George, died in 1891, aged 27, after a long illness.

Eliza became one of the most successful businesswomen in the Territory's early history. She was among the first women to be registered as a taxpayer when the South Australian Government started to levy taxes during 1884*. As a midwife and a nurse to the Palmerston Community, everyone knew her. Her training was more through experience than schooling, but this was not an unusual method for the time: Inspector Foelsche of the police, for example, was an accomplished dentist.

---

*   Eliza Tuckwell and her daughter Eleanor were two of the 82 South Australian women who registered to vote in 1894, thus becoming some of the first women in the world to become voters (after New Zealand in 1893) (James, 1989).

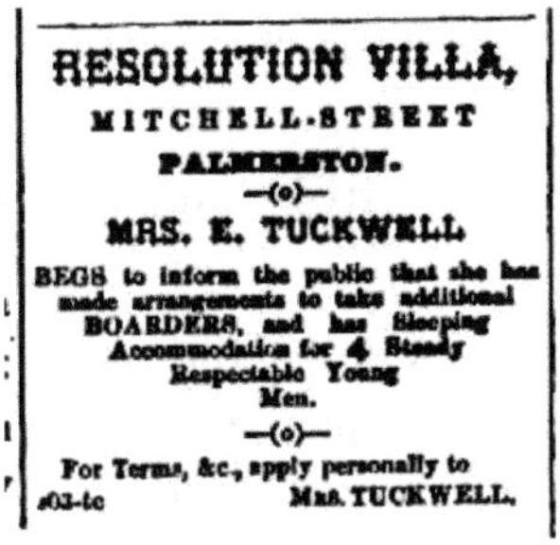
RESOLUTION VILLA,
MITCHELL-STREET
PALMERSTON.
—(o)—
MRS. E. TUCKWELL
BEGS to inform the public that she has made arrangements to take additional BOARDERS, and has Sleeping Accommodation for 4 Steady Respectable Young Men.
—(o)—
For Terms, &c., apply personally to
MRS. TUCKWELL.

Figure 14: Mrs Tuckwell's advertisement for the Resolution Villa (*NTTG*, 5 Sept 1883).

When the Resolution Villa was destroyed by the Great Hurricane of 1897, her soon to be son-in-law, the prominent citizen V. V. Brown (who married her daughter, Eliza Sarah Tuckwell, in 1901), assisted Eliza to start again, and she was soon back in business (Carment, Maynard, & Powell, 1990). As time went on, Eliza Tuckwell became a well-respected elder, known to everyone as 'Granny' Tuckwell. She died in August 1921, when 85 years old, after 43 years in the Territory. She had nine great-grandchildren (*Northern Standard*, 9 August 1921). Eliza is buried with Ned in the Goyder Road Cemetery in Darwin. Their daughter Eleanor married Tom Styles, who managed the underground work at the Zapopan Mine near Pine Creek. Their family dynasty contains several important historic and pioneering individuals, such as the nurse and unionist, Eileen Fitzer.

A new gaol

By the 1880s, the old town gaol was inadequate for use by an increasing number of prisoners. In 1882 John Knight probably designed the new gaol buildings—he certainly oversaw their construction—on a seaside block at Fannie Bay (Carment et al, 1993). On 9 September 1882, Government Resident Price called for tenders:

> TENDERS are required for building a GAOL at Fannie Bay, the Contractor providing all labour and materials. Walls of stone, timber of cypress pine, which may be obtained from Indian Island [in Bynoe Harbour].

The fence, on a separate tender, was to be made of timber and iron, twelve feet high (4 metres). The Fannie Bay site was chosen, not only because it was away from town, but because there was no land available on Goyder's plan for a gaol (de la Rue, 2004), but 31 acres of Fannie Bay had been retained for government purposes when the land was surveyed by J.P. Hingston, in 1877*.

Once tenders were let, the gaol was built swiftly—until it ran out of building material:

> … I am sorry to say that through some official blundering the works at the new gaol are almost suspended in consequence of necessary building material, which has to be imported from South, not having arrived. This is a serious calamity, as the old gaol is totally inadequate to the criminal requirements of the district. There are now thirty-six prisoners packed in a building which has only accommodation for sixteen. This state of things in a tropical climate is simply horrible torture, and would, were it summertime, doubtless lead to an epidemic amongst the criminal inmates. Especially nice for Europeans—of whom there are three, one sentenced and two waiting for trial—to be packed like herrings in a barrel with Chinese and aboriginals. Pah! the very thought of it is sickening (*Register*, 18 July 1883).

The prisoners were transferred from the decrepit prison in Smith Street the next year—there were 18 Chinese, 10 Aborigines, and three Europeans, along with four gaolers. In 1885, gallows arrived in Darwin on the *Guthrie*. The *Times* was heartless:

> The Government sent up a gallows to hang malefactors on, by the *Guthrie*. Now, as we shall in a few months require one, they'd better send a hangman (*NTTG*, 17 January 1885).

The Fannie Bay Gaol, with modifications, was used as the Territory's major prison for 96 years. It is now a museum.

John George Knight

John Knight was attracted to the Northern Territory by the gold rush, but on arrival was recruited to the civil service, and appointed as Secretary and Accountant to the Government Resident, and

---

* … some of the land was used for a clay brick works. Bricks were needed for the stamp-works on the goldfields and were used in the gaol, in parts of the hospital, Vestey's meat works, and in private houses. The clay was dug from the current Lake Alexander recreation lake site and the bricks baked at kilns near where the Darwin Sailing Club now has its premises (Boland, 2016, Gibson 2011).

Figure 15: Theatricals at The Residence 1886 (L to R) Mr John Knight,
Mrs Hilson, Mr Green, Miss Parsons, Mr Ward, Mr Whitelaw, Mr Howse
(LANT ph1060-0074).

Superintendent of Works in 1873. In 1876, he became the Gold
Warden, and in 1880 was appointed the Clerk of the Court at
Palmerston, as well as, during the 1880s, Deputy Sherriff, Clerk of
the Licensing Bench, Curator of the Property of Convicts, Registrar,
Accountant, Special Magistrate, Justice of the Peace, Crown Prosecutor,
and Official Receiving and Returning Officer (Carment, 1990).

Knight was a man of many skills, and a showman too—he liked
to dress up and perform in amateur dramatics with other members
of Palmerston society. He was also responsible for the excellent,
well-received displays about the Territory at the Adelaide Jubilee
Exhibition in 1887, and the Melbourne International Exhibition in
1888. He did the Territory proud, particularly in Adelaide. At the
Melbourne Exhibition, he decided that the whole 'colossal affair,
covering a roofed area of 36 acres' was too large for Australia. In a
letter to Adcock, he wrote that:

> … there is nothing like the spirit and go in it that there was
> in the Adelaide show of last year, and one cannot help feeling

Figure 16: The N.T. exhibit at the Adelaide Jubilee International Exhibition 1887–88 (S. Solomon, SLSA B 10212/29).

that the Exhibition era is played out (*North Australian*, 20 October 1888).

In Adelaide, he was awarded a First Order of Merit medal for the 'mineral trophy and ball of Territory gold'. Perhaps the better prize for him was an opportunity to spend some quality

Figure 17: Knight received a trophy for this display at the Adelaide Jubilee
Exhibition, for 'a cake of retorted gold from Olaf Jensen's Eleanor Mine at
Pine Creek' (S. Solomon, 1887, SLSA B 10212/60).

time with his family in Melbourne—as they never joined him in
the Territory.

In 1889, Knight, acted as government resident and the next
year was finally appointed to the position. Unfortunately, on
10 January 1892, he died of an asthma attack brought on by bronchitis

Figure 18: 'Knight's Folly' or the 'Mud Hut' was built by John Knight using prison labour in 1884. It was destroyed by fire on New Year's Eve in 1933. The Government Offices are on the high ground above the house (Foelsche 1887, SLSA B-5060).

and influenza. He was 68 years old. He is buried in the Goyder Road Cemetery and remains the only N.T. government resident to die in office.

Knight the architect

Most people lived in basic accommodation—and dwellings that were not suffering the ravages of rot and termites were few indeed. In 1884, for example, John Knight was living in a most inappropriate residence for a senior civil servant:

> ... The cottage at present occupied by Mr Knight, S.M., is almost the last of the wooden buildings imported in 1873 which still hangs together, but so tender is the structure that its occupant has—on three occasions—fallen through the floor, the last time being almost dangerously injured ...

Luckily, John Knight was in a position to do something about it:

Figure 19: Palmerston Town Hall and Solomon's Mart (later Brown's Mart) buildings, as seen from Mitchell Street (Anon, Roger Knott Collection, LANT, ph0002-0080).

Figure 20: The Mining Exchange designed by John Knight in 1885, now Brown's Mart Theatre, Smith Street, Darwin (Foelsche, c1887, ph0002-0074).

Mr Knight, who is an architect by profession, and originally the architect of the Houses of Parliament in Melbourne, has designed a novel residence (the whole being built of concrete), and the first two-storied house erected in Palmerston. The site is not a happy one, being on the side of a steep bank, but as there was no better available spot within view of the sea, there was no alternative but to take it. To suit the employment of the material used, the building, when completed, will present some of the characteristics of the Norman style. The double verandah having massive piers and arches all formed in concrete, so that little will be seen of the plain walls which now shows with somewhat undue prominence. The roof is flat … and finished with an embattled parapet (*NTTG*, 5 January 1884).

The house was called 'Aspendale'. It was designed to suit the climate and built on the hill above Kitchener Bay. Constructed of 'Egyptian' bricks and concrete, it was a two-storey, one-room-wide residence, with large verandas on each side. It was an unusual building for Palmerston and a source of the community's gossip for years. It was dubbed the 'Mud Hut', or just as disparagingly, 'Knight's Folly'. Controversially, the house was built using prison labour—'blackfellows and Chinese, under the direction of the European prisoner' (Fergusson).

The other building which Knight is well known for today was a commercial premise built for Vaiben Louis Solomon, in 1885. It was constructed of local porcellanite stone, like the town hall across the street, and was originally known as Solomon's Mart. In September 1887, it was bought by Victor Vowles Brown to house Port Darwin Mercantile and Agency Company. It later housed the offices of the Eastern and Australian Steam ship Company, Lloyds, and the Northern Territory Mining Exchange. Eventually the name changed to Brown's Mart, and it still exists, albeit renovated after several destructive cyclones and various incarnations, as the Brown's Mart Theatre in Smith Street.

Gallery
Changes in 'The Camp'

Figure 21: The store built by Goyder's men is removed to build a house for Gilbert McMinn. SS *Edinburgh* is moored offshore (1881 Foelsche, LANT, ph1060-004).

Figure 22: McMinn's house is complete, 1881. The 'government quarters'
are behind the fence (centre) (LANT, PRG-280-1-2-240).

Figure 23: The 'government quarters' at Port Darwin. Alfred Searcy was one of its residents from 1883 (c. 1886, LANT PRG-280-1-2-238).

Figure 24: The Camp in 1887, McMinn's house, in the foreground, is now much enlarged (Foelsche, nla.obj-141843057-1).

Figure 25: Chinatown houses in the 1880s (LANT PRG-280-1-11-69).

Figure 26: Chinatown houses in the 1880s (1886, NLA, 1227-1993-11).
nla.obj-420573274.

Chapter 2
A Chinese territory

The Chinese mostly left home after their new year celebrations, so arrived in Port Darwin at the beginning of the dry season, when there was no water in the goldfields. No one had told them, as they were boarding their transport ships in February, that panning was impossible in the dry season. As a result, many became destitute, and some starved. To avoid a catastrophe, Government Resident Price introduced a system of relief work in 1878 and 1879. It was therefore mostly Chinese labour that built the Government experimental garden, lengthened the jetties, cleared mangroves and tree stumps, repaired roads, and constructed porcellanite rock gutters along Smith and Cavenagh Streets*. When many fell sick from fever, Price had a temporary hospital built in their camp—which soon became known as 'Chinatown'—at the southern end of Cavenagh Street.

Many Chinese men returned to China if their mining ventures failed, but only if they could afford to. Some found enough gold to fund a business in their hometown and went home in triumph. Others stayed and earned wages in the mines or farms by working for other people. Many died: in 1880, about 10% of Chinese miners perished of a fever. Their bodies littered the roadside. Unnamed corpses were buried without fanfare—the cemetery at Rum Jungle, for instance, has at least seven occupants listed as 'unknown Chinese' (see

---

*   The stone was quarried from a site near the modern Quarry Street, in the suburb of
     Stuart Park.

Figure 27: The skeleton of a Chinese man who died next to an OTL pole
(SLSA PGR130/1/16/36). In 1880, about 10% of Chinese miners perished
of a fever. Their bodies littered the roadside.

Figure 28: Chinese diggings near Yam Creek. Hundreds of men dug small
shafts to the alluvial deposits about two metres underground. After 140
years, the ground is still a warren of their holes.

www.gsnt.org.au). Some corpses were simply rolled into abandoned
holes on the digging fields and covered over.

The first gold rush was over all too soon. But, even without it,
the early 1880s was an exciting time for those lucky enough to select
the right claims, and the cheap labour necessary to run the mines kept
coming. Most of the easy alluvial gold was found in the 1870s, so
miners then needed to follow reefs and extract gold from ore bodies.

Figure 29: A house site at Yam Creek on the hill overlooking the diggings
(Whelan 2020).

This required stamping batteries, ore transport systems, and larger investments. Mines were getting deeper and bigger. Prospector Adam Johns, who had arrived in the Territory in 1873, discovered the Union Reefs and 'Saunders Rush' with his partners (Philip Saunders, A. Grant, S. McBride, and S. Meaker). Johns then built one of the first stamping batteries in the area. The partners were also the discoverers of tin near Mount Tolmer. Johns managed the operations of Spring Hill for three years and supervised the erection of the entire Zapopan Company's plant (*NTTG*, 19 September 1896).

The Chinese diggers who arrived in the late 1880s were more likely to earn wages than be independent, but in the early years there were many making good money in the goldfields, much to the displeasure of the newspaper editors:

> … The Chinese on the Margaret Rush are making money fast*—30, 50, 80 oz. nuggets are being picked out every

---

* Fred Goss noted that the Margaret Rush was all alluvial, but… 'mostly nuggets. The proportion of fine gold was small. I saw one nugget… about, I think, as large as my

37

Figure 30: Adam Johns' homestead and battery on the Union Goldfield,
(1879, Foelsche SLSA B10142).

day. The last one found is valued at £600, being over 6 lbs.
in weight, and strange to say the field is monopolized by
Chinese.

... These human locusts are picking the eyes out of the
country: they fill our gaol; they are buried at our cost and
enjoy a free breakfast table. When the dry season is over,
they will be flocking here in thousands to our shores without
contributing a fraction to our revenue (*NTTG*, 26 June 1880).

The 'Almighty' Ping Que

The Chinese population grew to be more than six times the European
numbers. Chinese leaders like Ping Que, who spoke excellent English,
were able to build up huge wealth and influence in many business
areas.

Ping Que had learned the business of gold mining in Victoria,
where he arrived in 1853. He was a naturalised Australian by the time

---

fist. The find was soon exhausted, after a few months it was never heard of again
(Goss, 1956).

Figure 31: The Union (Foelsche 1879, ph1060-0058)

Figure 32: The Union Extended Gold Mine with shaft and drive (LANT, Foelsche, 1888, ph0001-0033).

he moved to the Northern Territory and the Union Reefs in 1875. John Knight, as gold warden, reported to the government resident after a visit to the Union area:

> Lambert Smith and Ping Que are now the principal workers
> at the Union and are turning out a fair quantity of stone.
> They pay their coolies one pound and provisions. Ping
> Que manages his countrymen very well and works them
> to make his mining pay which is more than can be said of
> other employers of coolies. He added, the most enterprising
> miner in this district (the Union) is Ping Que, an intelligent
> Chinaman who speaks good English. He employs about
> fourteen coolies (*NTTG*, 27 May 1876).

Ping Que's team of Coolies had little luck for the first two years. Then, in 1877, they followed a rich lead and crushed as much as 227 ounces of gold out of 400 tons of rock. Ping Que then regularly retrieved an ounce of gold for every ton his men could crush at Adam John's battery at the Union. He employed more people, even travelling to Singapore to engage them. John Knight described him as the 'the most enterprising miner in the Territory', and suggested the government employ him to return to Singapore to employ more Coolies to fill the labour shortage that most mines sometimes experienced.

Ping Que was well-liked. By 1880, he had expanded his businesses in a variety of directions: apart from owning several mining claims on land extending from Pine Creek to the Union, and the Margaret River and Saunders Rushes, he managed several other claims and had joint ventures with leading prospectors such as Adam Johns[*]. He also bought 600 cattle, employed slaughtermen, and sold the beef. In 1880, with J.W. Tennant, he became an owner

---

[*] Adam Johns, J.P. mined in the Northern Territory and Western Australia for many
    years. He and Philip Saunders were the first prospectors to find gold at Hall's Creek
    in the Kimberley in 1883. He was the Chairman of the Northern Territory Mining
    Board when he died, aged 46, on 19 September 1896: 'In the afternoon, while
    driving in company with Mr P. Greet to Brock's Creek, the buggy capsized in the
    creek and Mr Johns was killed instantly' (*NTTG*, 19 September 1896). He is buried
    in the Brocks Creek Cemetery.

of the Pine Creek Hotel. He became a committee member of the Port Darwin Camp* Progress Association and was a leader in the push for retribution parties used to punish Aborigines who committed crimes against Chinese workers. He even provided £20 to fit out a party to punish natives and helped fund the Miners Hospital built by the warden, John Knight, at The Shackle. He was a generous man (Jones, 2003).

Respect for Ping Que was so high among the Europeans that in September 1883, he was appointed, under the Northern Territory Gold Mining Act of 1873, a member of the Mining Board (Jones, 2003). The highest praise that he could be given in those times came from Adam Johns, who referred to Ping Que as 'the whitest man in the Territory' (*NTTG*, 12 May 1877). To Sowden he was the 'almighty Ping Que' (1882).

Ping Que travelled home to China in 1886, and news came back, much to the shock of those in Palmerston, that he had died, aged 49. The *Northern Territory Times* was moved enough to publish their first obituary of a Chinese man:

> … It is with sincere regret that we have heard of the death of Ping Que who was well known for twelve years in connection with mining enterprises on the Union Reefs. Many years of hard work and sterling pluck and enterprise earned for Ping Que the respect and goodwill of every Englishman with whom he was brought into contact. He was far and away the smartest mining man we have yet met in the Territory. Whether he was overseeing underground work or looking after a battery the work was always done heartily and well. Ping Que will be missed by many who have profited by his experience and advice. For ourselves, we can only express sorrow at the unexpected death of one of the pluckiest and straightest men it has been our lot to meet in the Northern Territory (*NTTG*, 15 May 1886).

---

* Port Darwin Camp was 200 kilometres from Port Darwin. Its name caused confusion and it later became better known as Grove Hill. There is one headstone still standing in the Port Darwin Camp Cemetery, that of William Knight Hay, a drover from Queensland, who died in 1885.

Virtues not vices.

The hard-working Chinese workers naturally had to spend some of their money, and Palmerston's European merchants reaped the benefits. The Chinese were mostly an admirable group: Edward Price found them law-abiding and gentle. He was a little concerned about their opium smoking and gambling, but these were no threat to the European population; Alfred Searcy complained that 'it was their virtues, not their vices we had to fear' (Searcy, 1909).

But, of course, there were repercussions. The working-class Europeans in Palmerston found it hard to get work because Chinese workers would accept lower wages and had a reputation for working harder. Then, when Chinese shops began to open in direct competition with European stores, the European merchants also became disgruntled. European opinions of the Chinese changed quickly. By the 1880s, the Chinese were often viewed as dirty, disease-ridden, and dishonest, and Chinatown as filthy and smelly (de la Rue, 2004). The Europeans began to worry. The *North Australian* led:

> ... probably there is nothing more generally believed among
> all classes of our European community than the fact that at
> some time or other we shall be visited by one of the many
> terrible diseases which, in other parts, have been brought
> about by the careless, dirty, and sickening habits of Chinese
> (*North Australian*, 4 January 1884).

Chinatown had quickly become a permanent part of Palmerston. After it was designated as the Chinese camp, Chinese businesses quickly took out leases on land in Cavenagh Street and filled them with huts made of grass, bamboo, bark, and cast-off corrugated iron. In June 1880, the inevitable happened:

> ... A most disastrous fire broke out on Sunday, the 20th
> inst., in that portion of Palmerston known as China Town.
> On the eastern corner of Cavenagh Street, the Chinese have
> erected their usual class of dwellings, chiefly composed of grass
> and bamboo, one or two storekeepers have leased or rented

ground, and around these have squatted from time to time some 500 to 1000 Chinese.

Their close proximity to town has always been considered a nuisance by the European residents, and it has been a matter of surprise that their township has not been burnt down long ago it is so no longer, as now the fire has swept everything away, and only a few sheets of curled-up iron and ashes mark its site.

About a quarter-past one o'clock we were disturbed by a continuous sound of crackers and blacks calling 'fire!' It did not take long, a very few minutes, before the whole town had turned out. It was soon seen it was useless to attempt to save anything. Some Europeans did spend their strength for naught, while the calm chinkies watched them with a most complacent air, the only noisy inmates of this quarter being pigs, fowls, dogs, and cats. Of these many must have been burnt alive. In about an hour it was all over, and tho' the heat was suffocating, we began to make a few inquiries touching the origin of the fire, as the conflagration we had seen. From information received from the Chinese we gather that the fire broke out in a small hut at the rear of a Chinese store kept by one Yee Hee.

The man was cooking his dinner, and by some means the sides of the hut, composed of grass, became ignited, the wind blowing fresh from the south-east, carried the flames along with fearful rapidity through the loose grass and horehound weed, and in less than a quarter of an hour it was seen that China Town must go. Yee Hee had only just time to save himself and rushed into the street. Yee Hee held a large stock of rice and other goods usually sold to the Chinese; his loss will amount to from 12 to 15,000 dols [dollars]. There were two other stores, owned by Quong Song Ti and Ah Lok. Their property has been almost entirely destroyed. We hear from other Chinese storekeepers that the total loss will be about 30,000 dols., only a small portion of the stock held on consignment, in one of the stores, being insured in Hongkong,

It was most fortunate for the Europeans that the wind was blowing from the south. Had it been from the east, in all probability we should have had to chronicle the burning of the city.

We hope, after this warning, steps will be taken to prevent the Chinese from huddling together in such close quarters in the township (*NTTG*, 26 June 1880).

Dudley Kelsey remembered his part in another fire in his memoir, *The Shackle*. He and another lad had been hunting kangaroos and came on a Chinese fishing camp, where fishermen would dry their catch before shipping it to China. Kelsey said everyone used to complain about the smell that used to float over the whole town during the drying time:

> … this was a monthly occurrence and lasted several days—no one seemed to be able to prevent it. The Chinese had erected a large shed—a light framework thatched with grass all over it. Now, it was empty except for a few wooden bunks, and we thought it would be a good opportunity to set light to the hut. Did it burn! All Darwin saw the flames (Kelsey, 1975).

By 1882 Chinatown had been rebuilt:

> … Some substantial stores have been erected and are well supplied with goods which are kept in a very creditable manner. The first store … on the Esplanade, and is a substantial building of wood and iron, with a verandah extending over the entire footpath. This store was very neatly fitted up and presented a most cleanly appearance. This property belongs to Kwang Yee Lung, and Sam Sing is apparently the manager or working partner. Further on are the buildings built for a family hotel by one Colgan, but no license being granted, the various two-roomed cottages which formed the hotel frontage were taken possession of by the Chinese. A Chinese baker has established himself in one and is doing a very fair business. Thence are several restaurants and a seed and plant shop, the first of its kind. The enterprising Chinamen who brought his potted plants from Canton deserves encouragement and patronage … His plants are in large pots, and consist of camellias, oranges, lemons, and a large variety of others bearing sweet smelling flowers—very nice presents to those young ladies who have a taste for floral beauty.
>
> Next to the Family Hotel block a new iron store is being erected for Gee Gy, its dimensions being 27 feet by about 40

feet. This will be a very pretentious building and will present quite a southern appearance. Other storekeepers have been enlarging and beautifying their buildings, and among the most noticeable are those owned by Yot Sing, Sun Kum Loong, and Yee Kee. At the rear of the stores and restaurants on the eastern side of Cavenagh-street are many Chinese dwellings of a rather primitive type. They enjoy a good view of Francis Bay and the outlying shore... (*NTTG*, 1 July 1882).

Newspapermen's prejudice

By 1884, the 'primitive' dwellings had again increased in number—but fire was not the only danger. The editors of the *North Australian*, George Mayhew and Charles Kirkland, discovered that 'the most dreadful of all diseases is now busy seeking victims among us, and... has actually victimised three of our 'almond-eyed' citizens', because of the 'the careless, dirty, and sickening habits of Chinese'. The newspapermen's prejudice was almost a solid thing—their description stands in contrast to comments made by William Sowden, two years earlier:

> ... you observe the absence of foulness and dirt which prejudice had forewarned you to expect ... the houses ... are quite as clean and wholesome as those of the other quarter (Sowden, 1882).

Leprosy and smallpox

Mayhew and/or Kirkland found a guide and entered Chinatown to visit three Chinese men they had heard were suffering from leprosy. The first victim was:

> ... a man of rather an aged appearance, which, however, may have been brought on by the terrible working of the disease, and his place of abode is a wretched hovel which nobody but a Chinaman could exist in, there being just room for a man to crawl in and lay down.

> At the time of our visit, he was sitting outside and presented a really pitiable spectacle. His face has a most peculiar appearance, being a series of hollow patches, which are

discernible upon a close inspection, the flesh having wasted away in a state of decay; the nose, too, is gradually receding into an insignificant little hump in the place where an ordinary-sized Celestial nose once occupied a prominent position. Upon being asked to bare his legs and feet, the leper did so, and here was a queer sight indeed. The skin of both legs is wrinkled, dry, and loose, and what flesh is left appears to be as soft as jelly; the feet appear also to be wasting away, and perhaps the most prominent feature in connection with them is the presence of a whitish substance at the tips of the toes. The hands and arms are reduced to about the size of an ordinary broom-handle, the fingers being particularly thin and boney [sic], and are getting quite useless …

… we believe precautions will be taken, and the lepers removed to some isolated place, where they will he attended to at Government expense (*North Australian*, 4 January 1884).

The government did indeed take precautions. They first tried to expel him from Australia, but they were unable to get the unfortunate man onto a China-bound ship because:

… the steamers for China have been crowded, and as something closely resembling panic sets in amongst the heathen on the approach of a leper, the agents have not been able to secure him a passage (*NTTG*, 31 January 1885).

Doctor Wood J.P. then took the 'unfortunate wretch' to Channel Island, which lies about 12 kilometres from Port Darwin, near the mouth of the Blackmore River. Quarantining lepers on islands was a long-established European custom (Saunders S., 1989). 'A tent was erected, and other means taken to ensure the man's comfort as far as possible in his dreary isolation' and he was left there to practically fend for himself until a ship could be found to take him back to China.

He was joined by others before then, however. Dr Wood found another victim at the 12-Mile mining camp, and Dr Morice found a couple more in Palmerston.

An unofficial place a leper could be abandoned was Goat Island. The *North Australian* rejoiced in the death of an exile who was sent there in 1885:

… At last! The leper king of Goat Island is dead as a doorknob…
The poor unfortunate wretch we presume, died from the effects
of his disease. Howard, the boatmen who took over his supply
of rations, missed him upon his last trip, and on looking into
his hut found the leper lying dead. We believe the Chinaman's
remains were burned (*North Australian*, 1 May 1885).

Neither of the newspaper's editors was hands-on in helping the
ill, poor, or destitute and were regularly happy to be critical of the
unfortunate, or of minority groups. The *Times* did make the effort of
scolding the population over the plight of one man:

… A few paces from Ah See's carpenter's shop in Bennett
Street, is or was (we suppose it's all over now), to be seen
the spectacle of a living death, however paradoxical that
may sound. In a miserable hovel, slowly decaying before
a loathsome disease, without food (perhaps water) lies a
Chinaman. Too helpless to move, even for the most urgent
needs, deserted by his countrymen, he lies, a mass of festering
corruption, round which flies in millions form a sickening
halo. Yet we have heard the legend that this is a Christian
country and have seen a parson and a smug-faced interpreter
exhorting the Chinese to abjure their present form of worship
and be converted to a religion under the sway of which one of
their countrymen may die like a homeless dog and cared for as
little. Pah! (*NTTG*, 10 January 1885).

In 1889, a permanent quarantine station, or 'lazaret' was built
on Mud Island*, a few kilometres closer to Part Darwin, and a medical
officer visited once a week to treat the patients. The total number of
sufferers of the disease will never be known because Chinese victims
were often undeclared to the authorities. However, according to
Saunders (1989), there were 17 diagnosed patients in the Northern
Territory in the 1880s (and 95 patients in total before 1925). They
were sent to live in a 'lazaret'—a single galvanised iron building with
a veranda and a dirt floor. There was no freshwater supply, although
rainwater tanks were installed to catch water during the wet season.
Patients were given rations, fishing lines and a shotgun, but their

* Mud Island is the peninsula upon which now sits the Inpex Gas Refinery.

47

Figure 33: Mud Island Lazaret (without a veranda as recorded). A quarantine officer is on the right (P. Brown image, LANT PH01550048).

standard of care was extremely poor. In 1906, Dr W. Ramsey Smith, reporting on diseases in the Northern Territory, concluded that 'the Leper Station at Port Darwin is unsuitable for any being of the human species' (Smith W., 17 November 1906)*. The island became known as 'Living Hell Lazaret.'

Many residents of Chinatown fell victim to disease. In August 1887, a man who had been living in a hut on the corner of Woods and Bennett Street was suddenly expelled from his house:

> … Corporal Waters was attracted to the cries of a man in the street; he at once proceeded to the spot and found a Chinaman, who had been brought out into the road to die by his countrymen, lying on the ground (*North Australian*, 6 August 1887).

Dr Stow diagnosed smallpox, and the man—plus the four with whom he shared his house—were immediately transported to the quarantine station. They were towed in a dinghy behind the government launch and 'Dr Stow, Corporal Waters, and Constable

---

* The new Channel Island Leprosarium was opened in 1931 and over 440 victims of leprosy were sent there over the next 52 years, of which at least 142 died (www.pastmasters.net).

Martin underwent a thorough process of fumigation on return ...; and the boat in which the Chinamen were towed to the island was sunk near shore' (*North Australian*, 6 August 1887). The next day the police burned the house.

Another victim was found at the 10-Mile camp a day or two later. A man had been expelled from an opium den when he was found to be sick, and both he, and the two men who had handled him, were sent to quarantine. Other victims were found on boats, and a temporary quarantine facility was set up on Point Emery for people who did not yet show symptoms of the disease. The measures worked well, and although several other cases were found, smallpox soon disappeared—temporarily, at least*.

Opium

Opium was a scourge of the Chinese population. It was a legal drug, but it attracted heavy import duties†. Alfred Searcy, who took the job of customs inspector in 1883, spent much of his time searching for smugglers bringing the drug into the town (smuggling of gold out of Port Darwin, without paying the export tax, led to the other main part of his job). In *By Flood and Fire* (1912), Searcy recounted some of the events in Port Darwin after he arrived. His first success at catching smugglers occurred a short time after he began the job:

> ... One night, while watching for suspects on the jetty, I saw three Chinamen coming towards me, and one of them was surprisingly bulky. I caught hold of his coat to detain him, when he threw backs his arms, slipped out of the garment, and darted over the side, taking a dive of twenty feet into three feet of water above a rocky bottom. The coat was well-lined with tins of opium. Seizing the other men, who were too astonished to run away, I found they also carried quantities of the drug.

---

* Foelsche wrote that smallpox was the disease most feared by the Larrakia and other tribesmen. It was known from a time several years before white settlement. He knew a young man named Mangminone had contracted smallpox as a child and was heavily scarred from it (Foelsche, 1882).

† In 1888 the excise duty on opium was 30 shillings per pound.

In a moment of inspiration, I saw how pigtails could be made
to do good service for the state and grasping my prisoners by
theirs, I... drove them to the police station... (Searcy, 1912).

Smuggling opium meant big profits. Searcy later stumbled
across a group unloading a hidden opium shipment. Searcy was
attacked, tied up with a bag over his head, and left for the police to
find the next day. He was uninjured but:

... when the opium chest was examined ten cases of Chinese
delight were missing, which meant to the thieves a saving of
over seven hundred pounds of duty alone... none of the drug
was ever recovered... (Searcy, 1912).

Anti-Chinese sentiment

A worsening European attitude towards the Chinese is reflected in the
tone of anti-Chinese sentiment in the two Palmerston newspapers,
particularly the *North Australian*. As time went on, both became more
critical—even Chinese New Year was criticised:

... Who has not been a victim to the above celestial
celebration? Certainly, no one who has ever lived within
easy distance of a Chinese encampment during the festive
season... the few apparent features of enjoyment which our
yellow citizens seem to have any fondness for were freely
indulged in, to the delight and amusement of themselves, and
the chagrin and discomfiture of the whites who reside within
'cooee'. There is only one difference between a Chinese and a
European New Year celebration; Both are equally noisy while
they last, but the whites are contented to 'beat the old year out
and the new one in'; whereas a Chinaman never seems satisfied
until he has driven the old year out and the new one in, and
then thrown in a couple of days' gratuitous demonstration
by way of giving a sort of grace to the new arrival (*North
Australian*, 20 February 1885).

The Europeans conveniently forgot that, a decade earlier, the
Chinese were the saviours of the mining industry after European
diggers had abandoned it. They came to Australia to support their
families back home—few viewed it as permanent migration. Most

of their gold was sent home and when, or if, they amassed enough wealth, they returned home in triumph.

Many men also pre-arranged for their bones to be sent back to their families if they died.

Anti-Chinese sentiment continued to grow through the decade. On the goldfields, one problem was the sheer number of Chinese diggers keen to follow any rumour of a new gold find. The Europeans were frustrated—surely a white man who found a lode should be allowed to access it first … Calls for government control of Chinese movement around the country grew louder:

> … The Chinese population should also be restricted from
> flocking onto new goldfields which Europeans had been at
> much trouble and expense in discovering and prospecting
> (Uhr, NT. Reform Association, *NTTG*, 5 April 1884).

> … it would be well if the advisability of preventing Chinese
> working upon new discoveries for a term of three years from
> their being found, was fully considered, as there can be no
> doubt European miners will hesitate to come into the country
> or prospect for new fields, so long as the Chinese are permitted
> to swarm upon new fields without restriction (*NTTG*, 10 July
> 1886).

Chinese Immigration Bills were introduced in most states of Australia between 1888 and 1891, and long were the discussions about amendments (*Telegraph*, 17 September 1891). The restrictions they imposed did not work well. For example, a small alluvial field was found near Maudie's Creek, in the Katherine region, in 1889. Over a hundred Chinese arrived on the new rush within days. 'We understood that the Chinese were to be kept off newly discovered fields for a certain period' complained the *Times*, 'and also that they were not to be permitted to proceed further south than the Katherine River'. But:

> … both these rules seem to be utterly ignored by those who
> administer the affairs of the Territory locally, and it certainly looks
> as if the yellow-skinned pests are to be allowed to ignore all our hard
> fought-for measures of restrictive legislation. So long as the system

of encouraging the Chinese in their policy of contempt for our laws is allowed to continue, there will be very little encouragement for European prospectors to seek for new goldfields. Strange to say our white-skinned settlers object to play the part of jackal for the sole benefit of Asiatic interlopers (*NTTG*, 6 December 1889).

Charles Millar and his brother gave some hope to the Europeans in 1887 when they bought the entire line of reefs at Union Reefs and other mines around Pine Creek (Jones, 1990), but their manager, Mr Armstrong, employed Chinese labour. In 1890, he told Government Resident Knight that he had employed six Europeans in Sandhurst Mine on two-year contracts. However, three of them left after a few months. They 'gave him more trouble than all the Chinese together, those three whites having demoralised the Chinese by begging cigars and liquor from them and getting drunk in their huts' (Knight, 1890).

The Millars sold up two years later to a Chinese syndicate for a bargain price of £1000 without any explanation. Then, except for a very few Europeans like Adam Johns and Henry Allwright*, the goldfields were mostly owned by Chinese miners. Certainly, according to Knight, there was not a single mine where Chinese labour was not employed.

In Palmerston, Chinatown was thriving. In his 1888 report, Inspector Foelsche described the composition of the Chinese population:

> … they have 39 stores and greengrocer's shops, 3 carpenters' shops, 2 shoemakers' shops, 3 laundries, 5 tailoring establishments, 32 fruit and vegetable gardens… 6 gambling houses, 7 Chinese brothels occupied by 34 prostitutes. There are also 5 Japanese brothels occupied by 23 prostitutes. The Chinese population of Palmerston varies from 800 to 1000. Up country they have 11 stores and 23 fruit and vegetable gardens. The floating population is about 5000, employed in railway works, mining and as servants… (Foelsche, 14/8/1880).

---

*   Henry Allwright owned the Margaret Crossing Hotel at Port Darwin Camp before Ellen Ryan took it over, and was a merchant and miner, owning several mines. He died in Pine Creek in 1888.

Figure 34: Chinese market gardens, near Palmerston in 1885 (SLSA B61942).

On 11 January 1888, a committee elected by the Palmerston District Council, all eminent European members of the community*, drew up a petition against the Chinese. V.L. Solomon—who became a Member of Parliament in 1890—was voted to take the next steamer and deliver it to the southern governments, meeting with politicians such as Sir Henry Parkes in New South Wales. The petition aimed to get their support against the South Australia Government on the grounds, the petitioners claimed, that they had been ignored on these issues:

> On behalf of the European settlers of the Northern Territory of South Australia, we the undersigned desire to make this appeal to you on the subject of the Chinese Question with a view to obtaining your assistance towards having legislative measures introduced by the Government of South Australia to deal effectively with the Chinese, so that the privileges which they enjoy here and their alarming influx into our country, may be reduced to a more tolerable standard, if not absolutely abolished (*NTTG*, 25 February 1888).

---

* The committee was: Herbert H. Adcock (Chairman), V. L. Solomon, C. J. Kirkland, W. D'Arcy Uhr, and G. W. Mayhew.

The petition included 'particulars' about the Chinese in the Northern Territory which, it was felt, the southerners should know:

> ... the number of Europeans scattered over our area of 423,620 square miles does not exceed 900, whereas the number of Chinese now in the country is variously estimated between 5,000 and 6,000, and they are arriving here at the rate of from 2,000 to 3,000 per annum.

> ... the Chinese are fast gaining a monopoly of all descriptions of labour, of all trade work, of agricultural pursuits, and of mining. They are exclusively employed in the labour department of the railway construction work, generally at little short of actual slave wages, to the detriment of European labourers... At the present time, our goldfields do not employ 50 actual European working miners, whereas, by approximate calculation, the number of Chinese who live and work on the fields cannot be less than 3000, and they are increasing weekly as the hundreds arrive from China.

> ... with the completion of the railway to Pine Creek, and the continuation of the line overland to Adelaide, there is great danger that the Chinese will find their way in large numbers to our interior, and thence over the border into Queensland, thus escaping the poll-tax levied in that colony. There is no immigration tax levied on Chinese entering the Northern Territory (*NTTG*, 25 February 1888).

From Sydney, Mr Solomon was pleased to telegraph that he had 'personally interviewed Sir Henry Parkes, and other influential politicians, and the editors of the leading papers, all of whom have promised the movement their warm support' (*NTTG*, 24 March 1888).

The reappearance of smallpox during 1888, gave the anti-Chinese lobby ammunition, as Port Darwin was 'continually invaded by smallpox' during 1888:

> ... commencing with the *Whampoa*, which arrived on January 15th, and ending with the *Changsha*, which arrived on February 15th—within a period of a month—six steamers arrived either with smallpox cases actually on board, or having had smallpox patients on board, after leaving Hongkong, which were landed at Singapore or Sourabaya... (Parsons, 1888 Report).

The Governor-General, Sir William Robinson, declared an emergency:

> ... All ports in China and Chinese dependencies, the Malay Peninsula, Singapore, Timor, and all the ports and islands in Netherlands-India are infected with smallpox, and it is probable that such disease may be brought from such places to the Northern Territory of South Australia, and I... do further proclaim, order, and direct, that from the date hereof, all ships or vessels arriving in the Northern Territory... shall be liable to quarantine within the meaning of the said Act, and shall, in every case, be detained, and be ordered to such quarantine station, Port Darwin, as may be directed by the Health Officer in the said Northern Territory, until they receive a certificate from the Health Officer (*NTTG*, 14 April 1888).

In 1888, Government Resident John Langdon Parsons found in the quarantine requirements an opportunity to discourage Chinese from coming to the Territory:

> ... Quarantine on vessels arriving from any of the ports mentioned in the above proclamation, will accordingly be required at Port Darwin for twenty-one days after arrival, except as regards persons not being Chinese arriving by vessels having no disease on board, who will be granted immediate pratique if not from Hongkong.
>
> A poll-tax of ten pounds per head will be imposed, subject to Parliamentary sanction, on all Chinese arriving in the Northern Territory, and having left therefore after the 1st of March 1888. Or being now in the Northern Territory and leaving for any part of the Northern Territory more than two hundred miles south of Port Darwin (Parsons, 1 March 1888).

Of course, the Chinese objected, but right across the Australian states and territories, similar anti-Chinese movements were gathering pace. The Territorians were latecomers to the movement but, in 1889, the *Times* took racism to a new level:

> ... We strongly advise the immediate formation of an Anti-Chinese league, with branches at all the principal centres of population, its object being to make the strongest protest and opposition to any further introduction of coloured labour into

the Northern Territory.

'Australia for the Australians' should be our watchword, and to those who want Chinese cheap labour, and Chinese or black fellow colonists, we say, go and reside with them in their own country. White men can live in the Northern Territory; white men constructed our telegraph line through an unknown country; white men have made the Northern Territory what it is now; white men have found out the mineral wealth of the country, and last of all, white men are determined to stick to the country, and resist all the attempts of self-interested capitalists, to make it a refuge for cheap coloured labour, for the sole benefit of their own pockets (*NTTG*, 11 May 1889).

The 1890s did not look good if you were Chinese in Australia, as the pressure continued. The peak population of Chinese in the Northern Territory reached an estimated 6,122 in 1888, compared to 1,010 Europeans. Every year after that the numbers dropped (Jones 1990). At federation, there were 2,690 Chinese and 1,055 Europeans[*].

The Northern Territory was late to the anti-Chinese movement because they were an essential part of Territory development throughout the 1870s and early 1880s, and everyone knew it. Things changed as the economy stumbled and Australia moved towards federation (Jones, 2003). The Immigration Restriction Act of 1901 was among the first Commonwealth legislation enacted[†]. This became known as the 'White Australia Policy', which effectively ended all non-European immigration by setting impossible entrance examinations in a range of European languages (Asian immigrants could be asked to sit the test in Lithuanian, for example).

---

[*]   According to Jones (1990), it was not until 1911 that the European population was larger than the Chinese (1,729 to 1,542) and not until 1924 that the numbers of European miners exceeded Chinese miners (90 to 70).

[†]   Fortunately for Darwin, many Chinese were naturalised and had become Australian citizens before the Immigration Acts started. Many of their descendants still live in the Territory and they are an important part of society.

Chapter 3

On the Overland
Telegraph Line

The OTL

In June 1870, news arrived in Palmerston that the South Australian government had won the contract from the British Australian Telegraph (B.A.T.) Company to construct a telegraph line from Port Darwin, 2,897 kilometres south to Port Augusta. The B.A.T. had already undertaken to lay an undersea cable from Java to Darwin by December 31, 1871, and the South Australian government agreed to have the Overland Telegraph Line ready by then or face severe penalties. It was a coup for South Australians. They had been awarded the contract, even though an attractive alternative route, east to Normanton in the Gulf of Carpentaria, was promoted by the Queensland Government. A telegraph line south already connected Normanton to Brisbane, and Normanton was closer to Port Darwin than Port Augusta—in fact, less than 2,000 kilometres.

South Australia was so keen to win the contract that the government promised the line would be completed within 18 months, following the overland route pioneered by John McDouall Stuart in 1862.

Government Resident Douglas was told that the OTL was to be his priority and everything else—experimental gardens, pastoral developments, even a gold rush—was to be delayed until it was up and running (Cross J., 2011). This was a great frustration to Douglas who was looking for government help in starting a gold industry. The government's answer was:

> ... As the discovery of a goldfield at this time would greatly interfere with the very important work at present in hand, it is considered undesirable to take any steps in that direction until the telegraph line is completed (*Advertiser*, 26 April 1870).

The Postmaster-General and Superintendent of Telegraphs in Adelaide, Charles Heavitree Todd, took charge of the project.

Todd knew that the economy would swell when Adelaide became

Figure 35: Charles Heavitree Todd in 1872 (SLSA, B 12209).

the entry and exit point for news and information between Europe and Australia.

Harriet Douglas, a daughter of the government resident, 'planted' the first pole in Smith Street, Palmerston, on 15 September 1870, and nearly two years later the cable was joined at Frew's Ironstone Ponds on August 22, 1872. The connection was celebrated by smashing a brandy bottle of cold tea on the post—no one was going to volunteer their brandy. It was one of the most outstanding engineering feats of the nineteenth century. Australia was now connected by cable to the world. The work had cost nearly four times what had been expected—£470,720—but then Adelaide was now Australia's centre for telegraphic communication.

John Archibald Graham Little, J.P. was appointed Telegraph Stationmaster on 1 August, 1871. He remained in this role for 34 years. It was he who sent the first telegraph message through to Adelaide from Palmerston on 22 August, 1872:

… WE HAVE THIS DAY, WITHIN TWO YEARS,
COMPLETED A LINE OF COMMUNICATIONS TWO
THOUSAND MILES LONG THROUGH THE VERY
CENTRE OF AUSTRALIA, UNTIL A FEW YEARS AGO
A TERRA INCOGNITA BELIEVED TO BE A DESERT.

He was also delighted to transmit the first message from London
to Sydney in October. Newspapers listed the route of the telegraph
line (in miles):

Adelaide to Port Darwin (land) 2,200
Port Darwin to Banjoewangie (sea) 970
Banjoewangie to Batavia (land) 480
Batavia to Singapore (sea) 560
Singapore to Penang (sea) 381
Penang to Madras (sea) 1,213
Madras to Bombay (land) 600
Bombay to Aden (sea) 1,664
Aden to Suez (sea) l, 308
Suez to Alexandria (land) 224
Alexandria to Malta (sea) 819
Malta to Gibraltar (sea) 981
Gibraltar to Falmouth [Cornwall] via Lisbon (sea) 1,250
Total 12, 650 (*Journal*, August 24, 1872).

Little also took on the roles of 'senior and inspecting officer' of
the line as far south as Attack Creek, deputy sheriff, 'sub-collector of
customs, and several other duties' in the growing town (Carment,
Maynard, & Powell, 1990).

Gold

The Telegraph Line Construction Team discovered alluvial gold
in holes they dug for the telegraph poles at Yam Creek, on 2
December 1870. Government Resident Bloomfield Douglas was
excited by the find but was told to focus on the OTL. The news was
suppressed because the OTL workers were needed—if they joined
a gold rush, the telegraph line construction would slow down,
and the government would be forced to pay heavy penalties to the
B.A.T.

Figure 36: Staff of the Darwin Overland Telegraph Office in 1888:
Back row L-R. 1 Albert McDonald, 2 Tom Morris, 3 a temporary officer,
4 Fred Killian, 5 Florence Bleezer, 6 (...) Burgoyne, 7 Dudley Kelsey, 8
Jim Shanahan, 9 Fred Price, 10 A.P. Ward, 11 George Reid, 12 Mr Lawrie,
13 Percy Bryant. Front row L-R. 1 Mr Cleland, 2 Cecil Marsh, 3 John G.
Little, 4 Ted John, 5 ? (LANT, ph1134-0001, 1888).

Consequently, the first prospecting party did not arrive until
1872, and the rush began. Douglas sent enthusiastic reports about
gold finds to Adelaide. Then he travelled to the telegraph construction
camps on the Roper River, just as they were winding up, and spread
the word about the discovery at Yam Creek. He organised George
Deane*, who was in charge of the government horses, and also recruited
two newcomers who were overlanding horses and cattle northward:
Matthew Dillon Cox and D'Arcy Wentworth Uhr. They were able
to provide safe passage to any of the workers wanting to seek their
fortunes. Almost single-handedly, he started the Territory's gold rush.

Territory gold was harder to find than that in Victoria. By the
1880s, the first rush was over, and reef mining overtook alluvial gold

---

* George Deane was a member of the First Northern Territory Expedition with
Goyder, in 1869 (Pugh, 2018b).

Figure 37: Our House Hotel, Stapleton 1879 (Foelsche, LANT, ph0754-0011).

panning as the most productive method. Most miners then worked for a company, and as Chinese miners were willing to work for a low salary, most miners were Chinese.

The Overland Telegraph Line ran through the middle of the goldfields. Repeater stations were built at Southport, Stapleton, Adelaide River, Yam Creek (The Shackle), Pine Creek, Katherine (Springvale), and at intervals to Port Augusta. Each station needed to be staffed by telegraph officers and their assistants so that messages could be repeated for transmission in either direction, 24 hours a day.

The Shackle

The Shackle* Telegraph Office at Sandy Creek was also called Yam Creek, despite the latter being several kilometres north of the station.

---

* Frederick Goss, a telegraph operator, described a 'shackle' as a 'contrivance made of specially shaped insulators, fixed about twelve inches apart by iron straps. The telegraph line is cut, and each end is fastened around one of the insulators. This is a permanent arrangement, but of course no current can pass. To overcome this a piece of line wire, about eighteen inches long is fixed to the telegraph line, one end on

Figure 38: The Shackle Telegraph Office (1879, Foelsche, ph0001-0029).

All three names—The Shackle, Sandy Creek and Yam Creek—were subsequently used for the settlement, despite the obvious confusion that created. The telegraph officer was John (Jack) Kelsey. He had arrived in Port Darwin in 1873 as a lad with his family. His brother, Dudley Evan Kelsey*, joined him as his assistant in 1882 when he

each side of the shackle, thus forming a bridge by which the electric current passes over the gap. Now when the operator wishes to 'speak', he unfastens one end of the bridge and leaves it clear of the telegraph line - then he attaches his instrument, by its two wires, one each side of the shackle and the instrument and its wires take the place of the bridge and he can do his speaking. When finished, he closes the bridge, disconnects his wires and instrument; the whole only occupies two or three minutes. In outback places, these shackles are placed in the lowest part of the sag in the line between two telegraph poles. This would be nine or ten feet from the ground. By throwing a cord or bridle rein over the wire, he can pull the shackle gently down to within his reach and when finished he can let it go easily back again. These shackles are placed at all permanent water holes or camping places, but in any case, not more than ten miles apart' (Goss, 1956).

*   The Kelsey brothers were sons of John George Kelsey, one of the early councillors of the Palmerston District Council. According to Mrs Kelsey's (then Henderson) obituary, Kelsey was the first to build a wooden house in Palmerston, in 1873 (*Northern Standard*, 27 July 1927). He was also a gaoler in the Fannie Bay Prison from 1883.

turned 17. Decades later Dudley wrote an autobiography that was published in 1975 by Ira Nesdale. It is from him that we learn much about life on the OTL (Nesdale, 1975).

The Shackle was Kelsey's first station appointment out of Darwin[*]:

> ... when I arrived, the population consisted of seven
> government officials (3 police, a goldfield's warden, the
> Medical Officer, Dr Wood, my brother, myself). Others were
> Mrs Ryan (proprietress of the hotel), Miss Freeman (her
> sister), and a few Chinese gardeners.

Of course, everyone originally lived in tents, but by 1873, when the Miners Arms Hotel was opened by Edward Williams, there were two general stores and a blacksmith's shop, and many corrugated iron shacks. A second hotel, the 'British and Foreign', was opened in December 1874 by Mrs A. Traversi[†] (with a 'good billiard table' and a French cook). Both hotels were eventually run by Mrs Ellen Ryan.

By 1873, 1500 people were living near The Shackle. There were fewer in 1881: the census in April counted 96 Europeans, including three women, and 807 Chinese men and two Malays (Donovan, 1981).

Charles Nash

In 1881, a young teamster named Charles Nash was appointed as gold warden. His was a controversial appointment because he was a teamster rather than a miner. He had been working in the area for several years, but there were rumours of the influence of his father, who was a member of the South Australian Parliament.

---

[*] The name Palmerston was officially changed to Darwin in 1911 in a response to common usage and because the address of Palmerston in New Zealand particularly caused confusion regarding postal addresses (see 'Our Queer Nomenclature', *North Australian*, 26 January 1886). Kelsey always used 'Darwin' in his memoir.

[†] Amelia Traversi, by then a publican, had previously owned 'Mrs Traversi's Temperance Bar' across the road from the bank in Palmerston. She sold 'cordials of every description.'

Nash had discovered and brought back the body of a murdered colleague, a teamster named James Ellis, in 1878. 'I could smell the decomposition of the body and therefore knew he was dead', he said:

> ... In the morning with the assistance of Messrs Berwick and Stretton*, I drew the body out of the water and then found that the deceased had a severe wound at the back of the ear, and also at the back of the head, the left arm was very much bruised apparently from warding off blows. (*NTTG*, 26 January 1868).

Nash was promoted to chief gold warden in 1887 and he continued to help the lawmen[†]. The 'McKinlay River Correspondent' for the *North Australian* informed their readers:

> ... I have to inform you of the exciting capture of Tommy Dodd at Burrundie on Monday afternoon by Constable Power, assisted by Mr Warden Nash. About twelve months ago this aboriginal murdered a Queensland blackboy at Mount Wells, and at intervals, since then he has visited Burrundie, of late making himself quite at home there. But the constable had his eye on him, and only waited until the nigger had full confidence in his own security. Then he made his grab, and Mr Nash was of very great assistance in placing the 'bracelets' on the murderer's feet, as it took all Power's strength to hold a slippery black of such strength as Dodd.
>
> Additional risk was added to the capture by the presence of a big crowd of Alligator blacks, whom Tommy called on to assist him. Great credit is therefore due to Constable Power and Mr Nash for securing the savage after a very tough tussle. Before leaving this subject, I may say that it's a great pity that proper chains and leg and neck irons are not provided at Burrundie (*North Australian*, 10 December 1886).

---

* William George Stretton (1847–1920) served in the South Australian Mounted Police from 1865 to 1869, then after 'apparently acting as chief storekeeper during the construction of the Overland Telegraph Line during 1871 and 1872, he returned to the Mounted Police in 1872'. He became chief warden of the goldfields in 1894, after Nash, and was an important civil servant in Darwin until his retirement in 1912 (Ling, 2011).

† Nash remained in the position of chief gold warden until 1894, when he transferred to Borroloola.

Figure 39: Burrundie Police Station. Only the floor remains. It has metal rings through which the chains of prisoners were passed.

The death of a constable

The Police station at The Shackle* was manned by Corporal Montagu, Constable Charles Luck and Constable Thomas Charlesworth. On 21 February 1884, Montagu was in Southport waiting for the mail-coach and gold escort, which was overdue. He telegraphed The Shackle and ordered Charlesworth to head out to look for the coach and render assistance as needed.

Charlesworth was not without experience. He was a 31-year-old South African who had fought with the Natal Mounted Police in the Zulu Wars. Nevertheless, he disappeared. His horses were found tied to a tree next to Peters Creek on the Adelaide River:

> ... The horses had saddles and bridles on and bells and hopples tied round their necks. In the saddle bag a cheque book and some correspondence were found, and these proved that the missing rider of the horses was no other than Constable Charlsworth [sic]. Summers ... distinctly saw evidence of a struggle having taken place to hold on to two trees in the middle of the creek ... next morning search was continued till 11 a.m. when the body of Charlsworth was

---

* The Shackle Police Station was built at a cost of £690 in 1881 (LANT A4797/1881).

discovered lying face downwards at the bottom of a tributary of Peter's Creek, fully dressed. There were no marks of violence on the body, except those caused by coming in contact with floating logs and trees. The body of the unfortunate trooper was taken into the Adelaide and duly buried, decomposition having set in (*North Australian*, 29 February 1884).

Dudley Kelsey thought that Charlesworth's horse had got him into deep water, and his heavy topboots and overcoat caused him to drown while being washed down the flooded creek* (Kelsey, 1975), although this did not explain how his horse came to be tethered to a tree.

Meanwhile, the mail coach arrived at Southport safely. They had merely been delayed by the flooded creeks and boggy roads.

Dudley Kelsey

Dudley Kelsey, as his brother's assistant, had a lot of spare time. Taxidermy was his paying hobby, and he spent much of his time shooting birds he could stuff. He also joined Constable Luck on some of his patrols. One day, when Luck was checking the Chinese diggers' miner's rights at Fountain Head, Kelsey tells of seeing numerous heads above ground, their owners working the mine beneath them, but the moment he and the constable appeared in the open, the diggings seemed suddenly deserted. The miners immediately hid in their holes, and then they would 'sneak away like a lot of rabbits'. A miner's licence certificate cost 10 shillings per annum, but collecting the fee was difficult. Parsons reported in 1885 that of the 2,000 Chinese diggers he estimated were in the goldfields, only 160 had paid (Parsons, January 1885).

Dudley Kelsey also helped Constable Luck on other missions:

... once ... a Chinese died from beriberi†—a disease that

---

* Drownings were common in the Top End during the wet seasons. They were reported often in the newspapers. For instance: 'The body of the young man, Gill, who was drowned some days back in the Ferguson River, while attempting to cross it, has been found by James Blair' (*North Australian*, 28 January 1886).

† The main cause of beriberi is a diet low in thiamine.

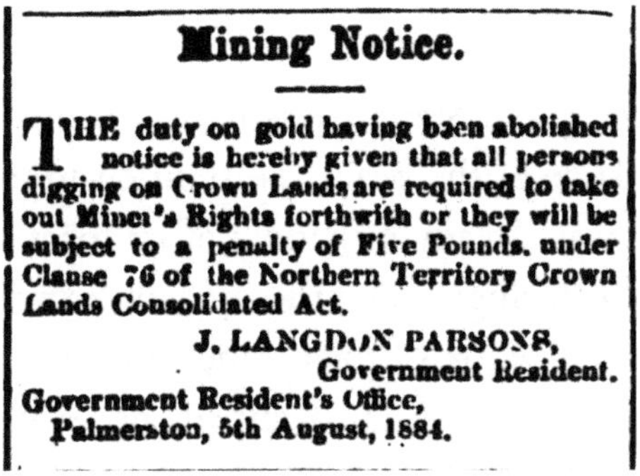

Mining Notice.

THE duty on gold having been abolished notice is hereby given that all persons digging on Crown Lands are required to take out Miner's Rights forthwith or they will be subject to a penalty of Five Pounds, under Clause 76 of the Northern Territory Crown Lands Consolidated Act.

J. LANGDON PARSONS,
Government Resident.
Government Resident's Office,
Palmerston, 5th August, 1884.

Figure 40: Miner's Rights notification 1885 (*NTTG*).

causes terrible swelling before death—and his friends had deserted him. Luck and I rode over to investigate and found him lying in a thatched humpy with little or no furniture in it.

In the town some distance away we sought help to bury the body but could find no one willing to assist. On our way back to the hut we noticed a head bob up from a fossicker's hole and found two Chinese miners huddled below. Charles made them come out and we got them to the hut, where they seemed terrified, and their Chinese vocabulary was let loose with real strength. Getting some rope, we made the two men pull their countrymen to the nearest digger's hole and let him down into it. As soon as our backs were turned the Chinese made off. Then, to avoid any infection, we thought it safer to burn the hut down, and this we did (Kelsey, 1975).

In 1885, Kelsey was transferred to the telegraph station at Southport; but both Southport and The Shackle were dying natural deaths as the railway passed them by. Instead, a new town was built:

... A new township has recently been surveyed at a bend of the McKinley River, named Burrundie. Some of the allotments were offered for sale at the Land Office, Palmerston, on Thursday, 11th December 1884. The new township will be the Government headquarters at the Reefs, and the Warden's Office and Police Station have been removed from The Shackle, Yam Creek. The Post Office and Telegraph Office will also be removed to Burrundie. The new township has also been selected as the site for the Goldfields Hospital, which is now built, and will in all probability be open by January 1886 (Solomon, 1885).

Southport

In the early 1880s, Southport Telegraph Station was managed by J. W. Johnstone, who was also a justice of the peace, assistant customs officer, and coroner*. Southport was already a shadow of its former self and it was abandoned in 1889. A single hotel run by Sam Brown and three stores still operated in the centre of town. The stores were branches of Palmerston businesses: Adcock's (adjacent to the jetty), Jolly's (next to Adcock's) and J.P. Allen's (across the road). Two Chinese stores remained open along Kersley Street: Sun Mow Loong's (on lot 222) and Quong Wing Lee's, next door. Plus, there was a saddler named George Bright in Cherry Street, a blacksmith named George Gawthorn, and E. Marker, a wheelwright. On Barrow Street, the telegraph station, and the police station†, were still manned—the latter by Constable Stott. Southport Chinatown consisted of about 100 homes on the southwest side of the town, next to the Blackmore River (Duminski, 2005).

Kelsey complained that Southport was 'rather quiet' except when the steam launches from Port Darwin and the inland coaches arrived. It was livelier in the wet season, as teamsters would camp there until the roads dried out. Kelsey writes of picnics, fishing trips, and playing the accordion for the occasional dances at the hotel. There were also sporting events:

> A cricket match between the Palmerston and Southport clubs will be played at Southport on Monday next. The following teams have been selected: Palmerston eleven: Christoe, Beresford, Kemp, Linton, Marsh, McDonald, Prince, Rundle, R. M. Stow, Solomon, and Wedd. Southport eleven: Adcock, Brown, N. Byrne, W. Byrne, Benison, Cole, Field, Gawthorne, Head, Kelsey, and Luxton. Emergencies: T. Marsh, and

---

* Johnson and his wife lived in 'a nice large house & nicely furnished and a number of Chinese servants' (Creaghe 1883).

† These days the Southport community is in a rural revival. The heritage-listed ruins of the foundations of the telegraph station, the police station, and a large well, can be seen on Barrow Street.

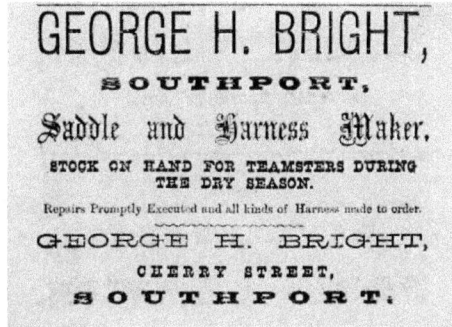

Figure 41: George Bright's advertisement in the 1886 Almanac (Solomon, 1885).

J. Turner. The steam-launch *Zulieka* has been chartered by the Palmerston Club, and will leave for Southport at six o'clock on Monday morning, returning to Palmerston the same evening (*NTTG*, 24 April 1886).

J.W. Johnstone

J.W. Johnstone, as the customs officer, collected the duties put on goods that were imported. Opium, a popular and legal drug at the time, especially among the Chinese community, attracted a high duty, so smuggling was common. One day, Johnstone questioned the large number of high heeled shoes being imported by some merchants, especially as he never saw anyone wearing them. On examination, he found they had false heels, within which was a small consignment of opium. The importers lost their product and were fined by chief customs officer, Mr Cate.

Johnstone was awake to a gold robbery in 1880. The gold, 202 ounces of it, had been stored in the Southport Post Office safe, but it had disappeared overnight. Constable Ferguson traced the theft to two Chinese men and arrested them, but Johnstone was suspicious and arranged for Constable Becker to search Ferguson's quarters. Becker found the gold and arrested Ferguson, who was sentenced to seven years gaol, some of it in irons after an attempt to escape. Kelsey said Ferguson remained in Palmerston after his sentence was complete, under an assumed name: 'He was keen on minerals; had great ability in many ways and was well-liked for many acts of kindness'. He

does not say what the assumed name was. As the only European prisoner, Ferguson led many of the building and construction tasks the prisoners were asked to do.

Dudley Kelsey was transferred back to The Shackle because the assistant who had replaced him had accidentally shot the Chinese cook when 'skylarking' about, and the man had died. Kelsey remained there for a few months until his brother got married, and in 1888, he transferred to Daly Waters Telegraph Station.

Surprise attack

The OTL Station staff were required to pass all messages that came from either direction, and the line was usually busy. The staff often could not understand the messages, as many were encrypted, and Kelsey found everyday life in the stations was monotonous. More appealing were the regular line inspections. Each station was responsible for about 200 miles of line—which was a big task, but Kelsey noted:

> … As a rule, the natives gave the linesmen no trouble, but it was necessary to be on guard constantly against treacherous, surprise attack (Kelsey, 1975).

He experienced such an attack just once, on the Ferguson River:

Figure 42: An 1885 horse team in operation (nla.obj-420571715).

… I sat with my rifle across my knee though the silent hours
[that followed] but was overcome with tiredness and fell asleep
and knew no more until hurriedly roused by [Joe] Barwis.
I saw him on his knees with his rifle poised—then he fired.
Several blacks disappeared in the long grass, fleeing towards
the river. Barwis was awakened suddenly by a feeling that all
was not right, and when he looked about, he saw the blacks
crawling towards us through the night. We looked to see if his
shot had taken effect, but couldn't find anything, but if Barwis
hadn't awakened in time, we would have been massacred
(Kelsey, 1975).

The isolated telegraph stations as far as Powell's Creek, which
is nearly 1000 kilometres from Darwin, relied on horse teams
reaching them from Port Darwin for their annual re-supply of food,
equipment, and the mailbags. The teams would take up to four
months to complete their journey, leaving after the end of the wet
season, and their arrival in the stations was the 'greatest event of the
year'. The mailbags would contain 'letters, packets and papers from
home and friends' and books, which would be read and re-read.
Stations ran their own cattle and sheep, and meat was the basis of
their diet. However, sugar, flour, rice, and salt were brought in by the
horse teams. If the stations ran out, they just had to go without.

On 14 May 1883, Emily Creaghe arrived at Powell's Creek after her exploration from Queensland with Ernest Favenc (see Chapter 17). Emily was the first white woman ever to have visited. Lindsay Crawford rode ahead to warn the staff of her approach, but no one believed them until Emily appeared. She said that the local Aborigines 'had an idea there was no such thing as a woman among white people, they thought we were all men'. She also described the house. It was made strongly, with 'high walls and no windows, as protection from the blacks' (Creaghe 1883).

Transporting goods was never without risk. The travellers often met Aborigines. Sometimes they were angry at the transgressions across their lands, or the white men would commit offences (usually over women) that required punishment. Some Aborigines would attack the Europeans with greedy intent, to steal food or other items. Creaghe pointed out that the Aborigines were terrified of men with guns because so many had been killed at different times:

> ... The S.A. government is very strict about murdering
> niggers, a man is liable to hang for it, if it is found out, so
> unless the blacks have killed cattle or sheep the white men do
> not harm them, & then they have to keep it quiet in case it
> should get to headquarters' (Creaghe, 1883).

Murder on the OTL

Another major threat to travellers was the long dry stages between water holes, especially during droughts. On 29 August 1883, a teamster named Martin was travelling south along the telegraph lines when he was murdered at Lawson's Creek, about 30 miles from Powell's Creek. Trooper Shirley followed it up and sent a telegram from Powell's Creek Station:

> ... I arrived here on Saturday and am leaving on Monday. The
> wet season has set in, and tracking is difficult. I expect to be at
> Readford's Camp, Attack Creek, on Friday, 19th inst. One of
> the natives who reported the matter is camped a short distance
> away. I shall try to secure his services as a guide. Readford had

no cattle with him at Lawson's Creek. The offenders are still travelling southwards.

Shirley went after the murderers, although he was already two months behind them, and the wet had started. He took a party of seven with him: Messrs. Allan Giles, George Phillips, John Rees, Arthur Phillips, James Hussey, and 'two blackboys'. They were last seen getting water at some crab holes, on 4 November. Every one of them, except Giles and one of the Aborigines, perished for want of water. The survivors managed to get back to the same crab holes for water on the evening of the 8th (*NTTG*, 5 Jan 1884). As soon as he could, Allan Giles wrote the story of their misadventure, not only for the newspapers but for the families of those who did not survive:

> ... I herewith beg to report particulars of the sad fate of the police search party, who all, with the exception of self and blackboy, perished for want of water, at distances ranging from 35 to 50 miles N.E. of here. All the horses also died.

> The horses were all done up on Tuesday evening, and four died during the afternoon in camp ... All the horses were done so we left them, and Shirley, G. Phillips, and the two boys proceeded on foot. I sent the boy at present with me on to bring back water from the crabholes, and Shirley sent the other ...

> On Wednesday evening I came to my senses about dark and started on tracks. Made on about three miles and was having a rest when I heard a voice calling about 200 yards from me. Went over and found poor Shirley under a little bush.

> He said that he came there to die, as he could not walk. I asked him if he knew anything of the others. He said only George, who was under a bush about 300 yards away, he thought, dead. I did not go to see, as Shirley could not go with me, and I was afraid I could not find him. Whilst we were talking, we heard a cooey [sic] and I answered it. Hussey came up. He said he had been camped close by all day but unable to come up, and that Rees and Arthur were behind somewhere, he thought dead ...

> Hussey and I decided to push on at once, and tried to persuade Shirley to come with us, but the poor fellow tried to walk and

fell, so we were compelled to shake hands, say goodbye, and leave him …We travelled on until sunrise, and could see scrub ahead of us, about two miles, when Hussey lay down. I begged of him to get up and not remain on the plain to die in the sun, but he only went about 200 yards further when he lay down again and no persuasion would induce him to move, so I was compelled to leave him under a little bush …

I made the scrub at about 8 a.m. and was then six miles from well. Managed to stagger on about two miles when I fell down and recollect no more till I was roused by boy pouring water over my head; he managed to get me along to within about two miles of camp when he left me in shade and went for more water, and I got into camp about 5 p.m. …

Started for here about 2 a.m. Saturday morning, and arrived yesterday morning about 9 o'clock, very thankful for my escape. I think the reason for my standing longer than the others is because I would not drink horse's blood, which the others did whenever a horse knocked up.

Can you kindly procure me warrants to bury bodies, and I can do so from here, and also recover some of the things, as rain has fallen yesterday and today. I could not rest easy with the thought that the poor fellows whom I have found such good mates are being torn about by dogs and birds of prey … A.M. Giles (*NTTG*, 17 November 1883).

Unfortunately, Giles was not of a mind to record the name of the 'boy', an Aboriginal man employed as a police tracker, even though he had saved his life.

Giles was ready to return and find the bodies of his companions by the next February. He was accompanied by Mounted Constable William Willshire* (1852–1925), who had come north from Alice Springs. Willshire found letters left by Mounted Constable Shirley, written when he knew he was dying:

… Returned today from eastern plains, having made a most careful search for the bodies of Rees, Hussy, and George

---

* Willshire became well known because he was the first policeman to be tried for the unlawful killing of Aborigines. He was acquitted. He also wrote a book titled *The Land of the Dawning: Being Facts Gleaned from Cannibals in the Australian Stone Age* (1896).

Phillips. Visited Shirley's grave, and discovered papers written by him stuck in a small bush near his grave, the first paper being addressed to Inspector Beasley in the following words:— 'Travelling allowance is due to me for all the time I have been out, please pay it to my mother, also give her and my sisters and brothers my dying love; I am too weak to write anymore; I died in executing my duty. (Signed) J. C. Shirley'.

On another paper addressed to Mr Michael, Barrow Creek, he says: 'Good-bye, old man, remember me to all on the line.—J. C'.

Willshire and Giles searched the area where the men were last seen, but had no luck:

> … Mr Giles, myself, and police black tracker searched one day and a half for the other bodies, but without success, as we were compelled to return to the nearest water, sixteen miles distant, our horses having been twenty-six hours without water, and ridden all the time on the burning plains. We erected black-painted crosses on Shirley and Arthur Phillips's graves, with their names and ages on… We remained at Rees Well expecting rain, so that we could continue the search, but the water dried up and we were obliged to return to Tennant's Creek … —(Signed) Mounted-constable Willshire. (*Chronicle* 23 Feb 1884).

The Kelseys

Meanwhile, back in the goldfields, Dudley Kelsey was sent to the telegraph station at the new town of Burrundie, under his brother Jack. He later worked at the Pine Creek station under J.W. Johnstone, but he returned to Burrundie to marry Miss Freeman, who was Ellen Ryan's sister. They set up home in one of the Burrundie railway cottages until 1891, and their son, Frank, was born there. The family then transferred to Darwin, where Kelsey was stationed for many years, except for some spent at Katherine Telegraph Station. Dudley Kelsey finally left the Territory to return to South Australia in 1901. He worked as a telegraph officer in the Adelaide office for the next 17 years. He retired to a vineyard at Watervale where his family looked after Ellen Ryan as an invalid, in her dotage. Mrs Ryan died in 1920,

Figure 43: Burrundie Railway Station, now deserted. There are few remnants of the town visible today.

and Dudley Kelsey in 1953, aged 88-years. His memoir was published by Ira Nesdale in 1975.

Jack Kelsey remained an employee of the telegraph and the railway companies and worked in various stations for 33 years. He was managing Pine Creek Telegraph Station throughout the late 1890s. His name appears as a justice of the peace and a coroner in various death certificates from the time. Jack eventually fell ill and took leave to seek better health in Adelaide on 12 March 1906. Unfortunately, he did not make it:

> … On the day the steamer left, Mr Kelsey looked so wretchedly ill and weak that many of his friends—who had gone on board to bid him good-bye—were impressed with the belief that he would never live to reach Adelaide, and as is known, this fear proved to be only too correct.…
>
> After leaving Thursday Island on the 15th March 1906, a change was noticed in Mr Kelsey's condition and his desire was to be on deck.… At midnight on the 15th the doctor was called, and the patient passed away at 5 o'clock on the morning of the 16th, being quite conscious almost until the time of death.…
>
> The first boat, conveying the Chief Officer, Purser, and men,

Figure 44: The remaining well at Burrundie.

first left the ship to prepare the grave…. A white azalea was also placed in the boat to decorate the grave. As this boat left the ship the ship's bell was tolled, and the flags were hoisted half-mast. On reaching the island the body was conveyed to the grave.

The cross was erected, and the mound covered with creeping plants, relieved by the white azalea. This cross can be seen distinctly from the deck of steamers passing in close proximity to the island. A more picturesque and suitable spot could not have been selected for the last resting place of our respected and esteemed late friend (*NTTG*, 20 April 1906).

Burrundie

Of the town of Burrundie, there is little to mark its existence these days: the remnants of the railway platform, a well, an explosives bunker, and a small concrete floor mark where the police 'cells' were—complete with metal rings through which prisoners' chains were locked. Outside the town, on the road to Mount Wells, lies the Burrundie Cemetery, with two fenced-in gravestones marking the last resting place of three of the town's residents: Ruth Beckwick, who died of amoebic dysentery, was the six-year-old daughter of Ralph

Figure 45: Burrundie Cemetery, the grave of G.E. Fitts, and R. Murray
1893.

Beckwick, the stationmaster: George Fitts, post, telegraph, and station master, aged 33, died of consumption, six months after arriving in Burrundie; and Robert Murray, a 43-year-old post and telegraph master from the Katherine station. Apart from these three, all other occupants of the cemetery remain in unmarked graves, hidden in the bush.

All this belies the success of life in the new railway town, at least for a few years. There was, for example, the Burrundie Turf Club, with races such as the 'Railway Stakes Handicap' and the 'Burrundie Cup'. It was formed in August 1888, with John Parsons as its patron, Gold Warden Charles Nash as president, and George Deane as the secretary. Punters would travel by train for a day of racing entertainment, although the complaint was that they were the same horses—with the same odds—that they saw at home in the Palmerston races.

Burrundie was substantial enough for a family to remain living there for years. Jean Buscall grew up there in the 1920s. In 1929, her family had not visited Darwin for six years, and they, at last, took a holiday there, by train, in 1929. Her letter to the *Weekly Times* described the trip from Burrundie to the capital:

… We caught the train at 9.30 a.m. from Burrundie, and
passing through Grove Hill, Fountain Head, Brock's Creek
and Howley, we arrived at Adelaide River at 12.30 p.m., where
the train stops for an hour while all the passengers have lunch.
We then continued our Journey past Stapleton, Batchelor
(late Government Experimental Farm), Rum Jungle, 46
Miles, Darwin River, 20 Miles, 10 Miles, 2½ Mile, arriving at
Darwin at 5.15, where a friend of ours met us with his motor
car, and we were driven to the Victoria Hotel, where we stayed
while in Darwin. We had not been to Darwin for six years,
so we were quite anxious to get about as much as possible
(Buscall, 28 December 1929).

Figure 46: Members of the parliamentary party who visited the Northern
Territory in 1882: from the left: Josiah Howell Bagster, Luke Turner, John
Langdon Parsons, Henry E. Bright, and Professor Ralph Tate
(SLSA B-5881).

Chapter 4

The South Australian parliamentary visit of 1882

In January 1882, the South Australian Minister for Education, John Langdon Parsons, led a three-month exploratory expedition to Palmerston and the goldfields. Parsons was accompanied by three members of parliament and Professor Ralph Tate, the Professor of Natural Sciences at the University of Adelaide.

> ... The object of the visit, briefly stated, is to enquire as far as possible into the present actual state of the Territory, to mark as far as practicable its mineral and other resources, and to note its present and probable future requirements in the way of public works, and such other matters which it is the province of the Government to see carefully attended to ...

The long, hot, Adelaide summer gave the party no inclination of what they were about to experience during the Top End's wet season, but Gilbert McMinn, who arrived in Adelaide on leave in time to offer advice, suggested that they would have no trouble travelling on horseback, as long as the Adelaide River, which is crossed 90 kilometres south of Port Darwin, was not in flood. In the end, one of the M.P.s, Henry Bright, who was a 'portly' man weighing about 110 kilograms, took one look at the river (which was not in flood), and taking the wiser path, returned to Palmerston, after just a day or two on the road.

A journalist from the *South Australian Register*, William Sowden, travelled with the minister. He had joined the paper in 1881 and quickly became the *Register*'s leading parliamentary reporter (Bridge, 1990). Through his lively reports, which were syndicated in all the major papers, the southern population learned exactly what the expedition got up to, and much of the gossip they heard on the way. Sowden later collated the reports in a book, *The Northern Territory As It Is* (Sowden, 1882). He was a clever writer, and he was happy to add a little sensationalism to his articles: for instance, his European readers must have breathed a collective sigh of relief to learn that the cannibals of Papua preferred to roast Chinese men because Europeans tasted too much like tobacco.

The expedition was well organised and ably supported by Government Resident Edward Price, Inspector Foelsche, the surveyor David Lindsay, and the gold warden, John Knight.

The *Menmuir*

The expeditioners were lucky to arrive. Travelling north from Sydney on the steam ship *Menmuir*, they ran into cyclonic weather which nearly sent them to a watery grave. For three days they were battered by high waves and furious winds. Gripping to the walls of his bunk, Sowden 'cogitated on the form their obituaries would appear', especially when the engine stopped for a time. One of the ship's boats was washed off the deck and had to be cut loose. In the process of letting it go, the chief officer was dragged overboard. But, fortunately for him; 'instantly a big wave came and washed him back close to the gunwale, and just as it was retreating, a seaman on the deck grasped him by the heel and pulled him in' (Sowden, 1882).

They were all much relieved when the *Menmuir* reached the calm waters of the Barrier Passage, and no further incidents marred their journey. Of interest was a stop at the uninhabited Booby Island, which had long been a 'post-office' where ships would leave messages or mail, and emergency supplies for ship-wrecked sailors. Many lives were saved in the early days, but since then, wrote Sowden, 'natives from the islands, as well as unprincipled Europeans, were in the habit of stealing the food so charitably left', and the Torres Strait Post Office ceased to be.

A few days later the ship sailed past the Tiwi Islands, and Sowden wrote about them in a way that demonstrates the European Australians' attitude towards the land and its original inhabitants. He described the islands at length because:

> … they are absolutely unproductive bits of South Australian Territory, supporting no one but the swarming tribe of blacks… the island is overrun with them, and they are as fierce as the bulky mosquitoes that congregate in the thick mangrove-lined coasts… The hostile Melville natives had better make the most of their opportunities; ere long we shall have to civilise them… (Sowden, 1882).

The *Menmuir* arrived in Port Darwin on 21 February 1882. The minister was warmly received by Government Resident Price, who joined the party on board the ship for their farewell banquet, where Captain Ellis was awarded a bag of sovereigns as thanks for his excellent seamanship.

In Palmerston the next day, the party sat through speeches of welcome from the leading members of the community: 'Messrs. P.R. Allen, Joseph Skelton, V.L. Solomon, Jas. Pickford, and J.G. Kelsey'. They then spent several days readying themselves for the overland section of their expedition, and on 23 February, they boarded a steam launch and motored up the Blackmore River to Southport, accompanied by John Knight and David Lindsay.

Southport, a commonplace little village

Travelling through the mangroves, the party speculated on the future. Sowden could see a time when 'the smoke of factories should begrime the scores of thousands of toiling mechanics'… (Sowden, 1882). He was not impressed with Southport. It was a small thriving township which 'would ever be the port of shipment for the south-western hundreds'. There was a telegraph office, a police station, a smithy, a saddlery, a cemetery, two public houses and branches of all the major importing businesses based in Palmerston. The population, said Sowden, included about 30 Europeans, more than a hundred Chinese people, and many Woolwonga and Larrakeeyah [sic] people*.

Chinese gardeners grew vegetables, and fishermen caught rock-cod and bream to sell in one of the 12 Chinese stores. There was neither a church nor a schoolhouse, but sly grog shanties abounded. Southport was, according to Sowden, a 'dull, shambling, dingy, fifth-class, disordered, commonplace little village'. However, he expected it would come into its own during the dry season, as through its port moved all the miners and mining equipment needed on the inland goldfields.

Travelling the goldfields

David Lindsay organised horses for the party. There were 22 of them: 'knock-kneed and lame, and bruised and spavined, and flea bitten...' but they were the best that were available. The party set off under heavy grey skies on 24 February and spent much of the next three weeks either broiling under the tropical sun or soaking wet in heavy rains.

Their first stop was Tumbling Waters, where a small gold mine—that had started with good prospects a few years earlier—now lay abandoned. Then on to Collett's Creek Hotel for lunch. The hotelier, R.E. Holmes, had recently been murdered here 'for too great attention to a lubra'. Nevertheless, Sowden thought the food was adequate—Collett's Creek had a flourishing Chinese garden, growing all sorts of vegetables.

As they travelled on, they stayed most nights in public houses that were scattered throughout the mining areas. They were 'a mockery of accommodation', but dry at least. They included the

* This is at odds with the 1881 census, which counted 92 Europeans and 209 Chinese at Southport.

hotels at Rum Jungle, The Shackle, Paqualan's Hump, Pine Creek, and Stapleton. They followed muddy roads that were difficult to pass on horseback, but almost impossible with a dray. They met six Chinese men travelling with five horses and a lightly loaded dray who had taken six days to travel 36 miles from Southport—and all they were carting was about 'eight hundredweight of rice.'

The incipient township of Stapleton

In the 'incipient township of Stapleton', the Professor of Natural Sciences, Ralph Tate, was excited to discover a type of tall bamboo he claimed was undiscovered. Stapleton had the only fenced cemetery on the goldfields, which was under water during the party's visit. They discovered that dead miners were called 'worm banquets' by the residents, and they were buried without fanfare or religious ceremony.

Stapleton Creek marked the beginning of the goldfields, but by 1882 many of the early mines had already petered out, and miners had moved on—or died. They passed mines called Virginia, Dean's Mine, and Terrible, on the way to Adelaide River, where there was a small public house on the south bank. Sowden correctly prophesied that the place would become the most important along the route of any future railway line.

The 'portly' Henry Bright, M.P., already exhausted by the journey, turned back to Palmerston at this point*. The party continued without him. Whilst most accommodation was in the goldfields' hotels, on at least one occasion they camped in an abandoned hut on the side of the road. They called in at each mine they passed, and the minister interviewed every miner he met.

---

* Parsons later entertained The House at Bright's expense: 'As we endured one little trouble after another—passed through one morass after another, and endured the pelting rain—and as we thought of those timorous ones who promised to go with us and then turned back, we thought that when they read the account of our experiences, those gentlemen would hold their manhood cheap when anyone spoke who had been to the Northern Territory (Laughter, and hear, hear.)' (Parsons, 23 September 1882).

Figure 47: The Virginia Mine in 1880 (Foelsche, LANT, ph0347-0006).

They saw the Chinese miners at Bridge Creek, where 37 out of 90 miners were struck down by malaria soon after the township had been settled. It was a 'slow, intermittent, prostrating affection'. Many of them had already died, and 'even the strongest man in the place [had] lustreless eyes floating in a sea of yellow' (Sowden, 1882).

Bridge Creek Hotel was owned by John W. Murch and his wife Emma*, and they too would die within the year. Emma, who was not home when the party visited, was one of the few women to live on the goldfields in 1882. Sowden had seen only two white women since they had left Palmerston.

Port Darwin Camp

The party's next major destination was the Port Darwin Camp—via the Howley, Margaret Creek, Yam Creek, Sailor's Gully, and Stuart's

---

* Both John and Emma Murch died in the hotel during 1883 (Emma on 9 August and John in September). Their deaths were not suspicious, so there was no inquest. Their personal effects, including jewellery, household effects, plates, cutlery, pictures, and dress material, reached 'good prices' at the intestate auction held in March 1884 in the hotel (North Australian, March 1884). Emily Creaghe arrived the day Emma died and mentioned in her diary that several were people making her coffin.

Map 5: A section of Professor Tate's map of the goldfields, showing the telegraph line, The Shackle and Yam Creek (nla.obj-231439653-1).

Gully mines. Professor Tate collected plants and insects everywhere they went and even found 'genuine pre-Adamite flint fossils' when bathing in the 12-Mile Creek. Tate preserved 99 different plants on the trip and sent them to both Adelaide and the Victorian Botanic

Gardens, and Kew Gardens in London. One of them, a small herb from near the 12-Mile Camp on the McKinlay River, was new to science and was named *Clerodendrum tatei,* after the Professor (RBGV, 1982).

Port Darwin Camp was large enough to boast a justice of the peace, and a 'medical attendant' who cared for patients among a string of Chinese-owned shops, a Chinese temple, and a 'homely' public house. One afternoon a group of about 50 Woolwonga men performed a corroboree in honour of Minister Parsons, then participated in running races and spear throwing competitions.

Chinese on the Union

The Union claim, near the town of Pine Creek, was said to be over the richest gold-bearing land in the region, but both were in serious decline in 1882. This is where an industrious Chinese miner and leader named Ping Que had come during the 1870s, directly from the goldfields in Victoria. He had quickly claimed or bought up mining leases and, as the alluvial gold was mostly discovered and removed, had turned to reef mining, where gold was extracted using a battery (gold was removed from pulverised ore that was 'battered' to dust). When the parliamentary party arrived, about 80 Chinese men were still on the Union: the 'surface-scratching' miners had moved on. The ground was riddled with mines, and riding horses across it needed great care.

Dead and dying miners

As in Bridge Creek, many miners had died on the goldfields during the epidemic of 1880, and men continued to fall sick and die. Getting rid of the bodies was a never-ending problem:

> ... This country—which has been pretty thoroughly turned over—was once the scene of races between the troopers and the Chinamen. The former would find a corpse lying neglected on the diggings and would chase the reputed relatives and compel them to take charge of the body of the deceased. But if they got hold of the wrong man, and could not quit their

unsavoury find, they would take it up and place it in the
centre of the gambling house… (Sowden, 1882).

The Europeans continually complained about Chinese corpses.
The Chinese did not bury their dead respectfully, they said, and often
not at all. Most Chinese preferred to let their friends and relatives
decompose quickly, so they could gather the bones and take them back
to China or bury them in a 'lucky place'. The lack of understanding
of this cultural practice meant it was another source of complaint
from the Europeans about the 'Celestials'. The latter did not want
to be buried deep in the ground if they died, they wanted their
bones cleaned and transported. And even then, there were further
complaints—some men were accused of smuggling gold out of the
country in the skulls of their dead mates (Cross J., 2011).

Batteries

The 10-head Pine Creek Battery and, nearby, a 14-head battery
known as 'The Standard', had been recently bought by a Mr Jansen,
for £2,000, from the Telegraph Company—which was a considerable
discount from the original costs of about £15,000. Mr Jansen, the
batteries' happy new owner, was now increasingly rich, crushing the
ore from his mine, the Eleanor, and from charging other miners for
its use. The batteries employed Chinese workers who would work for
£2 per week for an 8-hour daily shift. The few Europeans who worked
in the area were paid £5 per week.

The Parliamentary Party were stymied from travelling further
south by the flooding of the Ferguson River. In fact, the floods were
so bad that the minister telegraphed Adelaide with the news that:

> … at Pine Creek, Mr Sowden had a narrow escape from being
> drowned. Coming back from Jansen's, he was washed off his
> horse and had to hang on to a tree until the creek went down
> (Parsons, 8 March 1882).

Instead, the party toured the western goldfields area, passing the
Union Mine. They met John Noltenius and John Landers and their

partners in the Extended Mine. There was no forewarning that these gentlemen would later take up copper mining at the Daly River Mine and be murdered.

The travellers spent a Saturday night and a Sunday at the 12-Mile and witnessed how the miners spent their rest day:

> ... In the morning, a rifle match took place, the while a smith shod some horses. Then quoits were thrown in one or two cases by inebriated men. In the evening most of the residents of the place gathered in a little cottage not far from the quarters of the Ministerial party and carried on a drunken orgy all through the night and into the early hours of the Monday morning. The language used would put an irate trooper to the blush. Every third word was the sanguinary adjective, and a sentence of ten syllables I heard garnished with six expletives (Sowden, 1882).

Tin and copper had been discovered near Bamboo Creek, and several mines were in their early days of development. A Mr Walker* and Mr Tennant had already dug a 10-foot hole in a creek bed and, although the Minister was dubious, were confident of success.

The party turned back to the Port Darwin Camp from there and travelled via Mount Wells, Lorance's Creek and Spring Hill. They visited Manuel's Gully, Arnheim, Pay-Me-Well, New Era, the North-East Clifton Mines, and a dozen other sites whose names have slipped from the Territory's memory. As they passed, the Parliamentary Party even had a new mine named after them—The Parliamentary!

Near Mount Wells, John Knight nearly met his end when he was knocked from his horse by a tree branch:

> ... Mr Knight rode fifteen stone, and did not fall a feather weight, and a staved-in helmet and a scalp wound testified to the providential nature of the escape... (Sowden, 1882).

Northern Territory history would have taken a different route if John Knight had not survived.

---

* The remains of the Bamboo Creek Mine and Walkers Creek are popular sites to visit in Litchfield National Park.

Alluvial mining

In 1877, huge numbers of Chinese miners had rushed to a gold discovery at Margaret Creek. For a few years, it became the centre of alluvial mining by the Chinese:

> ... Matters are remarkably quiet on the new rush. The European population is getting smaller gradually. They have satisfied themselves that there is no use sinking deep holes down the flat, and a good many have left for other places where they are certain of getting a little gold. The McKinlay, I think, is the favorite, and between here and there any amount of auriferous country untried. Nuggety ground was never a poor man's diggings, as fine gold is not evenly distributed in it, and the chance of a prize stands at long odds. The Chinese are still drawing a few in the lottery, but the average yield of gold is said by the Chinese bosses to be falling off. They are not, however, always to be depended on for truth, and the coolie miners are becoming careful about divulging their returns. A miner found a nugget on Saturday morning, but neither the police nor your correspondent could ascertain its weight. A storekeeper, however, towards evening informed me that it weighed between fifty and sixty ounces clean (*NTTG*, 10 August 1880).
>
> ... Big nuggets, some as heavy as 25 lb. and more, were got from an average depth of 4 feet. About 2000 Chinamen were at work... (Sowden, 1882).

By 1882, most of these men had gone, but the nearby claim of Port Darwin Camp at Grove Hill was now being mined by Quong Wing Chong. In Sowden's opinion, Chong was second to the 'great' Ping Que on the goldfields. Ping Que also had a mine nearby, worked by three men, and the parliamentary party were told that they had recently taken £500 worth of gold out of a single bucket.

The Shackle's last legs

Returning to The Shackle, the party rested for a day or two. The Shackle was on its 'last legs—and feeble, tottering shanks' they were too, according to Sowden.

Figure 48: The Miners Hospital at The Shackle in 1879. It was built by John Knight and partly funded by Ping Que (Foelsche, LANT, PH0111-0026).

Aside from the telegraph repeater station, there was a small building that held a magistrate's court, and when John Knight lived there as the gold warden, he built a hospital, mostly at his own expense but, since his departure, the hospital and all the other buildings had been slowly turned to dust by the termites. Many of the huts were made of little more than bark and grass, and these disappeared very quickly.

The police station was still manned. Sowden was impressed by Corporal Montagu: he described him as a 'right good corporal'*.

Many more mines were mentioned by Sowden in his book. Some were household names in the 1880s, such as Princess Louise, John Bull, and Fountain Head. The latter was opened by the Honourable Thomas Reynolds, but he drowned in 1875, in the *Gothenburg* disaster—dragged to the bottom by the weight of gold in his belt. Reynolds had tilted his lance at the government resident's job whilst

---

* When Montagu later appears in this book, readers may conclude that there was little 'right or good' about him ...

Figure 49: Brock's Creek Gold Mine, 1887 (Foelsche, SLSA B9760).

still an MP, but there was something shifty about him and he never stood a chance (Pugh, 2019).

The government resident who Reynolds wanted to replace was Captain Bloomfield Douglas, who threw it all in any way in 1873, to join the gold rush himself. The 1882 Parliamentary Party passed by Douglas's Hill, where the captain dabbled for 12 months to little avail, before returning to Adelaide.

Brock's Creek

They stayed overnight at Brock's Creek Hotel and dined on the ubiquitous pork and chicken, but also on 'native companions' (brolgas) with its 'flavour of stewed mackintosh.'

Brocks Creek Mine was named after William Brock, an overseer for the telegraph line construction party, who discovered gold there in 1870. By 1885, Brocks Creek was a Chinese township of 400 men, with bark and grass huts, the 'Kwang Sing Di' temple, and market gardens.

93

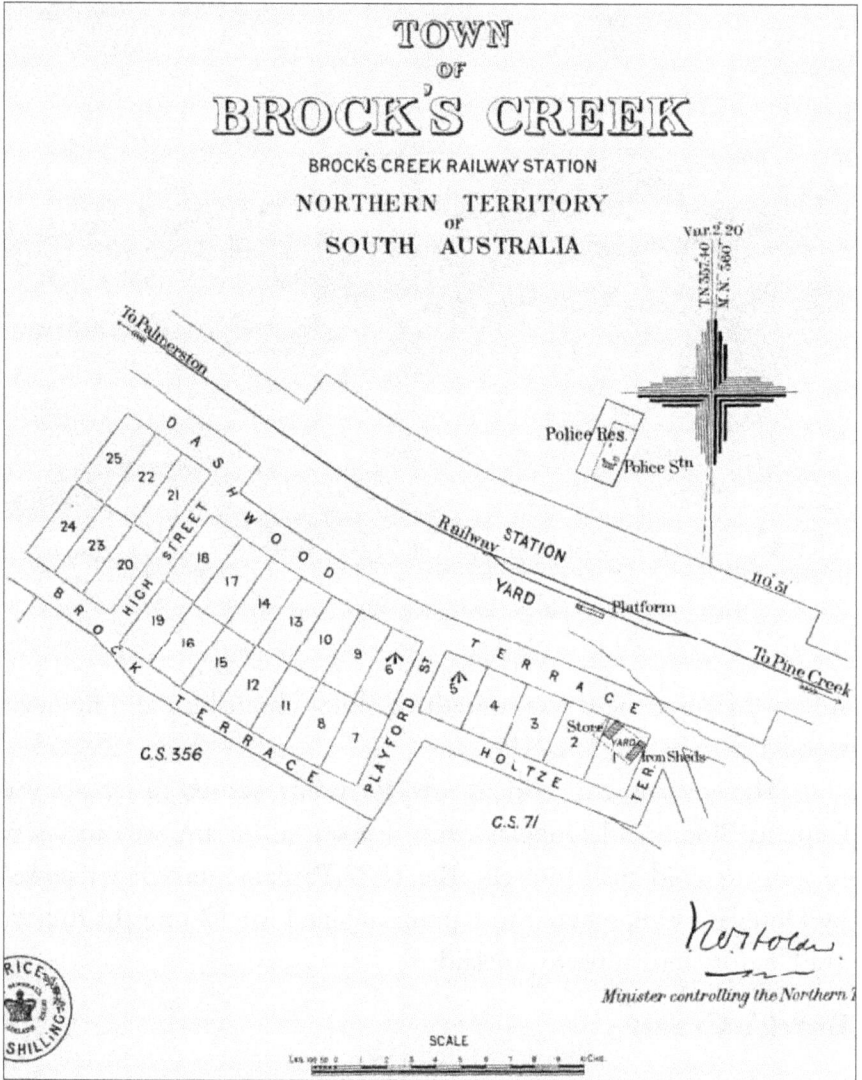

Map 6: Brocks Creek, N.T., in 1898.

The temple was guarded by two stone lions brought especially from China. Unfortunately, they could do little to protect the town: in 1895 there were still five stores trading, but the population had shrunk to 280. Then, in November 1895, much of the settlement was destroyed by fire, and most residents moved to other diggings.

A few struggled on, and several elderly Chinese men were still living there in the 1940s. However, after Darwin was bombed in 1942, they were evacuated south (Pearce & Alford, 2016). The town closed and the lions, which still stood at the temple entrance, were collected by soldiers as mascots for the army camps. One eventually became a garden ornament in nearby Tipperary Station homestead. Fortunately, they were recognised after the war and brought together again in Darwin. They now stand at the doors of the Chinese Temple* in Woods Street, Darwin, guarding once again.

Cheap labour

The party slowly made its way back to Palmerston via Rum Jungle (Batchelor). They visited the 'magnificent estate' of Poett, MacKinnon and Co's coffee plantation (Sowden, 1882), where the managers were planning to import a group of Tamil labourers from Ceylon because they believed they would work for two shillings a week. The £1 per week they were currently paying to their six Chinese employees was too high a price. Worse, Chinese carpenters could demand £3 10s per week! Unfortunately, within three years, the 400,000 coffee plant seedlings were dead, the shareholders abandoned the business, and the company closed.

The rates of pay for imported labourers was a common topic of discussion in 1882. The sugar plantations of Queensland needed labour too. Government Resident Price wrote, almost enviously, about their solutions:

> … Mr Bass, of Bundaberg, was in possession of written offers from Indian merchants to procure experienced agricultural labourers at a cost of £16 for passage and a wage of 22s. per month for a five years' agreement. The meeting generally was of opinion that Polynesian labour is more acceptable; and it was suggested that a Joint-stock Company should be formed for systematic recruiting, especially at the Solomon Islands, by means of two steamers, one of these to be employed solely

---

* The temple is known as 'Hall of the Ranking Sages'.

Figure 50: Henry Poett's coffee plantation, Rum Jungle, 1883
(LANT ph0002-0047)

at the islands, and the other to be engaged in quick trips to
Maryborough… There is an impression among some of our
largest employers of black labour that the coolies would not be
tractable, and that on account of their caste prejudices in the
matter of food the cost would not be much less than that of
European labour (Price, 4 January 1882).

As the parliamentary party returned to Southport, each
reviewed what they had learned. The Minister and the M.P.s had
enjoyed hundreds of meetings with mine-owners, business operators
and government employees. Professor Tate had made the most of his
time and collected a huge number of biological specimens to ship
to Adelaide. William Sowden was well-sourced in material for his
articles. He concluded:

> … For legitimate enterprises, and for well-directed speculation,
> there is no better field that the Northern Territory presents, and
> granted a railway, I warrant that our reviving white elephant will
> soon develop into one of the most useful animals any colony
> could wish to be blessed with (Sowden, 1882).

Professor Tate reported that the development of the ore bodies was still in its infancy*. He also concluded a railway was needed to 'cheapen carriage and make the country accessible to mining and other speculators'. The Professor joined the others in the call for cheap labour:

> ... To reduce the working expenses of our gold mines, it is imperative that we employ cheaper labour—that of Chinese or negroes. (Sowden, 1882).

Minister Parsons was most impressed by what he saw. He expressed his opinion to the Government in Adelaide with:

> ... some degree of confidence... that at last, after many years of despondency and discouragement, the colony of South Australia might congratulate herself that she had really turned the corner of difficulty, and might look forward in the future to carrying on the government of the Northern Territory without the necessity of incurring fresh loans for the purposes of government...

and:

> ... Whilst this is a source of great satisfaction to the Ministry; and to myself in particular, I believe it is a satisfaction which is shared in and felt to the very fullest degree by every member of this House... (23 September 1882).

Minister Parsons became one of the staunchest supporters of the Territory, particularly for the building of a railway line. In fact, it was he who introduced the Palmerston and Pine Creek Railway Bill to the Legislative Assembly†, on 17 July 1884. Two years later, after he was appointed the Government Resident of the Northern Territory, the railway was built on his watch.

---

*   Professor Tate's report was published as an appendix to Sowden's book, *The Northern Territory: the way it is*, in 1882.

†   Oddly, the bill was opposed by Mr Bright, who was the MP who turned back from Adelaide River when the journey became too physically demanding for him.

Darwin: Growth of a City

Chapter 5
Gilbert Rotherdale McMinn

Gilbert Rotherdale McMinn (1841–1924) arrived in Adelaide as a nine-year-old in 1850. After school, he was trained as a surveyor. However, in 1864, he joined the First Northern Territory Expedition as a labourer, on a salary of five shillings a day. Despite his qualifications, he went to Escape Cliffs for adventure and to join his brother, William, while hoping to win a position as a surveyor. When he did, his salary jumped to 16 shillings 6 pence per day. McMinn then worked at Escape Cliffs under James Manton until the expedition was recalled. In 1866, he returned north with George Goyder as a first-class surveyor and assisted with laying out the new town of Palmerston. He remained there in 1870 and became surveyor-in-charge of several of the central sections of the Overland Telegraph Line, from Marchant Springs to the Alice River. He also had a role in the building of Alice Springs Telegraph Station.

Figure 51: Gilbert Rotherdale McMinn (SLSA B10363).

In 1873, McMinn was appointed senior surveyor and supervisor of works for the Northern Territory on a salary of £350 p.a. He was, therefore, the senior civil servant to welcome George Scott as he arrived to take over as Government Resident in 1873, and it was he who toasted 'The Various Interests of the Territory' at Edward Price's welcome dinner in 1876.

McMinn was interested in all aspects of Territory life. It is to him we owe the fact that Government House still retains its original stone walls, built by Tuckwell and Ryan in 1870, because McMinn convinced John Knight to leave them in his 1878 renovation. Knight wrote of it in a letter:

> … The only remains of the former building will be the largest room, which, being of stone, was left standing. The rooms, although few, are large, and in case any future Resident required a greater number of rooms, can be divided by a wooden partition without any alteration being required to doors or windows (Knight 1878).

Tragedy struck for the McMinn family on Christmas Day, 1880 when Mrs Anna McMinn unexpectedly lost her life:

> … It is with unfeigned regret that we have, at the commencement of the New Year, to announce the death of Mrs McMinn, the wife of our esteemed friend, the Acting Government Resident, who departed this life on Christmas night, at the early age of twenty-seven. Her loss will be keenly felt by those who knew her, as one of those kindly, unassuming women so rare in our midst. Four days before her death, hopes were entertained of her recovery; but it was not to be. She rapidly faded away, leaving her husband and two young children to deplore her loss. The funeral took place on the following day when the majority of our townspeople wended their way to the cemetery to pay their last tribute of respect to her memory (*NTTG*, 1 January 1881).

Anna (nee Gore) and Gilbert had already lost a son, William, aged 7 months, in 1878. Eventually, McMinn fathered at least eight children: he had five more with his second wife, Madge Marsh (aka Fleetwood-Marsh) whom he married in November 1884.

McMinn got on well with Government Resident Price and stood in for him in Palmerston whenever he was absent. Price's appointment coincided with an economic boom right across South

Australia, and in 1884, he 'left a more prosperous region and a decidedly more contented community than the one he had joined eight years previously' (de la Rue 2004). The 1880s saw the pastoral industry emerge and it looked like it would become the backbone of the Northern Territory economy. Cattlemen were the pioneers of settlement throughout the interior. It was in this atmosphere that Price resigned and handed the reigns, temporarily, to Gilbert McMinn.

Acting Government Resident McMinn

McMinn stepped in as the acting Government Resident in March 1883, and he stayed in the job for 14 months. He is given credit for building the old courthouse, cell block, and police station on the Esplanade. At the same time, several businesses built expansive premises in Mitchell and Smith Streets, and the names of Jolly and Luxton, Adcock, and Allen & Co, and others, went up in big letters on their street facades. Mr O'Connor built a soft-drink factory in Smith Street, and both the Family and Exchange Hotels were rebuilt before they collapsed from termite damage. Then pearl shell was discovered in the harbour, and McMinn oversaw the beginning of a whole new industry. Pearl shell (for buttons) was followed by pearl fishing (for pearls), and the crocodile and buffalo leather industries. As Government Resident Price had advised him, it was this broadening of the range of industries that would ensure the Territory's future. It is a process that continues today.

As was tradition, in May 1884 there was a banquet held by the community leaders to farewell McMinn at the end of his time in the position and to welcome Parsons. The job of toasting the outgoing Government Resident fell to Councillor J. C. Millson:

> … Mr Chairman, Mr Vice-chairman, and Gentlemen.
> The toast which I have to propose is that of our late Acting Government Resident, Mr G. R. McMinn. I am sure that everyone in the room is well acquainted with the doings of Mr McMinn during the time that he has occupied the responsible position of Acting Government Resident so that there is no need for me to enlarge upon them tonight … The bulk of you

have been in the Territory since he took office, and I am sure
I embrace your thoughts when I say that he has earned the
esteem and respect of all (hear here.) Socially, I do not think
that anyone could speak more highly of Mr McMinn than
myself. I think the least we can do is to give him every honour
tonight (hear, hear) … (*North Australian*, 16 May 1884).

McMinn then replied, and downplayed the rumours that he
was upset about being overlooked for the role more permanently,
especially since he already had a high opinion of John Langdon
Parsons:

> … Whatever good qualities you may give me credit for
> possessing, you would certainly never give me credit for
> being a good public speaker on an occasion like this. During
> the fourteen months of my administration here I have
> endeavoured to do what was right and beneficial to the
> interests of the country, and I leave it to you to say whether
> or not I have succeeded. There was a statement going about
> concerning myself which I wished to correct, and that was that
> I intended leaving the service on account of the appointment
> of Mr Parsons. It is so far from being a fact that immediately
> on my hearing of the appointment, I wrote to Mr Parsons
> telling him how glad I was, and also telling him that he would
> be welcomed here by all. I feel proud of being associated here
> with men like Mr Parsons, and if called upon at any future
> time to fill the position I have just vacated, I would do so with
> pleasure. I thank you all for the leniency and courtesy shown
> towards me since I came into the office of Acting Government
> Resident (*North Australian*, 16 May 1884).

McMinn remained on salary as the senior surveyor in the
Territory and was a justice of the peace. But, as a senior civil servant,
he appears to have become a 'spare wheel' in Palmerston, and an
expensive one at that.

The South Australian Government was entering a recession,
and the Northern Territory salary costs needed trimming. The survey
department budget was cut by £1,250; the government cutter, the S.S.
Palmerston was sold; civil servants lost their professional allowances;
and Dr Morice, Protector of Aborigines, was retrenched.

At the same time, the expanding pastoral industry needed a resource town in the gulf country, and the town of Borroloola was established in 1885, following the explorations of Ernest Favenc.

Gilbert McMinn was given the option of either resigning or becoming the first special magistrate in the new town—at a reduced salary of £550 per annum. He took the latter option and worked in the Territory for a further five years.

He left the Northern Territory with Madge and their children in 1890 and lived his final decades in South Australia and Victoria.

His career of more than twenty-five years in the north was remarkable—he was among the first surveyors to arrive, had surveyed much of the Palmerston area in 1869, as well as the central section of the Overland Telegraph Line (he was the first European to discover Simpson's Gap, through which he ran the line).

McMinn died from heart failure in St. Kilda on 18 October 1924, aged eighty-three. (ADB, 1967).

Chapter 6
Drovers

The overland route first taken by Ludwig Leichhardt across Queensland into the Northern Territory in the 1840s was followed by other men, who pushed mobs of cattle and horses westward towards new pastures. They were called drovers. They quickly became larger than life characters of Australian folk stories, songs, and bush poetry, when they were heralded by Banjo Patterson, Henry Lawson, C.J. Dennis, and others. Australians in 'dusty dirty cities' soon dreamed of the 'sunlit plains extended,' and the iconic Australian bushmen became a part of the Australian psyche.

The overland routes through western Queensland and north from South Australia were soon well-trodden. Droves consisting of thousands of sheep and cattle were pushed across the country to feed a growing population. First in was Ralph Milner, who brought 2,000 sheep north from South Australia to feed the work crews constructing the Overland Telegraph Line in 1870 (Rose, 1964).

The first horses and cattle were brought from Burketown in Queensland by Dillan Cox and his overseer, Darcy Uhr, in 1872, although they lost most of the horses in the bush near the Roper River. Cox planned to sell the cattle in the goldfields and breed the horses for military use in India, and he drove the animals to Palmerston.

On 27 October 1872, Cox applied for a pastoral lease on the land then called Douglas Peninsula, but now known as Cox Peninsula. The application was never ratified, but Cox ran his station, Bowerlee, unofficially until his early death. This was caused by a stab wound, given to him by a nephew in a fight.

The second cattle drove arrived in Palmerston on 19 October 1874. George de Latour brought them overland from Townsville and yarded them at Knuckey's Lagoon, about 20 kilometres from Port Darwin. They were then sold for meat at more than £20 a head and none were left to breed and establish a local cattle industry. On his overland return to Queensland, de Latour picked up a 'large mob of horses', which were probably those lost by Cox, and sold them in Normanton. He then returned to the Limmen-Bright region to look for more horses*.

Mr de Latour was interviewed in depth by the *Brisbane Courier*, about his knowledge of Port Darwin and the country he crossed (20 November 1876). His descriptions were wide-ranging and positive, though he was not impressed by the hotels: 'The less said about the hotels the better' he said, 'their appearance, accommodation, and general management not being worthy of commendation'.

The early drovers shot their way through any resistance in the Aboriginal lands they crossed and established droving routes that were used for decades to transport animals across the country. Others developed routes further west, to Western Australia, and became the pioneers of the Kimberley region.

The first cattle stations

The first cattle station formed was by Travers and Gibson, called Glencoe Station, with Mr Burkitt as its manager. James Warby brought in the first cattle in 1879, following the overland route used by D'Arcy Uhr, and Nat Buchannan brought in more a few months later. Glencoe Station was close to Yam Creek and the goldfields, and a ready market was found for any meat that was produced.

---

* George de Latour and his son were both murdered in New Hebrides in 1913, and 'the body of the son was taken away and eaten, amidst great rejoicing' (*Sydney Morning Herald*, 13 October 1913).

Figure 52: Glencoe Cattle Station (now called Delamere Station) (Foelsche, 1883 SLSA B 46806).

Figure 53: Springvale Station on the Katherine River (SLSA B-10129).

Springvale Station, on the Katherine River, was owned by Dr W.J. Browne, a retired pastoralist from South Australia. In June 1879, it was established by Arthur Giles, and his brother, the Overland Telegraph Line explorer, Alfred Giles. Alfred was married to Mary Augusta Giles, the first woman to settle on a pastoral property in the Northern Territory (James, 1995). Alfred Giles brought 12,000 sheep from the Flinders Ranges by following the Overland Telegraph Line, and Arthur brought 3,000 cattle, in mobs of 500, from the upper Darling River region to Springvale. Other stations soon followed, often aided by a nucleus of cattle herds that began to form around each telegraph station on the line.

The Territory's land rush continued into the 1880s when nearly 1.3 million square kilometres of land across the Territory were applied for as pastoral holdings. They were huge areas of land, marked by lines on a map. Their quality was a matter of luck for any pastoralist who applied for them, unseen. Some stations fell in stony deserts and were never taken up, but many of the others were carved out of the bush and soon became famous names to Territorians, such as Elsey (known across the globe to readers of *We of the Never Never*); Victoria River Downs, Newcastle Waters, Marrakai and Daly River Stations.

The cattle industry was poised to enjoy a boom that would last through the early 1880s. Integral to the industry's success was the availability of cheap Aboriginal labour, paid for by rations of flour, tea, sugar, and tobacco. The sheep industry did not do so well. Dr Browne's flock of sheep failed to survive, and there was very little wool ever exported. Browne had lost $50,000 by the time he left the Territory in 1887 (Cross J., 2011).

In 1884, Glencoe Station was stocked with about 7,000 head of mixed cattle and 400 horses, but it was by no means the largest cattle station. That was Victoria River Downs, at 41,155 square kilometres. Situated on Bilingara and Karranga native lands, VRD was taken up by Charles Fisher and Maurice Lyons—who also bought Glencoe Station in 1881. The two stations were then stocked with 20,000 head of cattle that Nat Buchannan brought in a single drove from Queensland. It was the largest cattle drove in history. Within a few years, VRD alone ran over 30,000 head of cattle, and by 1907, it boasted nearly 70,000.

Red-water fever

A major problem for the pastoralists in the 1880s was red-water fever, a disease carried by cattle ticks (*Boophilus microplus*) that causes the appearance of blood in the urine*. It arrived from Queensland, first appearing in Territory herds in 1882. It killed thousands of Territory cattle over the next decade or two, and in many stations, the boom came to an end before it really started. The 'Chief Inspector of Sheep' in 1887, thought the disease was caused by 'miasmatic vapours', but could not explain why these vapours had no effect during the 1870s (*NTTG*, 10 May 1887). No one was sure of its cause until 1894, when a Queensland Government bacteriologist, Mr C. J. Pound proved that 'red-water is occasioned by ticks' (*NTTG*, 28 December 1894). It was only then that scientists could begin working on a cure.

Local knowledge

Local knowledge in the dry stages of droving was invaluable, and Aborigines played an important part in keeping the drovers and their cattle alive. Barney Lamond and his mate Jack Horrigan were station workers who travelled with a mob of about 20 horses to the Kimberley from Queensland in 1885, looking for work with the Duracks. They first crossed the tablelands to Tennant Creek from Queensland. It was a good season, because, Lamond wrote, there was always plenty of water, and the seeding spinifex gave his horses a feed as good as oats.

---

* Red-water fever (aka 'tick fever', or bovine babesiosis) is a cattle disease caused by blood parasites transmitted by the cattle tick, *Boophilus microplus*. It kills cattle: during an outbreak, about 5% of at-risk animals will die, and pregnant cows may abort. Sick cattle also lose condition, and the live cattle export can be closed for 12-14 months or longer. Red-water fever caused the closing of the Territory market to Java for 7 years, from 1896 until 1903.

The travellers stopped in Tennant Creek for the annual races—attended by cattlemen from hundreds of miles around (including many who had 'never been to Alice or Port Darwin'). They then followed the Overland Telegraph Line north as far as Newcastle Waters, and Lamond left the camp there to scout ahead, across the dry country to the west. From him comes a record of one way that Aboriginal knowledge was used by the drovers:

> … We went out to the Thirty Mile camp, left our pack and
> spare horses there, went for a ride around to the west, and cut
> a well beaten pad, evidently made by blacks, leading into the
> desert and back west for water. We followed the pad until it
> came out on a bit of a plain, about a mile or so across. There
> were about twenty black women and children walking in a
> line along the track carrying water coolamons. Each woman
> had one under each arm, full of water, and fastened in a loop
> around her shoulder by a rope made from their own hair. Each
> coolamon held a gallon of water.
>
> We cantered up towards them—the wind was against them
> and they did not see or smell us till we were right beside them.
> They rushed into a heap, one on top of the other. The water
> went into the air—the children, boys, and girls on top of the
> women, all trying to hide their heads. Such a heap of arms and
> legs! After a few minutes they commenced to untangle and
> some of the old women could understand what we wanted.
> They had been used to mixing with the station blacks and
> were a bit civilised. We explained that we wanted two boys
> to go out with us to find water, so that we could get across
> to the big river. We promised them, if they would go with us
> for a few days, to bring them back to the waterhole and give
> them some tea, sugar, flour, and tobacco. They seemed quite
> willing to come, so we went back to where we left the horses,
> accompanied by two boys about fifteen years old … (Lamond,
> 1986).

The boys guided the drovers to several 'native wells' but they were dry. Luckily, the horses drank heartily from a trench filled by a sudden thunderstorm, but they quickly decided that there was not enough water around to get their party across. Back at the waterhole*, they paid the boys off, as promised, and returned to their main camp. They eventually travelled west after following the Overland Telegraph Line north as far as Katherine.

An insidious practice

William Sowden discovered another way Aborigines were employed when he was travelling with the South Australian Parliamentary Party in 1882. He met a drover in a little 'homely' public house near Yam Creek:

> … At the Port Darwin Camp there was brought under notice a custom which is too much in vogue amongst people who drive cattle over from Queensland. We met one of them who had a little black, dressed in boy's clothing, travelling with him as servant. It transpired that this little fellow was really a girl, and what her life may be, I know nothing of.
>
> In the particular case I refer to I believe it may be comfortable enough, for I believe the master is a good-hearted man, but in most cases, these feminine boys are the victims of their masters' debasing passions. That is the fact, and I do not see why the matter should be minced. There has been too much mincing of it already. Some of these thoughtless bushmen have, in the stealing of their black servants, had 'brushes' with the male relatives of the latter and shot them down.
>
> The natives make reprisals, and sometimes kill guilty, and at other times, innocent men. The whites resident in the district then have a 'revenge' party, and shoot down a score of blacks or so, and call it English justice.
>
> The Queensland Government can scarcely be blamed for this because in the sparsely populated districts, they cannot get at the offender. Whether they can prevent the practice of females going about the country clad in male attire is another question. Whether we cannot do something in the way of missionary enterprise is also a question which I will simply

---

* Lamond said the boys disappeared as fast as they could, and it was not till later that they found out why. The drovers rested before moving on but Lamond had to return to the waterhole to collect some spurs he had left behind. He surprised a party of Warrigal men: 'nine niggers, fully painted, and armed with spears and cundys [sic: clubs], standing just where we had been sleeping'. Lamond and his mate felt lucky to be alive (Lamond, 1986)

dismiss with the comment that half that we give to foreign missions would suffice for the work, in the way of which at present there is absolutely nothing done. They live and die like sheep, only that their lot is even more degraded. And the whites degrade it.

Experienced men throughout both colonies tell you that they never knew a so-called native trouble arise but that a lubra was at the bottom of it, and the conscientious will not take part in 'revenge' engagements. How long is this blot on our civilization to remain?

And there is just one more suggestive query—where do all the half-caste children go? They are born; the women remain with their English masters after they are born. Where are the children? You can't see half-a-dozen the Northern Territory over. Why? (Sowden, 1882).

Aboriginal women played a more important role in the development of the Northern Territory pastoral industry than they are often given credit for. As Searcy wrote:

… these women are invaluable to the white cattleman, for, besides the companionship, they become splendid horsewomen, and good with cattle. They are useful to find water, settle the camp, boil the billy, and track and bring in the horses in the mornings. In fact, it is impossible to enumerate the advantages of having a good gin 'outback' (Searcy, 1909).

Aboriginal girls were abducted and used in this way right across the top of Australia, from the Kimberley to Townsville. Emily Creaghe, Australia's first woman explorer in the north, gave an account of Mr Shadforth bringing in a new girl to Carl's Creek Station in western Queensland, in 1883. She was a 'wild black gin' who was dragged behind a horse with 'a rope around the gin's neck & dragged … along on foot, he was riding', to the homestead. She was then chained to a tree near the station house and kept there until she was thought to be 'tame'. 'This seems to be the usual method', she noted, adding that it rained all afternoon (Creaghe, 1883).

The Honourable Ted Egan AO, the 18th Administrator of the Northern Territory, revealed the insidious practice to the modern

public through his 1981 song, *The Drover's Boy*. Egan's song is even
more poignant when we understand that he was referring to drovers
working in the 1920s, forty years after Sowden described the 'little
black, dressed in boy's clothing' in a remote pub on the Territory's
goldfields. Generations of women were taken from their homes,
willingly or otherwise. How many people died when they or their
families resisted, will never be known.

> ... In the Camooweal Pub they talked about
> The death of The Drover's Boy
> They drank their rum with the stranger who'd come
> From the Kimberley run, Fitzroy.
> And he told of the massacre in the west
> Barest details—guess the rest,
> Shoot the bucks, grab a gin,
> Cut her hair, break her in
> And call her a boy—The Drover's Boy
> And call her a boy—The Drover's Boy.
>
> So, when they build that stockman's hall of fame
> And they talk about the droving game
> Remember the girl who was bed mate and guide
> Rode with the drover side by side
> Watched the bullocks, flayed the hide
> Faithful wife but never a bride
> Bred his sons for the cattle run
> But don't weep for The Drover's Boy
> Don't mourn for The Drover's Boy
> But don't forget The Drover's Boy
> (Ted Egan 1981, reproduced with permission).

In the vast spaces of western Queensland, the Kimberley, and
the Northern Territory, men lived rough, isolated lives, and were
largely unbothered by the laws of the city folk. However, many fell
afoul of Aboriginal law, which few understood—and paid the price.
Unfortunately for the Aborigines, the white man was backed by lethal
technology and confidence in their right to overrun the country.
Retributions against the 'treacherous natives' were often as swift as
they were terrifying.

Chapter 7
Murders and massacres

There was a murder of a teamster near The Shackle in 1878. A coroner's inquest, held at The Shackle Police Court, found that 'James Ellis was wilfully and brutally murdered by some native blacks, unknown, on the 16th day of January 1878' (*NTTG*, 26 January 1878). An ominous rider that followed the verdict pre-empted tragic events that unfolded six years later:

> … The jury respectfully desire to call the attention of the
> Government Resident to the fact that it would be futile to
> look for the actual perpetrators of this barbarous outrage,
> and that the only available retaliation is to give a lesson to the
> tribe. They, therefore, recommend that instructions be given to
> the police to track and disperse the natives and that volunteers
> be allowed to accompany the troopers. The jury feels that if
> this outrage on the high road be allowed to go unpunished,
> the lives and property of those living in the country will be at
> the mercy of these savages (*NTTG*, 26 January 1878).

In 1884, Harry Houschildt, Henry Roberts, John L. Noltenius, John Landers, and Thomas Schollert, a cook, worked the Daly River Copper Mine, near Mount Wells. These men were all experienced miners—their names appear in mine lists throughout the 1870s, and Kelsey—who knew them well—said they were among the 'first prospectors in the country'. None of them was a new chum.

On 15 August, Houschildt left the camp with his 'boy'—a Woolwonga man named Nammy—and several other Woolwonga people. Houschildt had business at the Union. It was usual for him to be accompanied by Nammy and they were on good terms:

> ... Houschildt always treated prisoner [Nammy] very kindly; he always provided food for prisoner; prisoner had been Houschildt's boy about two or three months, and had gone on expeditions with him before, so he would know how he would be treated ... (Roberts, *NTTG*, 27 December 1884).

Houschildt

They set up camp an afternoon's ride from the mine. Unwisely, though perhaps it was his habit to behave in this way, Houschildt showed an interest in one of his guide's wives and was murdered.

Nammy was arrested and told the story of the murder at his trial. He admitted that he was involved and that:

> ... Waloo brought lubra to Houschildt's camp; Houschildt told prisoner [Nammy] to tell Waloo to go away, and let lubra stop there; after Waloo went away, Houschildt said to prisoner, 'You leave lubra long me; I give her to you tomorrow'.
>
> Houschildt and lubra slept together in mosquito net; prisoner slept little way away; Houschildt got up and told prisoner to look out long horse; he did so, and saw the horses were all right; prisoner then went to sleep; afterwards Waloo came and woke up lubra, who woke prisoner up; Waloo went away; lubra asked him to go with her to blackfellows camp; when he got there, only one old man there; while he was at blackfellows camp, Boola came to him and told him Waloo had speared Houschildt; he went over to see Houschildt's camp, when Loweridgee speared Houschildt in the head, and Dolby struck Houschildt with a spear in the thigh; Chorock threw another spear; prisoner [Nammy] tried to wake Houschildt up after the other blacks went away; he threw a stone to wake Houschildt up; he no wake up; he then struck Houschildt with a small spear in the left arm; he did not wake up... he went to blacks' camp and asked Waloo what for he growled at Houschildt; he said, because Houschildt had taken his lubra prisoner ... (*NTTG*, 19 December 1885).

The Daly River Mine murders

It got worse: Houschildt had left his colleagues at the mine on 15 August, and they remained unaware of his murder. On 3 September, they were visited by several Woolwonga men looking for food:

> ... Suddenly, while the first three were at work in the mine and the cook was in the kitchen, they were attacked by a gang of natives, and before they could secure any weapons of defence, Schollert was speared and killed on the spot, Roberts received a blow from a pick-head which rendered him insensible, and the other two men sustained frightful injuries from the spears of the natives, which eventually resulted in their death (*Chronicle*, 24 January 1885).

Henry Roberts survived and retold his story at the trial:

> ... I was at work at the copper claim; I was sorting ore. Noltenius, Landers, and Schollert were there; Landers and Noltenius were working about ten yards from me; I could see them; Schollert would be about 60 or 70 yards from me at the kitchen; the large building on the photograph is the general dwelling and store; ... on the morning of the 3rd September the blacks made an attack upon us; at about half-past ten; I heard Landers call out, and looked up and saw him swing a hammer at some natives ...

> At about the same time I was struck on the right side of the head, near the temple, with some weapon which I believe was the head of a pickaxe; there were four natives working near me at the time; I do not know their names; I do know them by sight; none of them are the prisoners; I was rendered insensible by the blow: when I regained consciousness I went to the camp; when I got to the camp I found Schollert dead in the store; I took notice of the body, which was lying on its back, in the middle of the store, with the face turned towards the door; I did not at the time observe anything to show the cause of death; there was a little blood on the forehead but no wound; I found Landers* in the camp leaning on one of the bunks;

---

* In the N.T. Archives lies a desperate letter from an E.F. Sanders to the Government Resident asking if it was his brother who had been reported murdered, as the southern press was reporting. The G.R.s reply was that it was Landers, not Sanders who was the victim (LANT A7538/1885).

he had a large spear through his body, which entered his back and came out in front about 6 inches in front; it was a double-barbed spear; I took the spear out; the wound bled a great deal; Noltenius was there too; he also had a spear through his side; Noltenius then bound up my head; the spear in Noltenius had broken off in the body; I got one portion out; that spear also entered the back; afterwards, Noltenius and myself got a rifle and double-barrelled gun and walked round the camp; before doing that I washed the wounds and took Landers into the kitchen where he laid down; Noltenius was in great pain; we afterwards came in

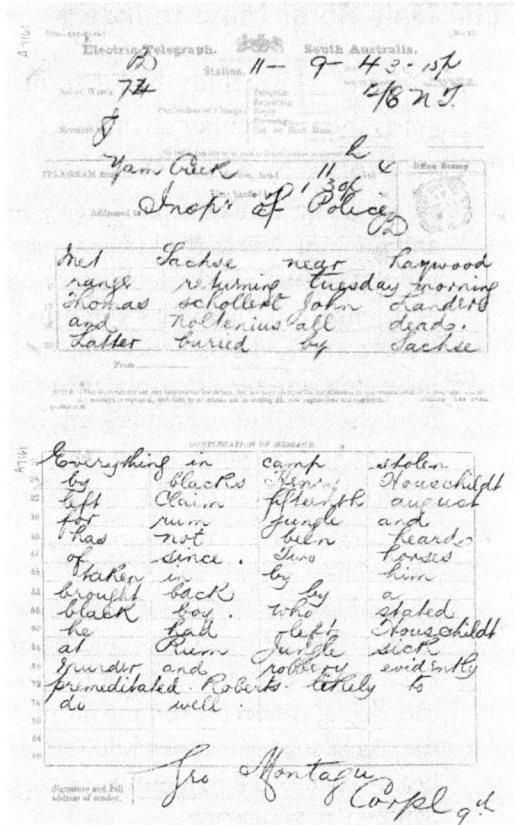

Figure 54: Corporal Montagu's telegram to Inspector Foelsche reporting the Daly River Mine Murders, and his meeting with Francis Sachse, before Houschildt was found (LANT, NTRS 790, A7161).

and laid down on the bunks: about two hours afterwards a spear was thrown into the camp and struck between my legs as I was lying down; after this occurrence we made preparations to leave the camp; we left about 5 o'clock in the evening to go to Fisher and Lyons' cattle station, which was about 35 miles distant: we went about 500 yards and camped, Landers being unable to travel (*NTTG*, 27 December 1884).

Roberts reported the attack to Francis Sachse, the manager of the cattle station, who then immediately travelled to the copper mine. His testimony, in front of Justice Pater, described the scene as he found it:

> … as I approached the claim I noticed a body about 40 or 50 yards from the track; could not identify it, as it was in a putrid state; I had been directed by Mr H. Roberts where to find the body and I found it in the position indicated; one hand and one foot were missing from the body; Roberts had given me information as to the whereabouts of Landers' body; it appeared to have been moved; there was a large hole on the right loin; knew a man named Landers; I believe the body was the body of Landers, from the size and color of the hair; I received information about another person; after finding Landers' body I went to the camp, which I found had been plundered and was in a wrecked state; I expected to find Schollert's body in the store but to my surprise it was not there; there were no rations there; I went to the claim and found a dead body in a putrid state; then started back to find Noltenius; that was on September 8; found him about 9 miles from the copper claim, in a very weak state; he was quite sensible; after giving him a little stimulant I examined him; I felt a swelling about three inches to the left of the navel; I cut the skin, and a point of a spear jumped out; the spear point produced is the piece; I washed and dressed him; as I turned him over I observed a large hole just over his left hip such as would have been made by a spear; I tried to move him, but he asked me to sit him down, which I did, and after a few minutes he suddenly expired; I then buried him; I think the wound over the hip was produced by the spear of which the piece produced is a portion; he had no other injuries; I believe he died from the injuries he had received … (*NTTG*, 27 December 1884) .

A Woolwonga man, also named Tommy, was then put in the witness-box. He claimed the white men at the mine had been killed for their food:

> … My name Tommy; live at Rum Jungle; sometimes stop at the Daly River; I knew Noltenius; see him good while ago long Daly River; he work at the Daly River dig gold; worked longa copper claim; I know Tommy, Ajibbingwagne, and Daly; do not know Jemmy; I knew Jack Landers, Noltenius,

Tom the cook, and Harry Roberts; when whitefellow stop copper claim blackfellow kill 'em whitefellow, because no more give 'em tucker, only tobacco; blackfellow first time sit down longa camp, talk kill 'em whitefellow tomorrow; in the morning get up, have 'em breakfast, talk more kill 'em whitefellow; Tommy take 'em one spear; Ajibbingwagne one spear; another man named Nango take two spears, then go long copper claim; all go all about copper claim; I see Tommy take one stone spear long kitchen kill 'em Tom the cook, longa kitchen; speared him longa back; stone did not come out; bamboo came out; Tom the cook run long big fellow house; lay down inside; Nango take two spears longa Landers; took one wood spear; spear Landers longa back; he fell down where grass house was; Ajibbingwagne run after Landers, and speared him in the side; Nango also speared Noltenius, after he came out of a hole, with a whitewood spear in the side; did not see where Noltenius go; Roberts was working longa stone; Daly came up and hit him with a hammer on forehead and on neck: Daly run away; think Roberts dead then; blackfellow go back Ionga camp; sleep at camp that night; before they went away. Ajibbingwagne threw another spear longa house, where whitefellow were; next morning come up and look about house; see Tom the cook lie down inside dead, blackfellow then take 'em tucker all about; flour, rice, sugar, tobacco, sardine... (*NTTG*, 27 December 1884).

On death row

The jury found Tommy, Ajibbingwagne (aka Jimmy), and Daly (and later, Nango) guilty of the wilful murder of Johannes Lubrecht Noltenius, at Daly River Copper Mine. They were sentenced that afternoon by Justice Pater:

> ... His Honor, addressing the three men, said, 'you have been found guilty by a jury of the murder of Noltenius, and I believe the jury have arrived at a right conclusion. The law imposes upon me the duty of passing the sentence of death upon you, which is that you be taken to the place from whence you came, thence taken to the place of execution, there to be hanged by the neck till you be dead, and that your bodies be afterwards buried at the place of execution

or some other place which the Governor may direct, and may God have mercy on your souls' (*NTTG*, 27 December 1884).

A special meeting of the Executive Council was held in Adelaide in August 1886. It resulted in all those prisoners still on death row for the Daly River murders having their sentences commuted to penal servitude for life*. The prisoners, except Nango, were taken to South Australia and held in the Adelaide Stockade at Dry Creek (*Kapunda Herald*, 10 August 1886). Nango died in Fannie Bay Gaol on 22 December 1886 of a 'subacute attack of beriberi', under the care of Doctor Wood (*NTTG*, 25 December 1886).

Although Inspector Foelsche travelled into the bush and arrested the ringleaders of the murders successfully, there were two other expeditions raised after the attacks. They were shockingly different to Foelsche's expedition and have become deeply ingrained in the folk-law of the region where they occurred.

Houschildt rescue party

The second was a civilian party known as the 'Houschildt Rescue Party'. The men involved were armed by the Government but not accompanied by any police. They were led by the miner Philip Saunders and W.K. Griffiths†, a storekeeper from Port Darwin Camp. Their party was supplied with ammunition for use in 'self-defence' but did not have to account for its use. They later explained the high cost of their expedition by the fact that they were joined by more volunteers than expected, and therefore needed more equipment (LANT A7318/1884).

---

* This included Ajibbingwagne, Daly, and Nango. Another man, Candelanah, who murdered a Chinese man named Ah Foo, at Port Essington on 20 April 1885, over tobacco, was also sent south (*North Australian*, 11 December 1885).

† W.K. Griffiths was one of the first to take up reef claims at the Union, and he held several claims that were worked 'on tribute' by the Chinese miners on that line, up to the day of his death in 1892, including mines such as Princess Louise. He began storekeeping at Grove Hill and ran a battery there that 'had monopoly for years of the crushings of that district' (*NTTG*, 8 April 1892).

The civilians travelled to the Daly River by the steamer *Palmerston* and then went into the bush. The ship's officers remained on board, moored in the river, to await their return. They later said that they heard gunfire in the distance *for the whole of one night*. However, Saunders said that his party failed to kill any natives and the matter was dropped. Despite calls in the newspapers for an inquiry, it never happened. Dr Robert Morice, M.D., the Protector of Aborigines for the Northern Territory, who was fired from his position because of 'insubordination' during the trial, wrote 'I think that their butcher's bill will compare most favourably with that of Corporal Montagu' (*Register*, 17 November 1885).

Montagu's retribution expedition

Figure 55: John Little
(LANT, PH1134-0001)

The third team was led by Corporal George Montagu from the Yam Creek Police Station at The Shackle. Montagu was already experienced in retribution expeditions, as 10 years before, in 1874, he was sent out from Daly Waters Telegraph Station to hunt down those responsible for the killing of Charles Johnstone. This was at the same time as a raid of terror 'led' by Chief Telegraph Officer John Little in revenge for the death of Johnson (who was his brother-in-law). They hunted Aborigines for nearly two months. As many as 40 Mangarrayi men, women, and children may have been killed during this reprisal.

In September 1884, Montagu was clearly in command of one of the expeditions sent out to hunt down the perpetrators of the Daly River Copper Mine murders. Other members were Mounted Constables Charles Luck, MacDonald, and Cox. Whatever happened on the journey, Montagu found himself in all sorts of strife after his candid report was published. In it he wrote:

… I do not know what other parties have done, but I believe the natives have received such a lesson this time as will exercise a salutary effect over the survivors…

… One result of this expedition has been to convince me of the superiority of the Martini-Henry rifle, both for accuracy of aim and quickness of action …

What he meant by this was minutely examined by a Board of Inquiry, chaired by Arthur Baines. The board included the Honourable R. Baker (the Minister of Justice and Education), the Rev. F. W. Cox, and Mr C. B. Young. The meeting was held behind closed doors, but the transcript was published anyway. Part of it was as follows:

… Did any of your party give you any information as to natives being shot? Yes, that the natives who attacked McDonald and Cox, and one or two others that resisted, were shot …

Did the natives provoke you to the use of firearms? Yes, by resisting examination of camp and identification of natives.

Did you see any members of your party shoot natives? Yes, I saw [Mounted Constable Charles] Luck shoot one in the water.

Before leaving the lagoon on the Mary River, did you make examination to see if there were any dead or wounded natives? Yes, I saw two bodies in the water, and I believe two other bodies sank …

What do you mean by saying in the report 'None of those who took to the water were known to have got away, and I believe; the natives have received such a lesson this time as will exercise a salutary effect on the survivors in time to come'? Are we to understand by this that of all the natives you saw, only those who were pursued by Constable Luck escaped, and that all the others present at the lagoon were shot by your party? Because they were not seen to have got away, and because the few who were shot would be a salutary lesson to the survivors.

What did you intend to convey by the report when you say, 'One result of this expedition has been to convince me of the superiority of the Martini-Henry rifle, both for accuracy of aim and quickness of action?' Does this imply that it was owing to the number of natives who were shot rapidly that you formed this opinion? If not, what other reason had you for making this statement? My opinion of the Martini-Henry rifle was formed because while on the expedition we shot game, and sometimes at stations, had rifle contests; also, because I was informed that had it not been for the rapid action of this rifle, McDonald, and perhaps Cox, would have lost their lives ...

What was the feeling in the Northern Territory? Great commiseration for the murdered men who were well known. The people in the Northern Territory are often disposed to think that a severe lesson on the natives is better than bringing them to justice at Palmerston, which the natives don't understand, and the result of which the other blacks don't know. I did not hear of the shooting of any women or children from members of my party.

Why do you suppose there were twenty or thirty men in the water? Made a guess afterwards. Some of them might have got away before the police came up. Do not think that more than four or five were killed; one who was killed was about to throw a spear at MacDonald, and another killed had thrown a spear at Cox. Two others sank. I saw the water discoloured with their blood ... (*NTTG*, 23 January 1826).

Montagu's responses to the board were more considered than his written report had been, but the board concluded that he had led his men to the banks of a Mary River lagoon near Argument Flat and Marrakai Station, where several families of Woolwonga people were camped, and started shooting. How many were shot then by the police is a matter of conjecture. Modern analysis by Newcastle University suggests that between 70-150 people were shot (Ryan & Pascoe, 2019). Montagu's report documented 20–30 Aboriginal deaths (those in the water).

Montagu agreed that he could not know for sure if the perpetrators of the Daly River Copper Mine massacre were present at the lagoon, but he was sure they were Woolwonga people, and therefore of the same tribe. He gained support from the editor of The *North Australian*, who reflected many of the sentiments of Palmerston society of the time:

… As to the shooting of the blacks, we uphold it defiantly. Previously, it seemed to be an understood thing that men, women, and children were shot down indiscriminately. The Corporal's report now shews [sic] us that before a shot was fired at the lagoon where the 'terrible butchery' took place, the women and children ran into the bush, and the men took to the water. There were between twenty and thirty men, and of this number, only three escaped. No doubt, to persons unsophisticated in the ways of savages, to kill say 25 blacks in a waterhole sounds awful. Calm reflection and experience at once exonerate the police from all blame. The blacks opened the fight themselves and were one or two of our ranting Members of Parliament in Cox's place when the spear grazed his neck, we venture to say that they, too, would consider it high time to retaliate actively and effectively. The assumed brutality of the occurrence reads well when we remember the butchery at the copper mine, the treachery of the natives in that case. What more cold-blooded assault could be wanted than that committed by the blacks?

And is it not reasonable to assume that the massacre of white men was shared in by all members of the tribe who found an opportunity to act?

Taking this for granted, the most plausible method of dealing out punishment was certainly that of holding the tribe responsible, after it had been found impossible to capture individual offenders. The same thing is done all over the world… Instead of imperilling their lives in a fruitless attempt to take the natives alive, the police, taking the cue from the blacks themselves, opened fire upon them, and if it does seem to have been a cowardly proceeding to surround the natives in a waterhole and shoot them down while helpless and unable to defend themselves, this suggestion of cowardice is wiped out by the knowledge that had the positions been reversed, and the blacks been in the place of the police, the supposed cruelty, of which Adelaide hypocrites express such holy horror, would have been vastly heightened.

The whole thing merely resolves itself into the question—Is it just to hold a tribe responsible for murders committed by some of its members? We say emphatically, yes; provided, of course, that (as in the case of the Daly outrage) the proper murderer or murderers cannot be found (*North Australian*, 8 January 1885).

Two weeks later the board summarised their report for the Minister of Education:

> … That from the evidence of the mounted constables who were under Corporal Montagu in the Daly country, there is no actual proof of any natives having been shot, or that the dead woman, said to have been seen by the Corporal, was killed, or shot at by members of the Police Party. That from the evidence of Roberts and others examined, there is no doubt that the natives encountered on the Mary River were mixed up in the copper mine outrage, but there is no evidence to prove that any natives were killed, each member of the party, excepting Montagu, stating emphatically: that no dead bodies were seen, and simply that two were shot at in self-defence.
>
> In conclusion, the Board wish to state that they are unanimously of opinion that the natives were treated with leniency, and that there is no evidence to shew [sic] that slaughter or cruelty was practised by the police (*North Australian*, 26 January 1886).

The *North Australian* conveniently failed to mention that several perpetrators of the original Daly River Copper Mine murders were known and named: Nammy, Waloo, Boola, Yuba Yuba, Chorock, and Loweridgee. Nammy was already in custody and would shortly be tried and sentenced to death for the murder of Harry Houschildt.

When the Board of Inquiry handed down its report, Montagu and his colleagues must have been pleased:

> … The Board considers that Corporal Montagu's report, the publication of which made such a stir, was very ill-advised, and generally traverse his statements. They find that only two blacks were shot by the police and that those two were killed in self-defence (*Dispatch*, 18 January 1886).

Nammy's luck

Nammy was found guilty by the jury and sentenced to be hanged by Justice Pater. However, luck went Nammy's way. During the appeals process, it was found that the court had no jurisdiction to try a murder, and Nammy was released by September 1886, along with a Chinese murderer named Ah Kong (see Chapter 10). There was an outcry:

> … that they escape the gallows is bitter enough, but to expect us to admit them among us as free men is to encourage the harshest feelings against our rulers and a more intense hatred of the criminals themselves (*North Australian*, 10 September 1886).

After Nammy was released, he returned to his Daly River home. He was feared by the settlers for several years:

> … The released murderer Nammy… impudently walked up to the mine camp a few days ago with a fish as a conciliatory offering but he left suddenly when shown a loaded Winchester. If these escaped murderers come near the mine, we are surely justified in warning them off (*NTTG*, 18 December 1886).

> … It is well-known that Nammy and the other released murderer—released through political idiocy—have guns and ammunition in their possession, and from the Rev. Father McKillop and others who have lately been down there, we learn that it is boasted by some of the natives that they intend to kill all the whites in the locality during the present wet season (*North Australian*, 3 December 1887).

The 'notorious' Nammy never carried out any threats he was supposed to have made, and by 1888, he was working as a 'rouse-about' at the Adelaide River Police Station (*NTTG*, 1 December 1888). He last appears in the record as being part of a gang who stole 'flour, tea, salt, matches, beef, knives, spoons, blankets, bags, singlets and other clothing' from a camp at Pine Creek in 1895 (*NTTG*, 15 February 1895). Nammy was named because it was 'well known that some of the worst of the Daly River and Victoria criminals frequent this locality, now that there are but few Europeans here …'

Long Charlie had been arrested with Nammy, but there was no evidence against him, so he was released before the trial. He was, however, another Aborigine who caused the settlers some concern:

… AN OLD OFFENDER: The well-known Daly River native, Long Charlie, has again been causing some anxiety in the Daly River district. A few days ago, Charlie visited the Mount Tolmer Tin Mine and stole a revolver, persuading Mr Johns' boy to state that he had lost it. The boy was sent after Charlie to give him a caution, and the revolver was at once brought back to the camp. The following day the natives, with, it is believed, Charlie's assistance, succeeded in clearing Auld's camp out of rations and unless the settlers take the law into their own hands, and put this black scoundrel out of the road, there will probably be more trouble with the natives during the coming wet season.

It will be remembered that Long Charlie was one of the principal witnesses in the Daly River massacre case, when several admitted murderers were, owing to a South Australian legal muddle, let off the just penalty of their crimes; and the settlers, who know most about the affair believe that Charlie had as much to do with the massacre as any of those who were tried for the offence. Charlie and Nammy are a pair of as treacherous natives as can be found in the Territory, and it will be well for the settlers at the Daly and Mount Tolmer to keep a sharp lookout for them and rid the district of their presence at the first opportunity (*NTTG*, Friday 29 November 1889).

Perhaps someone did 'keep a sharp lookout for them'. They were never heard from again.

A postscript of the Daly River massacre story came from Dudley Kelsey, the telegraph operator at The Shackle:

… a few years after the murder at the Daly River, some natives came to Shackle Station; among them a young lad about 10 or 12 years of age. We noticed a number of small lumps on his buttocks and, when asked the reason, he told us that during the time the shooting parties were out, one came on some of his tribe. He was hit and dived under some thick undergrowth. All his friends were killed, but he wandered about in the bush till he came up with another tribe who took care of him (Kelsey, 1975).

Chapter 8
Port Darwin

When Port Darwin was originally settled, all ships needed to be unloaded by transferring people and equipment to a lighter, which would then be beached. This was very labour intensive and therefore expensive.

Animals could be swum ashore, though this was not without risk, as George Goyder found, when he brought the very first stock as part of the Northern Territory Survey Expedition in 1869:

> … Commenced landing stock, bullocks all landed successfully, but one very weak. Half the horses landed, black mare badly handled by men in the dingy [sic] and nearly drowned … in lifeboat to assist and took the mare safely ashore. Orders given by myself and captain that the dingy should not be used any more in landing stock… [and later] …returned to ship where we found that contrary to my express orders and those of the Captain, the ship's carpenter had again attempted to land stock with the dingy and the result was the 'Young Bobby' one of our best horses was drowned. But for the willingness and energy displayed by the Carpenter in landing stock, I should have censured him … (Goyder, 1869).

It took five years before any wharves or jetties were built (Bartlett, 1990). They were as much causeway as jetty, constructed from stones cut from Fort Hill. Three were started near Fort Hill. One of them, Cook's Jetty, was at right angles to the current, so it silted up quickly and was never used again. The second was a rock wall that jutted into the sea less than a metre. It was useless because it bore the full brunt

Figure 56: Fort Hill in 1888, showing the Gulnare Jetty (left of centre), the remains of the breakwater (left), 'the camp' (right of centre), and The Residency (extreme right, obscured) (Foelsche, SLSA B-5066).

of the tide in both directions. The best was the Gulnare Jetty* on the inside of Kitchener Bay. Sowden said it was so-called because the *Gulnare* had 'staved in her sides across it' and become 'part of it, with her ribs in the middle.'

Embarrassing jetties

The jetties were an embarrassment to the little colony in the early 1880s. Travellers arriving by ship at high tide would first see two long poles with empty nail cans hoisted up high. They marked the 'termini of the two apologies for jetties, and they [were] placed there to warn vessels not to run into them'. Anyone coming at low tide would see the cans as 'beacons at the edge of a sea of high-flavoured mud' (Sowden, 1882).

When Edward Price took over as government resident in 1876, he was not impressed:

* The 152-ton *Gulnare* was a small schooner that made five trips to Port Darwin under Captain Sweet. She was used to survey the Roper River but was later damaged while carrying parts for the Overland Telegraph Line near the Vernon Islands. She returned to Darwin and was decommissioned by Government Resident Douglas, stripped, and moored off the coast. In 1873 Douglas, very drunk and suffering temporary alcoholic insanity, climbed to the roof of The Residency and threatened to shoot the police because he thought they were after him as a debtor. Dr Millner managed to get him to dry out in the hulk of the *Gulnare*, moored off Fort Point. The *Gulnare* was then left to rot on the beach, just where the new jetty was built (Pugh, 2019).

… of the two jetties or causeways I can only speak favourably of one, and my opinion is that the money would have built a good ship jetty … a causeway built at right angles to a strong tide can have but one ending. Namely, silting up into a mud bank (Price, 1876 report).

Gulnare Jetty had a better gradient and less current passed it, though it was still underwater at high tide. It served the settlement for more than 10 years but fell into disuse when the new jetty was built from Stokes Hill, in 1886. It was resurrected in 1898-1904 as a passenger wharf whilst the Stokes Hill jetty was replaced, 'despite being made of loose, slimy stones said to be as slippery as an eel' (Bartlett, 1990). The 'walk along the top of the oily mass is quite amusing—a walk full of surprises … [with] occasional full-length tumbles' (Sowden, 1882).

A petition sent to the South Australian Parliament in 1880, signed by 111 members of the Palmerston community, explained the need for a better jetty than Gulnare: the delivery of goods from a ship cost 13 shillings per ton (by 1882, the cost had risen to 15 shillings a ton). Unloading ships onto a jetty would cost a fraction of this.

The 'finest railway pier of its kind in the colonies'

There was little response, and nothing much was done until suddenly, in 1884, advertisements were released in September in Adelaide, and November in Palmerston, calling for tenders to build a railway jetty. The railway was going ahead, and suddenly there was no time to lose. Some test piles had been sunk into the mud in July 1884 by J. W. James, a superintending engineer for the railway. He concluded that each pile would need to be sheathed in copper up to the high-water mark to protect the wood from *Toledo* worms. This would cost an extra £11,000.

The winning tender came from John Wishart in Adelaide. According to him, the jetty would cost £39,817 16s 8d, and would take 75 weeks to build, barring accidents.

Accidents and delays started immediately. Wishart chartered three ships to bring the materials for the jetty from Western Australia. One of them, the *Bittern*, hit a reef off Browse Island*, north of the Kimberley, in the Timor Sea. All hands were saved, but a significant cargo of jarrah piles and other timber was lost. The cargo was insured but, said the editor of the *North Australian*, 'it is extremely unpleasant to have to record such a mishap as that to the *Bittern*, and it does seem really as if some evil genius were presiding over our affairs' (1 May 1885).

The wreck caused a delay of about three months. The *Bittern*'s crew was rescued and brought to Port Darwin in time to help unload a second ship. One of the crew, Yu Wong, ran out of luck. On his first day of work after arriving, he was crushed by a heavy load of copper sheathing and killed (Bartlett, 1990). He was not the only one to die by accident on the jetty in the first years. A Malay man named Mariano died of a cracked skull when four logs slipped and fell whilst being unloaded from the *Cutty Sark*† in 1889. A Chinese timber gang led by Ah Hung and Ah Sam were cleared of wrongdoing, and the unfortunate man was declared dead by accident. The logs had fallen with such force that 'they crushed through the deck of the *Cutty Sark*, which is three inches thick, and smashed a heavy beam as if they were mere matchwood' (*NTTG*, 3 August 1889).

The jetty was nearly finished by early April 1886, and the first freight that arrived on it was 1500 tons of railway lines and fishplates. On 22 April, it was unloaded directly from the *Dochra*, placed in rail cars, and pushed on shore. The cost of unloading was 3 shillings 9 pence per ton, about a third of the cost of lightering. The jetty was, according to the *Times*, the 'finest railway pier of its kind in the colonies' (11 December 1886).

---

* Browse Island is uninhabited. It was mined for guano between 1870 and 1890. At least six ships were wrecked on reefs around it during this time (Admiralty Reference # 1642).

† The *Cutty Sark* was a famous tea-clipper. She set speed records in the 1870s, right at the end of the age of sail, before steamships became more common. Since 1953, she has been a museum ship on display in Greenwich, London.

Figure 57: The railway jetty with ships dressed 'in their holiday rig, and the display of bunting made quite a pretty scene'. The large ship is possibly the *Earl Roseberry*, the others; *Armistice, Mary Low*, and *Hersey* (Foelsche,1887, LANT, PH160).

The jetty was completed 'without the slightest notice having been taken of it, either officially or otherwise'. Captain Kerr, of *Earl Roseberry*, whilst unloading 'railway iron', was told that his was the first ship to dock after completion. He took it upon himself to arrange a celebration of the event. He joined with the captains of *Armistice, Mary Low*, and *Hersey* by dressing their vessels 'in their holiday rig, and the display of bunting made quite a pretty scene' (*NTTG*, 11 December 1886). Then, still displaying her bunting, *Earl Roseberry* was taken 'to the ballast grounds off Lameroo Beach' to load sand ballast and there, she was nearly lost. During a heavy squall, she dragged her anchors as far as Fort Hill. 'This vessel' said the *Times*, 'has been delayed for some weeks taking in ballast owing to the heavy weather and the unsuitability of the vessels employed in the work of ballasting' (*NTTG*, 25 December 1886).

Figure 58: The *Sandfly* NA1 Steam locomotive worked in Darwin from 1887 until 1950 (SLSA B53773).

Of the other two ships, *Armistice*, owned by the Millar brothers, returned to Adelaide for 'bridges and bridge work'; and *Mary Low*, which had taken 143 days to reach Port Darwin from Glasgow because her captain had fallen ill, returned to Britain for another load of 'materials for the Palmerston and Pine Creek Railway' (NTTG, 11 December 1886).

The final cost of the jetty was £51,600.

Even before it was finished, 25,000 tons of railway equipment had been unloaded. The *Sandfly*, a 10-ton C40 type saddle tank locomotive, arrived on the *Armistice* on 4 December 1886. It was assembled on the wharf and started its long service on 20 May 1887. It finally retired in 1950.

Figure 59: The jetty makes a curved sweep out to its end where there are three ships berthed plus *Tsinan* (1459 tons, anchored with steam launch *Victoria* alongside). The docked steamer on the left is the *Menmuir* (1247 tons), and the *Catterthun* (1406 tons) is on its right (SLSA B-6442), the large sailing ship is the *Falkland Hill* (1492 tons, with a cargo of cement for the Millars) (September 1888, Foelsche, ph0238-0094).

Darwin: Growth of a City

Chapter 9
The Palmerston–Pine Creek Railway

The need for a railway across Australia—a great 'Trans-Continental Railway'—had been discussed in Adelaide as early as the 1860s. In 1872, a group of 'substantial men' even offered to build it in exchange for 35 large land grants along the route, which covered an area of 200 million acres. The land grant system had worked well in the United States of America, and immigrants had flooded to distant lands along the railway corridor. There was much discussion about how it would be funded, and whether it should be a South Australian investment alone or whether all the colonies should be pushed into contributing:

> … A meeting of persons interested in the project of
> constructing a line of a railway across the Australian continent,
> between Adelaide and Port Darwin, [was] held at the rooms
> of Mr Cowderoy, Market-square, Sir. Marshal Singleton in the
> chair (*Register*, 13 January 1873).

Adelaide would become the 'London of Australia' if they went it alone, some thought, but others wanted the railway to curve through Victoria and New South Wales as it headed north. Squabbling continued for years. The turmoil of South Australian politics at the time did not help: The Ayers ministry collapsed in 1873 and Arthur Blyth took over and continued the debate. There was a vague offer of £20 million from a Mr Main of Ballarat, and a Mr Chapman in Melbourne optimistically promised he could provide 'a 3'6" line, including the provision of 20,000 emigrants, pro-rata as the line progressed' (Fletcher, 2013).

The Commissioner of Crown Lands and Minister in charge of the Northern Territory, the Honourable Thomas Reynolds, went to Port Darwin for a 25-day stay in 1873. He travelled via Ceylon and Timor to get there, and the total trip took 125 days*. There was a need for a faster form of transport. Direct steamships were one answer. By the 1880s, a steamer could travel from Adelaide to Port Darwin in just 18 days, but this was still slow and expensive.

South Australia experienced several boom years in the early 1870s, but then came a recession. The state's wheat and wool fell out of demand and depression loomed. Luckily, viniculture and copper mining continued to support them, but the railway idea was put on the backburner. It was brought forward only when there was concern about the slow progress of Territory development. In 1881, a private consortium—the Central Australian Railway Company—put out a prospectus hoping to raise £6 million by the sale of 12,000 shares at £500 each. In return, they wanted 57 million acres of land granted in alternate blocks along the line. The Bray government refused the project because they 'did not consider it … wise to allow any company to lay down the line on the principle which had been suggested'. Then, John Langdon Parsons, the new Minister for the Northern Territory, led the 1882 Parliamentary tour of the goldfields (see Chapter 4). The roads of the region were impassable in the wet season, and the ongoing mining industry was moving away from alluvial mining towards machinery-demanding reef mining. The possibility of a railway was mentioned numerous times.

Parsons returned to Adelaide and wrote the *Palmerston to Pine Creek Railway Act* of 1882. Parsons' idea was that land adjacent to the railway would be sold to finance the line (Fletcher, 2013). Both

---

* Reynolds succumbed to gold fever and returned to the Territory as a private citizen with big plans for his future at the Fountainhead Mine. Unfortunately, he drowned in the *Gothenburg* disaster in 1875 (Pugh, 2019).

Gilbert McMinn, the Territory's senior surveyor, and John Knight, the mining warden, supported the plan. All three of these gentlemen would spend time as Government Resident in Palmerston over the next decade.

The early 1880s were golden days for the Territory. Edward Price retired in 1884 and said at his farewell banquet that the Territory was doing better than South Australia. They were in a period of surplus: they paid 19% interest on bonds, and confidence was high. The government decided to call tenders for the construction of the Palmerston to Pine Creek Railway. It would be a state-funded investment, and the first stage of the line would eventually extend south, right across the continent.

Tenders were called for twice because the first lot were not accepted, even though the newspapers supported them:

> ... The lowest tenders for the Pine Creek Railway were put in by Messrs. Robinson, Hague & Jesser. The amounts were, with European labour, £721,086, or with coolie labour, £638,405. We regret that the first tender has not been accepted, as European labour would give a great impetus to the business of the Territory ... Our readers will doubtless be surprised and annoyed at the news contained in our telegrams to-day, that the railway tenders have not been accepted, and that new tenders will probably be called for (*NTTG*, 5 December 1885).

The Millar brothers

The winning tender came from Charles and Edward Millar.

> ... The Millar Bros., the successful tenderers for the construction of the Palmerston and Pine Creek railway, signed the contract yesterday. The price is £605,424, and the contractors are not restricted to the employment of European labor (*Port Augusta Dispatch*, 12 May 1886).

The Millar brothers were highly experienced in railway construction. They were ready to begin, and soon became a prominent part of Palmerston society. The line grew from the new jetty and, by

Figure 60: The Millar's house on Stokes Hill, Port Darwin (Foelsche, 1887, nla.obj-141844102-1).

1886, it was well on its way to Pine Creek. The Millars controversially used Chinese labour because they were cheaper than white men—and the Millars openly justified their policies by stating that white men could not work in the Territory heat anyway. But as the *North Australian* pointed out:

> …One thing is certain, viz., that the firm of Millar Bros. have no ambition to be employers of white labour in the Northern Territory while the Chinese are so convenient. Mr C. G. Millar… nothing that would suit his book better than to have every M.P. in South Australia believe him when he says that white men cannot work in the Territory. It is not hard for one on the spot to see how the wind blows, but surely it is not to be taken for granted that the statements made by a capitalist, railroad builder, and employer of cheap labour, must be accepted as being true as gospel… (28 January 1888).

The savings in employing the Chinese were remarkable. As one European worker wrote to the *Times*: 'a navvy on the railways in Victoria, New South Wales, and South Australia, gets from seven to

Figure 61: The naming of the first locomotive *Port Darwin* at the Palmerston
Railway workshops in Parap, July 1887 (LANT PH0370/0063).

eight shillings a day; Mr Millar, in this country, gets his men for three
and sixpence a day' (20 April 1989).

The first full-sized engine to go into service was ready in
July 1887. On a gala day, Mrs Pater was pressed into naming the
locomotive, in front of the 'largest crowd ever to gather in Palmerston'.

'I now name this locomotive *Port Darwin**,' she said, 'and wish
prosperity to the railway':

> … at the same time smiting the bottle of champagne over it;
> then, in the midst of hearty cheering the *Port Darwin* steamed
> out of the enclosure with the Union Jack floating from its
> tender (*NTTG*, 23 July 1887).

---

* For railway enthusiasts: The locomotive *Port Darwin* was a six-wheel coupled bogie
engine, with outside cylinders of 12 in. diameter, 24 in. stroke, lying at an angle of
16 degrees; wheels 3 feet diameter, except on bogie where they were 15 inches. The
footplate was covered with a neat cab for the protection of the driver and fireman.
The tender was four-wheeled, and capable of carrying 900 gallons of water, as well
as a liberal supply of fuel. The *Port Darwin* was manufactured by Beyer, Peacock &
Co. of Manchester (*NTTG*, 23 July 1887).

Figure 62: The official opening of the Adelaide River railway bridge on
3 December 1888 (LANT, Hilary Howe Collection, ph0314-0014).

There were toasts and speeches and refreshments set on long tables in the railway shed. Then:

> ... the ladies and gentlemen present returned to the
> christening platform, where a number of railway trucks were
> drawn up, headed by the *Port Darwin*. After everybody had
> been seated, the train moved off for a trip up the line, three
> cheers being lustily given for Mr Millar. The run, which
> was extended as far as the engine yard, was a most enjoyable
> outing, the line working smoothly and not the slightest
> mishap occurring to mar the occasion ...

Well, they had to admit to one mishap. Someone chose to celebrate a little too hard:

> ... An occurrence which, however, did not mar the
> proceedings, but rather added zest to them, took place after
> the return of the train to Palmerston. One of the Celestials
> who earns his daily bread by being 'a navvy on the line',
> attempted to celebrate the eventful day by diving into the
> subtle mysteries of 'Dry Monopole', and the charm of the
> beverage being, as may well be imagined, rather a novelty to

Figure 63: Adelaide River Bridge (Foelsche, 1889, SLSA B 5065).

the Mongolian, made him feel what is best described as 'fit'.

While in this happy comatose condition, between heaven and earth, and oblivious of wordly [sic] matters, he succeeded admirably in falling out of a truck on to his head in the railway embankment. A crowd of his countrymen quickly gathered around him and began to speculate on the nature of his ailment. The discussion, however, was quickly put an end to by a dusky aboriginal on the bank above, who delivered himself of the following: 'Him too much um gin; English feller all right; Chinaman no savee'.

The silence of the others gave consent, and the fallen follower of Confucius was escorted to his hearth by the rest of his tribe, to sleep off the effects of 'too much um gin' (*NTTG*, 23 July 1887).

Charles Millar then hosted a banquet in the Town Hall to celebrate the occasion. Mr Justice Pater was there as acting government resident, and community business leaders W.E. Adcock, V.L Solomon, and others, gave long speeches and toasts amid loud cheering. The confidence and anticipation the railway was delivering to Palmerston ooze from the newspapers of the day. A full description

143

Figure 64: Goods train at Port Darwin (SLSA B-53815).

of the banquet was presented by the *Times* on 23 July 1887: the toasts were flattering and entertaining, not least the toast to Queen Victoria, by Charles Millar:

> ... I beg to propose to you that toast which is the first to be honoured by every society of Englishmen, the health of Her Majesty the Queen. I have only to look round this room to know and feel that it is filled with loyal British subjects, men whose hearts throb, whose pulses quicken, on the mere mention of the name of the noble lady who has ruled the destinies of Great Britain and her dependencies for over fifty years, one whose whole life as maid, wife, and mother, has been so pure, so simple, so devoted to the welfare of her subjects, that to-day her name is held as an honor to womankind (*NTTG*, 23 July 1887).

Perhaps it took a while for some residents to realise how dangerous a moving train could be. The first fatality occurred just months after the railway was operational. Lee Sam Que was killed by a train hauled by an engine named *Silverton*. Justice Pater, at the inquest, was told that:

… his head was separated from his body, in the centre of the line… the body, which was a yard-and-a-half away on one side of the lines was cut open, and the two arms were very nearly severed from the trunk… part of the internal portion of body was scattered about the ground.

Dr Charles Lethbridge Stow concluded that the death of the deceased was caused either by his falling whilst attempting to mount one of the trucks whilst they were in motion, or he might have fallen off one of the trucks and been run over … (*NTTG*, 22 October 1887).

The railway opens

The opening of the railway, as it was handed over to the government, was a celebrated event right across the continent. There were Vice-Regal congratulations:

… The Palmerston and Pine Creek Railway was taken over by the Government today, and the Minister of Education waited on his Excellency and conveyed to him his own and the Government Resident's congratulations on the successful completion of the work. His Excellency was pleased to express his interest in the undertaking and sent the following telegram to Mr Parsons, Government Resident, Palmerston—I offer to all residents in the Territory my hearty congratulations on the successful completion and opening of the first section of the Northern Territory portion of the Trans-Continental Railway—[Lord] Kintore [Governor of South Australia].

The Minister of Education (Hon. 0. H. Gordon) dispatched the following telegram—J, Langdon Parsons, Government Resident, Palmerston. I reciprocate your congratulations on the completion of railway to Pine Creek. The Northern Territory owes you a debt of gratitude for your exertions in connection with this great undertaking. I heartily congratulate the residents and earnestly hope that the communication this day established between the mineral country and Port Darwin, will be followed by the best results. I have conveyed your congratulations to his Excellency the Governor who has been pleased to express his interest in the work and to telegraph you directly (*Telegraph*, 1 October 1889).

The construction of the line, which stretched 235 kilometres (146 miles) was an extraordinary feat. Subject to the times they lived in, the actual builders of the line were ignored in the congratulations—the labour of two or three thousand Chinese men went unacknowledged.

Even with cheap Chinese labour, the cost of the railway was significant:

> … There was a very large difference between the tenders with and without Chinese labor, and after several warm discussions in Parliament, it was decided to allow the contractors to employ Chinese. The contract was signed on May 11, 1886. The cost for the earthworks alone is £605,424, and for rails, sleepers, and fastenings, £189,462, The total expenditure on the line, including stations, &c., and a considerable sum for interest on the borrowed capital, is £1,086, 632, or over £7,300 per mile (*Telegraph*, 1 October 1889).

In 1888, a second Parliamentary Party toured the goldfields and Palmerston, much as had been done in 1882 (see Chapter 13). Minister Johnson shared the views of the Young Australia Party, to which he belonged, regarding the employment of labour:

> … Of the Chinese he would say nothing—all present were aware that the contract was an optional one and that they [the Millars] were not only justified in employing the cheapest labor but were compelled to do so, as a very heavy reduction had been made on the original estimates on that understanding. (A voice 'quite right, we don't blame your people').

> Messrs. C. & E. Millar imported some 125 Asiatics other than Chinese, but they had not turned out a great success, they were cheaper than Chinese, more amenable to discipline, and some few were as good as Europeans. Unfortunately, they had not the right class. Tamils were ordered but Singhalese had been supplied, and they were far inferior to the former for earthworks. The reason Tamils could not be obtained was that the Indian Government would not allow them to proceed to Australia, because no arrangement had been made by Australia for the appointment of an emigration agent here, authorised to protect their interests until this matter had been arranged it would be impossible to obtain the best class of Tamils for

Figure 65: Palmerston Railway Yards in 1889 (with Stokes Hill in the background) (Foelsche, LANT, PH0297-0033).

mining and other work. He ventured to say that when the mines are in full swing, those interested would find it absolutely necessary to have cheap labor for the drudgery, to enable the Europeans to apply their energy and skill to higher branches of mining than the pick and shovel (*NTTG*, 14 April 1888).

The railway was fully operational by 1889. Pressure was then placed on the government to extend the line as far as Katherine, but with the state now approaching an economic depression, this did not happen until 1923.

A Pine Creek journey

It did not take long for travel writers to report on the Pine Creek journey. The *Adelaide Observer* entertained their readers with:

> … At Port Darwin, a magnificent jetty was built about three years ago, and this is the starting place of the Palmerston and Pine Creek Railway. Leaving Palmerston along the railway line one goes through undulating country, the hills being encrusted with ironstone cement, the gullies containing rich alluvial soil.

147

Fifteen miles from Palmerston we pass on the left side Knuckey's Lagoon, which teems with fish and wildfowl. It is a great resort of Chinamen, who supply the Palmerston market.

Going on we come to a little rough country with granite boulders showing out, and then to an immense plain. Two miles to the right is Dean's Lagoon, which is well-populated with crocodiles and alligators, and in consequence, is noted for the scarcity of fish and wild game.

Proceeding south we arrive to within six miles of the Darwin. Here the line goes through a very rocky cutting and immediately crosses the Darwin River by a bridge of 340 feet … Then comes nice undulating country thickly studded with eucalypts and small trees, and then we soon pass Rum Jungle, a noted old hostelry of days gone by. A few miles further on the left of the line we pass the Darwin Pool, a remarkably large hole, which is some forty or fifty feet deep, and about 200 yards in diameter, being nearly circular.

To the right of this place is Poett's Plantation. This property was taken up for the purpose of growing sugar, coffee, and other tropical productions. A splendid feature of the property is the presence of a fine waterhole, in which one notices a very strong spring bubbling up, the water being at a temperature of about 70°.

The plantation, which has changed hands several times, was two or three years ago taken up by a Company. One man is looking after it as a caretaker, and the place, for want of proper cultivation, is going to ruin. I saw some coffee in the seed beds which was utterly useless for want of being planted out. There was, however, about half an acre of India rubber trees, which looked very healthy, but for the want of proper attention they were very straggly, and in some cases injured by the ravages of bush fires. It struck me that a plantation of these trees would pay for mercantile purposes, for they appear to flourish without any care or attention. Proceeding onwards through light cuttings and earthworks we pass on our right the old mail station where horses used to be changed on the overland route to Pine Creek. A few miles further on is a very fine flat called the Stapleton, which, I believe, would be a capital place for growing rice, as water is handy. The flat extends for miles, and

Figure 66: The 1888 railway bridge over the McKinlay River, near the town of Burrundie (Pugh 2020).

the soil is of a rich dark loam.

The next place of interest is the Adelaide River, on the banks of which is situated the hotel called the Q.C.E. (meaning 'Quiet, Comfort, and Ease'), which has for years supplied the wants of the travellers to the mining districts. It has ceased to be a house of call, as the railway station is a mile and half past it, so travellers have no need to put up there, for they now go right through to Pine Creek. This is only one public house out of many which has lost the custom of travellers since the opening of the railway. The Howley Creek is twenty miles further on, and then the line passes through low, undulating country for some miles further. Here the gullies which have been turned over by energetic gold-seekers are open to view. Burrundie, a small mining township, comes next, with its hospital, doctor's residence, two or three stores, and black smith's shop. Then there is the present terminus, Pine Creek. Two townships have been laid out by the Government along the line, which have been named respectively Knutsford and Playford, the former being situated at the present terminus. Some of the land has been sold to intending storekeepers, publicans, and others, and time will prove whether these places will be well populated (*Adelaide Observer*, 13 April 1889).

Chapter 10
Judge Thomas Kennedy Pater

Born in 1837, Thomas Kennedy Pater entered the legal profession as a barrister in London in 1859 but soon migrated to Sierra Leone, in West Africa, to practice law. He remained there for several years, before moving to Melbourne and then South Australia, where he worked with private law firms and as a crown prosecutor until 1884. On 19 March 1884, he was appointed Stipendiary Magistrate for the Northern Territory. In the following October, he became the Territory's first judge under

Figure 67: Justice Thomas Kennedy Pater (SLSA B505).

The Northern Territory Justice Act of 1885. His salary was £1,000 per annum (Obituary, 12 August 1892).

Pater, his wife Emily, and their two daughters, departed Adelaide on the *Menmuir*, in April 1884. On board with them were the new government resident, John Langdon Parsons, and Mr Richard D. Beresford, a lawyer (*North Australian,* 25 April 1884).

Controversy

Pater was soon embroiled in controversy in Palmerston. He was immediately disliked by the business leaders of the community, specifically those on the town council (Messrs. H. H. Adcock, V. L.

Solomon*, and V.V. Brown, plus D'Arcy Uhr), who were vocal in their worries about Pater's behaviour. The Northern Territory Reform Association met on 15 September and unanimously carried a motion that Pater was not fit to be a judge. The *Times* described him as 'a man of nervous, excitable temperament and hasty, violent temper utterly unfitted for the position of Judge' (Mildren, 2011), and the *Adelaide Observer* urged caution in the weeks before his appointment:

> … Mr Pater's heartless jocularity [and] his unnecessary harshness towards prisoners and his irritability towards witnesses are causing general dissatisfaction. It seems that he is unable to forget his changed position and fails to exhibit the dignity proper to the office. He combines too much of the Crown Prosecutor with the Judge and assumes too largely the functions of the Jury. Both [Northern Territory] papers comment strongly upon Mr Pater's demeanour on the Bench, and the general opinion is that the Parliament should pause before investing him with the powers under the proposed Bill.

The Council, Reform Association, and the newspapers were ignored. The Northern Territory Justice Bill was passed, and Palmerston had its first resident judge[†]. Up to the time of Pater's appointment, the courts were run by magistrates. These were usually the Government Resident, and/or various justices of the peace or stipendiary magistrates, such as Dr Ellison, S.M., and Gilbert McMinn, J.P..

The Territory had not seen a judge, in fact, since the circuit court of Mr Justice Wearing, who visited in 1875. He tragically drowned with his staff, and a seventh of the European population of Palmerston, in the *Gothenburg* disaster on the way home to Adelaide (Pugh 2019).

---

[*] V. L. Solomon may have resented Pater even before he arrived. The judge had to move into the Club Hotel on arrival because the residence that he was supposed to live in was occupied by Solomon and his family. The problem was solved by James Bath, a Secretary for the Minister of Education. He arranged for two bedrooms and a living room at Edward Hopewell's Club Hotel (LANT A6748/1884). Pater was then able to have a residence that suited his position, newly built at his leisure.

[†] From 1884 to 1911, there were four 'Judges of the Northern Territory' under the Northern Territory Justice Act: Thomas Pater, Charles Dashwood, Herbert and Mitchell. They had the full powers of the Supreme Court (*NTG*, 2020).

With Justice Pater on the bench, Richard Beresford, the Territory's only lawyer, was sometimes prosecutor, other times defence counsel. John Knight J.P., by profession an architect, was the prosecutor when Beresford defended the accused of the four high-profile murders at the Daly River Copper Mine. Tension rose between Government Resident Parsons and Justice Pater over this case, particularly over who should pay for the defence of the Aborigines accused, who were without money. Pater set a fee to be paid by the government, but Parsons did not want the criminals defended at all, especially by a lawyer (Reid, 1990). He wanted a 'speedy trial', and the murderers to be executed, quickly, near the scene of their crime and left hanging, swinging in the breeze, as a warning to their tribe.

Pater had a busy time in Palmerston. He and his wife and two daughters lived in a house on the Esplanade*, just a short walk to the courts. Judging by the number of court reports in Palmerston's two newspapers, Pater must have spent most of his time in the court. The crimes he tried were many and varied—from larceny, forgery and fighting, to being drunk in a public place, to murder. As well, he was in charge of licencing, and had the role of the coroner. Strangely, he needed 12 men in the jury for an inquest on a corpse, but to take a serious crime to trial, he only needed a six-man jury. Both were selected from among the business owners in Palmerston, and the same names appear repeatedly on the jury lists.

Pater in court

Pater's first case was an odd one:

> A diver was charged with disobedience to the commands
> of the owner of the boat on which he was employed. After
> hearing the case pro and con, Mr Pater decided to caution
> the defendant and ordered him to be taken on-board again.
> This was not what the defendant desired, for he repeatedly

---

*   Pater lived in a substantial stone and brick house of six rooms on Lot 648, opposite the cricket ground on the Esplanade. It was bought for the judge's use in 1884 for nearly £2,000. The house was destroyed by the cyclone of 1897.

expressed himself as anxious to go to gaol; but he was eventually taken to his boat. He was determined, however, to have his own way, and upon an opportunity presenting itself, he made his escape from the boat, found his way to the Police Station, and asked to be accommodated with a rug and lodgings, saying that he wished to go to gaol. Again, he was brought before Mr Pater, this time for continued disobedience, and the worthy S.M. decided that his request to be allowed to go to gaol should be complied with, the heaviest term of imprisonment being allotted him—three months with hard labour. The defendant was not so anxious to go when he discovered that he would be compelled to work, and it is very probable that he will not show such readiness to accept Her Majesty's liberality again when his present sentence is completed (*North Australian*, 16 May 1884).

Many cases in the Police Court were trivial, even before Pater arrived. For instance, before Gilbert R. McMinn J.P. in 1881:

… William Chancellor was charged with using profane and abusive language in a public place on Sunday last. From the evidence it appeared that some little girls, children of Mr Tuckwell, were passing defendant's hut, about two o'clock, when Mr Chancellor came out and used most abusive language, swore at them, and used very bad words. He kept on repeating the same words over and over again. Mr Burtt was in the neighborhood at the time and corroborated the girls' evidence. He heard what he termed loud and vehement vociferations, and very vile language. It seemed that Mr Burtt felt somewhat diffident in explaining the various expletives used by Mr Chancellor, but he need not have been, for most of them are in daily use in Palmerston. He was very much shocked when he heard the defendant tell the children their paternal parent might go to h---, as he didn't care a d--n for him!' (*NTTG*, 19 February 1881).

In another case a Mr Green* was having trouble with a servant, whom he had imported from Ceylon:

Thomas (a Tamil), charged with absenting from the service of

* Francis Mahon Green was secretary and accountant in the employ of Messrs. C & E. Millar during the construction of the railway.

F. M. Green before expiry of agreement, pleaded not guilty.
Mr Symes for prosecution.

Francis Mahon Green deposed: Defendant was in my service under an agreement now produced to serve me as a servant for three years from July 1st, 1887, at £2 per month; defendant left his service without leave last Wednesday night; there is about £3 due to him; he told me a month ago he was going to leave, but I told he could not do so; I accused him of stealing on the 9th September; it cost £12 to bring him from Ceylon, and it would take 5 months before I could replace him; Chinese labor would cost about £10 during that time; I would rather not take him back into my service.

Defendant was ordered to pay £3 compensation, £1 Court fees, and £2 2s for counsel, or in default 3 months' hard labour. The fine was paid (*North Australian*, 10 October 1888).

When murders occurred, such as when Sugar Manager Heath shot his foreman (McKinnon), Coroner Pater ran the inquest for the deceased, then sat in the criminal court as judge of the accused.

Luckily, capital cases were few and far between, but they did happen. In 1885, Ah Kong was found guilty of murdering James Lawless with a knife, at Port Darwin Camp. Lawless, a blacksmith, caught Ah Kong stealing and accosted him. In the struggle that followed, Ah Kong stabbed Lawless in the neck with a sheath-knife, completely severing his jugular vein.

Pater sentenced Ah Kong to be hanged. However, Pater's court did not have the right to try a capital offence at that time. The trial was 'bungled', and Ah Kong was held for a second trial. It was the same for Nammy:

… We regret to learn that the bungling over the first trial of the blackfellow Nammy who murdered Harry Houschildt, and Ah Kong, who murdered Lawless and was captured red-handed, has resulted in the verdict in both cases being made void. It will be remembered that the brilliant framers of the Act under which both these men were tried, omitted to provide for the laying of information and trying murder cases, consequently their first trial was declared void.

The men were brought up a second time after the law had
been altered, and their counsel pleaded that the men could
not be tried twice for the same offence. The point raised was
reserved, the men were found guilty, and sentenced to death,
but the higher court has decided that the defence put forward
is a good one, and both murderers will be released … (*NTTG*,
4 September 1886).

There was, of course, outrage among the leading citizens of
Palmerston. They met and resolved to forcibly expel Ah Kong back to
China, and he was subsequently put on the first boat available (*North
Australian*, 10 September 1886).

William Henry Whitton

Soon after that, in October 1886, Pater presided over the trial
of William Henry Whitton, who had killed Thomas Spellacy and Ah
Young at a cattle station on the Wilton River, on 9 March 1886. He
was found guilty of murder by the jury and:

> … His Honor in addressing the prisoner said: Prisoner at
> the bar, you have been found guilty of the wilful murder of
> Spellacy, and I have no doubt the jury trying your case took
> into consideration all the circumstances, urged by the learned
> counsel for your defence, on your behalf. I entirely concur
> with the verdict of the jury, and it only remains for me to
> pronounce the sentence provided by law for the punishment
> of the crime of murder. The sentence of the Court is that you
> shall be taken to the place from whence you came, and, after
> the time provided by law for appeal shall have elapsed, shall
> be hanged by the neck until you are dead, and your body shall
> be buried within the precincts of the gaol. May the Lord have
> mercy upon your soul (*NTTG*, 9 October 1886).

The sentence was never carried out—this time because there were
questions about Whitton's sanity. The death sentence was commuted
to imprisonment, and he was subsequently locked away in a lunatic
asylum in Adelaide. Nearly three decades later, in 1914, he died in
the Parkside Asylum. The *Adelaide Register*, always on the lookout for
a sensational story, found Whitton's arresting officer, an ex-Mounted
Constable William Curtis, then retired. They interviewed him

closely, and most of his story aligns with the court report of 28 years earlier, (although not the name of the victim, Thomas Spellacy). The nineteenth-century theories of phrenology and inherited traits of the criminal class had a boost when believers discovered that Whitton had a bushy mono-brow …

… With the death recently of William Henry Whitton, who had been an inmate of the institution for about 30 years, there passed away one of the most notorious criminals whose exploits have darkened the history of the Northern Territory …

'I regard the arrest of Whitton as my greatest achievement' remarked Mr Curtis. 'He was one of the worst outlaws in the Territory. A man of short stature, probably not more than 5 ft. 4 in. in height, he was something under 40 years of age when I managed to handcuff him on the Roper River. He was a man who would stop at nothing when hard pressed, and apparently thought little of taking human life. His features were noticeable on account of his extremely bushy eyebrows, which were unbroken across the bottom of his forehead. For daring the man could hardly be eclipsed. It was in regard to some cases of horse stealing that I first heard of Whitton. He was arrested to stand his trial and was sent from the Catherine [sic] River to Darwin in the charge of M.C. [Mounted Constable] Bay. He did not arrive at his destination without making a desperate bid for liberty'.

'While he and his guardian were resting at an hotel on the route, Whitton contrived to catch the trooper unawares and dash to where his horse was tethered. He jumped on the steed and made off with all haste. The mounted constable was equal to the occasion, however and procuring the only horse available, immediately followed. Eventually he overtook the fellow and brought him back in custody. The constable saw fit to overlook the incident at the trial, and Whitton was merely charged with horse stealing, an offence which was not proved against him. He, therefore regained his freedom.'

… 'It was only a few months after that I came into personal touch with Whitton', continued Mr Curtis. 'I was at Abraham's Billabong, about 60 miles west of the Roper River;

when a black tracker brought me a note from M.C. Power, who was in charge of a camp at Mount McMinn; to the effect that, murders had been committed at Wilton River Station; and I was required at the camp at once. I hurried thither, and on my arrival was informed that Mr Thomas Pellissey [sic] the manager of the Wilton River Station, and Ah Young, a cook, had been murdered.'

'A blackboy had come to the camp and said that Whitton had ordered him to say that the manager had suddenly gone mad and shot at and fatally wounded the cook, and that he had received fatal wounds in return from the Chinese. The blackboy's own version of the story was that Whitton approached the station, and as soon as the manager appeared at the door shot him in the groin. Immediately the cook came out of the house and was shot through the heart by Whitton. Mr Pellissey, though suffering fearfully, had not fallen. Propping himself against the wall, he had strength enough to keep holding a rifle. Whitton ordered the blackboy to get what was in the Chinaman's pockets (£80 was discovered there subsequently), as he feared that the wounded manager might shoot; but the boy was too frightened to go forward. Whitton then made off, taking the aborigine with him.

… I was set to watch Whitton who had been warned against leaving the locality, pending enquiries into the affair. While Power was away, I determined to arrest the man in view of the facts which had been brought to light, so one day I went to the Roper, where his camp was situated. There I found him lying on the ground, apparently dozing. At the first glance I could see that he had a revolver within reach of his right hand, and a rifle under his head. I crept up, snatched the two weapons, and forthwith taxed the man with the murders. I got one pair of handcuffs on him, and he exclaimed—'Do you think these things will hold me?' As the manacles appeared to be rather big, I determined to take no risks and used a smaller pair. I then conducted Whitton to the Burrundie police camp, and awaited Power's return with evidence …

'When M.C. Power reached Wilton River Station for the second time, he resolved to try to discover a diary, which Pellissey was known to have kept most methodically, in order to see if he had been able to record any reference to the shooting. Upon turning over some paper bark in the unfortunate man's trunk he came across the object of his search. The hoped-for clue was there, for in the diary was written in a shaky hand:—'To Mr Davis (owner of the station, who was at that time absent in China on a holiday)—Whitton shot me and the Chinaman this morning. Mind and have him hanged'. Underneath the above words was added the following: 'I have recovered a little, but I cannot reach a drop of water ... Sell my old black horse and send the proceeds to my poor old mother at Bendigo. Mind and have Whitton hanged' (*Register*, 19 June 1914).

Pater family tragedy

The Paters suffered a personal tragedy during their time in the north. Their eldest daughter—19-year-old Edith Mary—died of consumption in December 1886.

In 1885, Edith went to Victoria to complete her education and she fell ill whilst there. The best doctors were consulted, but her illness continued. Her mother rushed to Melbourne to be with her, but by then:

> ... the condition of the poor young lady was so much altered for the worse that the doctors pronounced the case as hopeless ... it was thought that a sea voyage might possibly re-kindle the little flickering vitality which remained ...

Emily Pater brought Edith back to Palmerston. She:

> ... seemed to rally for a while, but ... the once bright and beautiful girl gradually drooped and faded away. It is a very sad case indeed; here was a highly educated and accomplished girl of nineteen, the pride and hope of her parents, fitted by nature and training to enter the highest society, and with an apparently bright future before her, smitten down on the very threshold of life by an insidious disease beyond the physician's skill to cope with (*NTTG*, 25 December 1886).

Because Edith took several months to die, her death was not unexpected, but grief was felt across the small settlement. The funeral procession travelled from the Paters' house on the Esplanade to the cemetery on Goyder Road. The cortege included 12 carriages. All the mourners dressed in white, and the coffin was 'profusely covered with wreaths and flowers'.

In the procession were all the civil servants of the town and 'large numbers of the general public [who] also showed the last mark of respect for the deceased … all business in town was suspended until the funeral was ended' (*North Australian,* 24 December 1846).

Cutting costs

By the end of the 1880s, South Australia's economic recession meant the Government needed to curb their spending on the Northern Territory even further. John Parsons was a government resident with no legal training, and there was an opportunity to save money by once again combining the functions of government resident and judge. Ideally, Parson's successors would therefore all be lawyers.

Pressure was thus placed on Pater to leave as well, and the two positions of government resident and judge were once again amalgamated. On 18 December 1889, Pater sent a telegram to Adelaide stating that he had agreed to resign from his position as a judge in the Northern Territory on the condition that he be given a year's leave on full pay. The Government agreed to six months' leave (*Express and Telegraph,* 18 December 1889) and he returned to South Australia to become the city police magistrate. He died just over two years later:

> … At ten minutes to 1 on Thursday [11 August 1892], Mr
> T. Pater, S.M., the Police Magistrate of Adelaide, died after a
> short illness. On Wednesday morning Mr Pater was unable
> to preside at the Police Court owing to a sudden attack of
> paralysis in the legs, and on the first examination, his medical
> attendant, Dr Veroo, expressed the opinion that it was only a
> circulatory derangement. He found later on that the case was
> serious, and heart disease and apoplexy following on caused
> his death. Mr Pater died at his residence in Barnard-street,
> North Adelaide, in the presence of his wife and daughter.
> The deceased gentleman occupied the position of City Police

Magistrate for just over two years, and his occupancy of
the chief seat on the Bench gave very general satisfaction.
He brought to the discharge of his duties an extensive legal
knowledge and a long practice as a lawyer, which served him
admirably as a Magistrate; while his judgments were, as viewed
by the legal profession and the public, of an impartial nature,
and as a rule marked by a desire to promote the welfare of the
community. Mr Pater's distinctive personality, his original and
characteristic remarks to prisoners brought before him, and
his decidedly strong character assisted in making the Police
Magistrate a very conspicuous figure in his judicial capacity ...
(Obituary, 12 August 1892).

Figure 68: Maurice Holtze's residence at the Palmerston Gardens (Foelsche, SLSA B-9756).

Chapter 11
The Government Gardens

William Hayes

The first government garden was run by William Hayes, who was appointed gardener at the time of settlement in 1869. Hayes established an 'experimental garden' and grew food plants, but rarely ventured to undertake many 'experiments'. His produce mostly went to the tables of the senior civil servants.

By 1878, Hayes's garden was overshadowed by the Chinese market gardens, which produced better quality and a wider range of food.

Hayes died of diarrhoea on 19 June 1878. His death provided an opportunity to expand and improve on the government gardens. Providentially, there was a German guard at the gaol, named Maurice Holtze, who was also a botanist.

Maurice Holtze

Holtze had experience in the Royal Gardens of Hanover and the Imperial Gardens in St Petersburg. He and his wife, Evlampia, emigrated to Victoria in the mid-1870s and to Port Darwin a few years later, so were available when the vacancy in the gardens came up. He was recruited immediately. His work, and the changes he made, were of continuing benefit to the Northern Territory.

The original gardens were closed—they became the police paddock—and a new site was chosen near Fannie Bay. To get there 'you branch[ed] off from the telegraph line on the road to Southport

Figure 69: Ludmilla Holtze, daughter of Maurice and Evlampia (1890, ph0328-2170).

Figure 70: Maurice Holtze (NTL PH0391-0008).

and continue to ride for a mile through high grass and patches of thick jungle' (Sowden, 1882).

The 32-acre (13 ha.) garden was cleared of scrub and jungle by a team of destitute Chinese miners—employed on relief work by Government Resident Price in the dry season of 1878 for a shilling a day. By 1882, Holtze still employed 17 Chinese workers, but their salaries had increased to between 15 and 25 shillings a week—without rations, and they lived in small huts in the gardens. Holtze's salary was just under £5 per week (£250 p.a.) and he was provided with a substantial house that became a regular destination for members of Palmerston society.

The new gardens were established for the 'express purpose of raising plants of commercial value and distributing them over the colony'. Holtze, and his son Nicholas*—who took over in 1891—

---

* Nicholas Holtze earned some notoriety as a 14-year-old assistant at the Southport Telegraph Station. In 1881, he was lost in the bush for five days and the subject of a huge search effort to find him. He was eventually brought in safely by some local Larrakia men, who treated him well (*NTTG*, 10 December 1881). He was a clever lad, and by 1888, he was a relieving secretary and accountant and Acting Deputy Registrar for Government Resident Parsons (*NTTG*, 17 March 1888).

were the pioneers of tropical agriculture in the Northern Territory. They tested crops ranging from rubber to rice and peanuts to pomegranates. The potential of coffee, tobacco and sugar industries was examined, and seeds or seedling stock were provided to farmers in huge numbers.

Sowden wrote that the gardens were the 'greatest surprise' he had in the Territory. They were an 'umbrageous paradise'. He saw trees taller than the native trees outside the garden, even though they were 20 years older, bearing the 'most luscious fruit'. He toured 16 acres of sugar cane—in eight varieties—with canes two metres long—which was at least double the length that he had seen at Delissaville. All the stock for the sugar plantations had come from Holtze's garden. So too, did 8,000 banana palms and 13,000 pineapple plants—given to the planters freely, at the expense of the government.

Holtze's garden had termites, just like in the plantations, but he used arsenic to kill them rather than carbolic acid, as he found it more effective.

Moved again

In 1886, Holtze moved the gardens once again, to a site at the foot of some picturesque cliffs where the 'George Brown Botanical Gardens' presently grow. The old gardens were declared a recreation ground and they became the Fannie Bay Racecourse.

Three years later a *Times* journalist was impressed:

> … After the two previous unsuccessful attempts to establish a nursery for tropical and semi-tropical plants, and the abandonment of the gardens at the Police Paddock and Fannie Bay, the present site for the gardens was selected, and Mr Holtze at once set to work to transplant the most valuable plants to the new nursery. The present site … is very prettily situated at the foot of the cliffs overlooking the sea. The land, or a portion of it, had previously been occupied and cultivated by Chinese gardeners, and was partly cleared of timber and undergrowth, but at the same time, this advantage was counterbalanced by the fact that it had been somewhat

impoverished by the continuous cultivation of crops of vegetables, maize, sugar cane, etc. (*NTTG*, 16 February 1889).

Chinese gardeners forced out

The Chinese gardeners included Soo Hoo Yoke and Sam Sing, the storekeeper. Soo was a man who had already been in Palmerston for several years, working regularly in the courts as an interpreter for his countrymen, and dabbling in gold mining.

Soo was granted 'during the Council's pleasure', permission to farm the land Holtze later wanted. There was initially no rent to pay, but he was required to 'fix up a substantial trough outside the ground… and keep such trough continually filled with water, from a well or otherwise, for the use of cattle de-pasturing' (Kelsey, 11 October 1883).

In 1885, the Government changed the rules (under pressure from ratepayers), and Soo was charged just over £58 rent (£3 per acre) per annum for the 19 acres he occupied. He paid the first six months on time, but when he was 20 days overdue for his second payment, there was reason enough to evict him from his farm. This made way for government gardens.

A letter from Soo Hoo Yoke was published in the *North Australian* on 26 February 1886, and the editorial declared Parsons and the government to be 'mean, despicable, and unpolitic [and] unjust' over this decision (26 February 1886). He had taken the land under a permit from the Council when it was:

> … dense scrubby jungle, which I cleared and fenced at an expense of something over £1000; buildings cost fully £100; sinking four wells on different portions of the garden cost about—£25; cutting a large main drain from the foot of the rise to the sea… costing over £100… You will see by the foregoing rough schedule of outlay that before I could commence the cultivation of vegetables and fruit, I had to expend close upon £1,300.

He complained bitterly about his treatment:

… I should not have been able to carry on so long had I not
received pecuniary assistance from my Chinese commercial
friends who supported me on the understanding that as soon
as population came to the country, I should have a better
market for my produce. In addition to this the fruit trees
which I imported, planted, and nurtured for the past three
years, are just commencing to bear and the produce would
have proved a set-off in time against my great outlay. Should
the Government now deprive me of my outlay it means
nothing short of ruin (*North Australian*, 26 February 1886).

Soo Hoo Yoke was ignored by Parsons and was never
compensated for his loss. He was under 'considerable anxiety' and, as
he had predicted, ruined. In March 1887, he became ill, and returned
to China and died there, a broken man. The loss of the 'Government
Interpreter' was mourned by the *Times* (*NTTG*, 19 March 1887),
and a mining lease he held on the Mary River was announced vacant
in October the same year. He was forgotten by the population, and
never mentioned again by the newspapers, except by one—in 1915, a
journalist at the *Times* wrote a critical article titled 'Park Lands Piracy'
(*NTTG*, 13 May 1915).

A pleasant daytrip

Meanwhile, for the white population of Palmerston, the gardens
became a pleasant day trip:

One of the prettiest portions of the garden is at the base
of the overhanging cliff, which is almost hidden from view
by tropical foliage of every imaginable shade, from richest
green to a golden brown. Here a small artificial lake has
been constructed, and a few beds of flowering shrubs, pinks,
carnations, and balsams on its margin add a mass of richest
colouring, as a contrast to the dark background of the cliff
and fallen rocks, covered with overhanging creepers, ferns,
palms, and every form of wild jungle vegetation. At the foot of
the cliff, an ancient Banyan tree of enormous size spreads its
innumerable fantastic arms and gives a grateful shade from the
scorching afternoon sun.

… A very picturesque drive, bordered by an avenue of flowery acacias is now being laid out through the garden, towards the end of McMinn-street, meanwhile the fund of information to be obtained by a visit to these gardens will well repay the trouble of the walk. The distance from Palmerston to the gardens is only a trifle over two miles, and the area under cultivation is roughly estimated at 40 acres (*NTTG*, 16 February 1889).

The gardens became—and still are—a delightful place to hold a wedding. Perhaps the first was in November 1889: Maurice and Evlampia's daughter, Ludmilla, married Charles W. Hughes[*] in a quiet ceremony in the gardens. The happy couple then moved to Chillagoe in Queensland, and later to Kangaroo Island[†].

---

[*] Hughes is mentioned by Alfred Giles as being his relief manager of Springvale Station, when Giles was away on business (*North Queensland Register*, 9 January 1932). He was also a part of the exploration party crossing Melville Island, and a Councillor on the Palmerston District Council.

[†] Maurice Holtze retired to Kangaroo Island and lived his final days with Ludmilla and Charles Hughes. He died in 1923.

Chapter 12

Sugar

Port Darwin's first government resident, Bloomfield Douglas, may have been pleased when the whole peninsula on the western side of the harbour was named after him in 1870, but the name did not stick. In October 1872, cattle drover Matthew Dillon Cox, and his foreman D'Arcy Wentworth Uhr, arrived in Palmerston with cattle and horses they had brought from Queensland. On arrival, Cox applied for a pastoral lease over the whole of Douglas Peninsula and moved his herds there. The lease was never finalised, but Cox squatted in a station he named Bowerlee after the Government Resident's racehorse. Cox developed a strong friendship with Douglas, and he would stay at The Residency when in Palmerston, so the lack of a lease was never a problem.

Cox's Peninsula

Within a year or two, everyone called the peninsula 'Cox's Peninsula' and Cox sold beef to Palmerston's residents for one shilling a pound. The Peninsula is still called Cox Peninsula, and his cattle station, Bowerlee, was arguably the earliest in the Territory, although it was never 'official'. When Dillon Cox could not go droving, he asked his brother, Wynne Price Cox to bring a mob of horses north to Palmerston. They arrived in 1873, and the brothers planned to breed and export them to the army in India. Unfortunately, the drove was a disaster—most of the horses scattered across the Limmen-Bight Rivers area and the drovers were lucky to survive a torrid expedition (Cross J., 2011).

Dillon Cox possessed a quick temper (Wilson, 2008) and he fell into numerous brawls. On several occasions, he appeared in the Police Court for assault. Cox's nephew, Charles Bourchier, was similarly inclined. The two argued and fought on 13 April 1874. The fight ended when Bourchier stabbed his uncle in his side. He was charged with assault and immediately taken to court, where he was fined five pounds. In disgrace, he left the Northern Territory on the first available ship—and literally got away with murder—Cox died several weeks later from his wound, the knife having sliced his kidney.

Mrs Catherine Cox, his widow, continued to work the station with the help of Price Cox and Frank Cameron (another nephew). However, when Price, his wife and their four children were all drowned in the *Gothenburg* disaster in 1875, Cox's station died a natural death (Pugh, 2018b).

When Edward Price took over as government resident in 1876, he was keen to encourage the establishment of agricultural industries in the Top End. He encouraged George Coppenborg and Peter Ericksen to clear land along the coast at West Point to grow maize—which they did 'with fair success'. One industry he imagined early was sugar. The sugar industry was taking off in far north Queensland—so why not in the Territory? To encourage investment, the Government offered a reward of £5,000 for the first company who harvested 500 tons of sugar in the Northern Territory.

Figure 71: Sugar bonus advertisement in 1878. This ad was repeated in the Palmerston newspapers for years, but the £5,000 was never claimed (*NTTG*, 6 November 1880).

Northern Territory Sugar Cultivation Act of 1880

The South Australian government was pressured to release land to sugar farmers, particularly by Messrs. Spence and Ouston of Melbourne, Mr John S. Peterson of Melbourne, and Mr Benjamin C. de Lissa of Queensland. *The Northern Territory Sugar Cultivation Act of 1880* was passed. It allowed The government resident to allocate 100,000 acres of land to investors to plant cane. They advertised for people to take it on, received 30 applications, and chose men who were already in the colony. Spence, Ouston and Peterson were granted 10,000 acres each of land in the Daly River district, A.W. Sergison was awarded 5,000 acres on the Adelaide River*, de Lissa and others were granted land at Cox's Peninsula. It was at no cost, except they had to work it successfully† (*NTTG*, 23 April 1881). The Delissa Pioneer Sugar Company merged some of the land grants on Cox's Peninsula, and the community subsequently became known as Delissaville‡.

Delissaville

The *Northern Territory Times* recorded de Lissa's first actions on 23 October 1880:

> ... The Peninsula ... with its hundred thousand acres remained practically lifeless, till Mr D'Lissa [sic] arrived at Port Darwin; and within a few days of that event paid a flying visit to the land in question and saw almost at a glance that within hail of the finest port in these eastern waters

---

* A.W. Sergison was a passenger on the *Menmuir* in 1882 at the same time as the Parliamentary Party. He was returning with agricultural tools and horses. The 5000 acres of land he selected for sugar lies between Beatrice Hill and the Adelaide River, on the northern side of the current Arnhem Highway.

† Land granted on Cox's Peninsula for sugar plantation in 1881: B. C. de Lissa 10,000 acres; G.T. Bean (adjoining de Lissa's selection) 5,000; W.H. Bean 5,000; Arthur Bean 5,000; L. Scammell 6,000; J. H. Gordon. 5,000; Philip Levi 5,000; F. W. Stokes, M.P. 6,000; George Scarfe 3.000; W. Ross Sawers 3,000; plus, eight others at 3,000 acres each (*NTTG*, 23 April 1881).

‡ Delissaville is now the Aboriginal community of Belyuen. The name was changed in 1975.

there were tracts of agricultural land rich enough for the cultivation of sugarcane, and equally easy of access by land and by water.

Mr D'Lissa being a practical planter, as well as a scientific sugar maker, at once pegged out his selection and set to work, without an hour's delay, to clear and prepare his ground. He has scarcely been there a month and the transformation effected in that brief time has been simply marvellous.

The 'headquarters' are constituted by a fine, lofty house and store of galvanised iron, and a number of substantial huts are dotted about the clearing for the accommodation of the Chinese laborers. There are about eighty Asiatics and ten Europeans engaged in clearing the land, cutting, and stacking firewood for engine fuel, and digging holes for the reception of the cuttings of sugarcane.

Mr D'Lissa hopes to be able to plant one hundred acres before the wet season fully sets in, but he should think himself lucky if he succeeds in getting in half of that area. The soil is, of course, of variable quality, but most of it is good, pliable earth capable of growing any kind of tropical or subtropical produce. Mr D'Lissa has the energy of one of the latest improved compound condensing steam engines. He seems perfectly irrepressible and must either conquer all obstacles or burst! There are no half-way successes with him; and from what we saw of the manner in which he had subdued the wilderness in the course of three or four weeks, we cannot bring ourselves to believe that he can be capable of failure, especially when he has such a plucky and sterling coadjutor as Mr Charles Levi.

Should all go well, we hope to sweeten our editorial tea with native grown sugar within the next twelve months, to say nothing of the insinuating pine-apple rum, which so gladdened the heart of the Rev. Mr Stiggins (*NTTG*, 23 October 1880).

The sugar 'heads' were grown at the government experimental gardens in Palmerston by Maurice Holtze. The first crushing to collect the juice was carried out in 1881, under the direction of Arthur Bean, the company secretary, though not to the pleasure of Mr de Lissa:

… On the morning of Monday, the 28th of November last year, Miss Pickford, with characteristic grace, started the machinery for an experimental crushing of about ten tons of sugarcane, forwarded at the special request of Mr Bean, the Secretary of the Delissa Pioneer Sugar Company, for the purpose of ascertaining the quality of the sugar likely to be produced in the Northern Territory. The experiment was tried against the earnest protest of Mr de Lissa, who contended that cane which had been exposed to the weather for six or eight days was quite unfit to be put through the mill. The remonstrance proved to be well-founded for the cane when crushed looked like so many bundles of dried bamboo, yielding but a small percentage of juice, and, as was predicted, the total quantity extracted was insufficient to cover the coils in the boiling pans, so that after hours of anxious labour the liquor refused to crystallise and consequently no sugar could be made (*NTTG*, 1 April 1882).

The 'crude product' was put aside to wait for the ministerial visit and it:

… remained undisturbed until Monday, the 21st [March], when the Ministerial party paid a visit to Delissaville to inspect the property of the Pioneer Company. The occasion was thought to be a fitting one to see if the cane juice had solidified in the interval of four months, so the machinery was set in motion and two or three buckets of the thickest of the sediment were put through the 'centrifugals'. This beautiful piece of mechanism which revolves at the rate of 2000 revolutions per minute speedily transformed the dark treacley [sic] looking mixture into a fine bright grained white sugar, fit at once to be placed upon the breakfast table. In a few minutes it was thus proved that cane grown in the Northern Territory and crushed under the most disadvantageous circumstances still yielded a first-class sugar, leaving no doubt whatever that when cut at maturity and passed at once through the rollers, would turn out a sugar that no country could excel. The Ministerial party were delighted at this practical exhibition of the plant and machinery belonging to the Pioneer Company, which we shall now proceed to describe in a briefly detailed manner (*NTTG*, 1 April 1882).

Figure 72: Chinese workers among sugar cane (PRG-23-6-3-9).

The parliamentary party was fresh from the goldfields. Their visit to Delissaville was one of the last engagements for Minister Parsons before he returned south on the *Menmuir*.

William Sowden was amazed at how much work had been done in 18 months. 'Altogether' he wrote, 'there were 200 acres of cane, and there are 50 acres of maize' (Sowden, 1882). The sugarcane had at first suffered from termite damage, but by briefly soaking the canes in a solution of carbolic acid, the problem appeared solved. Sowden thought the canes were small but healthy, and de Lissa told him that he hoped they would 'spring up rapidly towards the end of the wet season.'

Slavery

Delissaville delighted the parliamentary party, but one aspect of it, hardly mentioned, casts a shameful shadow over the whole project. The overseer of the plantation was Charles Levi, who had been a partner with John Lewis, in the Cobourg Cattle Company in Port Essington (Pugh 2020). When Levi managed the Port Essington station in 1876, a visiting 'correspondent' was impressed by the station and how well the Aborigines worked for him:

> ... Great praise is due to the latter gentleman [Levi], for the work done and improvements made on the station (of which he is part owner), the amount of which cannot be realised unless actually seen ... A Palmerstonian going to Port Essington would be astonished at the amount of work that Mr Levi gets out of the natives. Besides the cook, there are only two Europeans on the station—all the rest of the work being done by the natives, who work as well as most white men.
>
> There is no begging or grumbling on their part. If they are told to do anything, they must do it at once and take their pay* in tobacco, &c., at the end of the week. Laziness or refusal to work entails immediate discharge, a proceeding which happily the captain has seldom found necessary to adopt (*NTTG*, 16 December 1876).

Levi's control of the Port Essington Aborigines continued. At Delissaville, an unnamed number of the Port Essington (Iwaidja) tribe lived on the opposite side of the creek from the 15 Chinese workers. The Chinese were paid £1 per week, but:

> ... these blacks, who have their lubras with them, are fed and housed, but do not receive a stated wage. They look and speak like intelligent fellows, and work as such in various parts of the estate. Mr de Lissa will allow no communication between them and the tribes around Palmerston. Some of them essayed to break through the ban a few months ago, but Mr de Lissa gave them such a fright, by means of rockets and such like, while not injuring them, that they have not tried to do so since. So now, whenever he goes to Palmerston, he distributes a bag of flour and some trifles amongst them; and if they hint at going over to their old ground, frowns upon them unutterably, frightening them effectually (Sowden, 1882).

---

* This situation continued for many years. Historian Samantha Wells noted: 'It was not until 1913, some four decades after settlement, that the payment to Aboriginal workers of 'a stick of tobacco and the scraps of the table ... for a day's work, such as cutting firewood, cleaning yards, and other work of a similar nature, was considered no longer acceptable' (Wells, 2003).

It seems that they were unpaid captives. No matter how willing they were to work for Charles Levi, this was slavery.

The Ministerial Party returned to Adelaide with samples of the sugar they had seen produced. It was put on display in Rundle Street, and the editor of the *Advertiser* was hopeful of seeing a new industry growing in the north of the state:

> … It is white crystallised sugar, somewhat dirty, owing to exposure for three months in an open iron tank, but otherwise it is a very fair sample, contains the usual quantity of saccharine, and possesses no foreign taste whatever, thus contrasting favorably with the Mauritius productions. It has been sampled by experienced connoisseurs, who pronounce it a dry grainy crystal, and who state as their opinion that if it can be produced clean and white it will become a highly marketable article. It is very interesting to know that sugar can be grown and manufactured in this colony, as it should open up a new and large industry. Those gentlemen who have interested themselves in the growth of sugar in the Northern Territory are to be complimented upon the successful nature of their venture, which now promises to become a national benefit (*Advertiser*, 21 April 1882).

Agricultural potential

After Minister Parsons had left Port Darwin, Sowden remained to explore the Top End further. He joined John Knight, then the Stipendiary Magistrate, and Mr Harrison J.P., and returned to Cox Peninsula to tour the West Point plantations belonging to Messrs. Ericson and Coppenborg*. These gentlemen were still growing maize,

---

* Coppenborg disappeared in 1886: 'We are sorry to learn that Mr George Cloppenburg [sic], who left the Robinson for Normanton, over 10 weeks ago, has not been heard of, and it is now considered certain that the poor fellow has perished. Mr Cloppenburg will be remembered by many of our readers as one of the hard-working pioneers of agriculture in the Territory. While engaged with Mr Peter Erickson some three years ago, planting on Douglas Peninsula, the work done by the two men in clearing and planting, was a marvellous example of what it was possible for two industrious, persevering men to do. George Cloppenburg was one of that class of settlers the Territory can ill afford to lose' (*NTTG*, 24 April 1886).

though by then were having serious issues with caterpillars. They had expanded their enterprise, and were now growing pigs, chickens, peanuts, sorghum, and rice. They also had 5 acres of sugarcane. Sowden thought the sugar plants were stunted and not making 'as much cane as they ought to have made'. However, he said, they looked better than the cane at Delissaville that he saw a fortnight earlier.

Professor Tate's opinion

The only scientist on the parliamentary party took it all in. He made observations of the climate and the vegetation around them, and drew his conclusions based on what he saw. No one listened to Professor Tate when he reported his understanding of the agricultural potential of the soil and climate in 1882. Tate could not recommend the place for agriculture. He reported that 'the dominant vegetation … implies, if not sterility of the soil, then certainly the absence of… atmospheric moisture, and conversely general exposure to the sun' (Tate, May 13, 1882). Unfortunately, the Minister of Education, J. Langdon Parsons, chose to disagree with him, and directly challenged Tate's conclusions:

> … In speaking of this [Tate's] unfavourable report on the agricultural resources of the Northern Territory, I wish to say at once I do not speak as a scientist, or as a practical cultivator of the soil, or a practical squatter. Now, no one respects more highly than I do the truly scientific man; no one bows down with greater submission to the certain ascertained results of science more completely than I do; but I feel strongly that the most scientifically unscientific thing in the world is unscientific science—and that the one thing we are to insist upon with regard to science before we accept the conclusions of it is that it is certain, that it is based upon investigation, and that the generalizations are warranted by the data. Apart from that the guesses of science are not worthy of any more credence than the guesses of superstition. We expect from scientific men that they shall be sure of the statements they make, and if the facts are not established, I say of all such statements that they are not science, at any rate (Parsons, 23 September 1882).

Parsons assured the parliament that he had spoken with 'practical' men who knew different. The scientist had been too hasty in his judgement and others knew better. He quoted a report sent to him from a Mr Thomson:

> ... The situation of the De Lissa Estate is well chosen. I
> consider the soil suitable for sugarcane. I consider the fields
> judiciously laid out; they lie well for drainage and irrigation.
> The kind of cane is very good; the misses are the result
> of bad planting. The weather is most favourable for our
> operations, and everything is progressing most favourably and
> satisfactorily (Parsons, 23 September 1882).

Professor Tate was right. However, Minister Parsons was never blamed for any of the mistakes and wasted efforts that came after.

After three seasons, the output of sugar from Delissaville remained so low that the company was in trouble. On 30 December 1884, the shareholders met for their half-yearly meeting in Adelaide. It was chaired by one of the landholders, George Scarfe. The shareholders heard that in 1883–4 'only 4 tons 10 cwt. 11 lbs. sugar' was produced. The cause, said Mr Biddles, the manager, was the soil. It had once been identified as perfectly suited for growing sugarcane, but in 1884, it was reported to be 'iron-stony, pebbly, and porous— and totally unfitted for the growth of sugarcane (*NTTG*, 31 January 1885).

The company directors sought further expert help, and Maurice Holtze, the government gardener, was asked to cross the harbour and inspect Delissaville. 'This he did without delay... and emphatically condemned the selection as a site for sugar growing'. Other reports came in also, and the directors were 'forced' to suspend operations immediately. Benjamin de Lissa was blamed:

> ... Your Directors sincerely regret the unsatisfactory result
> of the operations and expenditure to which the Company
> was committed by the purchase of Mr Delissa's interest
> in the Government concessions, and which but for the
> ignorance and infatuation displayed by him in making an
> unsuitable selection, should have been remunerative to the

shareholders… He represented that the land was eminently suited for sugar-growing … a sum like £20,000 being spent on the raising of five tons of sugar … [de Lissa] had either been very ignorant or had misled the shareholders and had spent their money recklessly … [for instance] de Lissa ordered twelve sets of harness when only two were required, ten carts when only two were needed, and had got two crushing machines when only one was necessary … Mr de Lissa's estimate for labour was quite as incorrect as for the plant. He calculated that it would be possible to obtain coolies from India; but as there was no agreement between the Government of this colony and the Indian Government, considerable delay arose, and from the aspect of affairs, the Directors came to the conclusion that it would not be advisable to bind themselves for any term. Hence it was found necessary to employ Chinese at a much higher rate of wages (*NTTG*, 31 January 1885).

The dream collapses

Mr. de Lissa had run out of friends and was told to move on. The *Times* thought he was terribly wronged by his backers, and the company directors struggled for an answer. They decided the only option was to wind-up the company, and then start another one with land from the Daly River Region, by buying the plant and equipment from the Delissa Pioneer Sugar Company and transferring it to the Daly. Spence and Ousten had surrendered their claim to the land on the Daly that they had been allocated in 1881, so 10,000 acres were available:

> … the whole of the valuable machinery, which is of the most modern and approved description, with the working plant, horses, tools, and other appliances necessary for the cultivation of cane and manufacture of sugar, will be offered for sale in one lot, and so afford an opportunity for the reorganization of the present shareholders or the formation of a new Company to purchase on what will undoubtedly be favourable terms, a plant that will place them in a position to commence operations at once, and avail themselves of the offer of the Government of selection on the Daly … (*NTTG*, 31 January 1885).

The demise of the Delissaville Sugar Company highlighted the possible success of other plantations in 1885. Otto Brandt, a member of the Palmerston District Council, had a 600-acre plantation at Shoal Bay:

> ... situated at a distance of about 14 or 15 miles from
> Palmerston, in a northerly direction, and comprises an area
> of 600 acres in extent. For the most part the selection is flat
> land, which in the rainy season is slightly inundated, but
> at this time of the year presents an outward appearance not
> unlike the hard, cracked soil of the Adelaide River. I mean
> these remarks only to apply to the ground in its virgin state,
> for where the plough has ripped through it, the broken soil,
> while still resembling to a certain degree that of the Adelaide,
> has a noticeable difference in one or two respects which, in
> my opinion, and in the opinion of many others better capable
> of judging than I, classifies it as a superior soil. It is on this
> flat land exclusively that the ploughman's labour has been
> expended, and the cane planted. Something like 70 acres are
> at the present time under crop, but... 20 acres of this were
> touched by a fire. Comparing the cane at Shoal Bay with that
> I have seen growing in other parts of the Northern Territory,
> I am inclined to give the former the 'cake' for healthy
> appearance... I know everyone will be pleased to see the Shoal
> Bay Plantation turning out finest white sugar, altogether
> unlike the dark, dirty stuff manufactured at Delissaville some
> time ago. (*North Australian*, 7 August 1885).

Brandt was desperately working to win the £5,000 offered to whoever could produce 500 tons of sugar. Its availability had been extended because no one had yet claimed it: but neither did Brandt— the most he could ever hope for was 300–400 tons of sugar per year. Any setback, like that he experienced in 1889, did not help:

> ... On the 28th of October 1889, the S.S. *Fleetwing* sprang
> a leak and was run ashore at Talc Head, while on her voyage
> to Palmerston, with 22 tons of sugar on board from Brandt's
> Plantation, Shoal Bay. The whole cargo of sugar was destroyed
> (*NTTG*, October 1889).

The price of labour

The price of labour was a 'tender spot' for the planters:

> … Mr Brandt has 125 Chinese and 11 Europeans at work on his plantation, and the scale of wages ranges from 2s. to 2s. 6d. per day for labourers and from 3s. 6d to 5s. for artizans [sic]. These wages he considers reasonable enough from the planter's standpoint, and he needs no Indian labour while the Chinese are free of a poll-tax; but if such a tax is instituted, he is impressed with the belief that Chinese labour would become very expensive, and the Government would then have to provide planters with cheap coolies. At the present low prices of sugar, which, if they do rise again, will never reach their former height, a sugar plantation can only be worked profitably by keeping the wages account down as low as possible, by cutting down to a minimum all other expenses, and by studying to obtain the highest possible percentage of juice from the cane (*North Australian*, 7 August 1885).

Each of the Delissaville, Daly River and Shoal Bay sugar plantations relied on Chinese workers. As resistance to the Chinese grew, labour became increasingly difficult to find and, as production rates were always poor in Territory soils anyway, the plantations were quick to close. Soon the only sugar grown in the Northern Territory was on a small scale: Chinese market gardeners continued to grow sugar cane in their gardens and small parcels of land around Palmerston.

In 1886, the Daly River planters and Otto Brandt at Shoal Bay were about the last sugar-men standing … Most of the land released for sugar plantations was resumed by the government:

> Notice of determination and resumption of land granted for sugar-growing and other products.

> To the under mentioned persons, and to all whom it may concern: Take notice that the respective agreements for selecting waste lands of the Crown in the Northern Territory for sugar plantations, dated 1st day of March 1881, and 1st day of June 1881, and respectively made between you and the Hon. Thomas King, the then Minister of Education, therein

contracting for and on behalf of the Government of South Australia, under the authority of the Act No. 191 of 1880, were, on the 1st day of December instant, duly and lawfully determined by His Excellency the Governor, and the lands mentioned in the said agreements were resumed, as provided in the said Act:-Benjamin Cohen de Lissa, George Thomas Bean, William Henry Bean, Arthur Bean, Luther Scammel, John Hannah Gordon, Philip Levi, A.W Sergison and Maurice Lyons, Frederick William Stokes, George Scarfe, William Ross Sawyers, William Benjamin Rounsevell, James Francis Wigley (representatives of), William Knox Simms, William Thomas Foster, T. Estcourt Bucknall, John Richardson, Arthur Rait Malcolm, Farquar Terry, Gordon McCrea.

Dated this 5th day of December 1885.

JOHN A. COCKBURN, Minister of Education.

Manslaughter at the Daly River Plantation Company

The new Daly River Plantation Company at first looked promising. They had bought their equipment from Delissaville for a song, and the land was free. But life on the Daly River sugar plantation did not always run smoothly. Up to 1886, Wright Woodward Heath was the manager. He lived on the plantation with his wife, Eliza, their adult son Walter, and a young daughter. Unfortunately, whenever Heath was away, the foreman, 41-year-old Donald McKinnon and Eliza enjoyed a passionate affair. They had already talked of her getting a divorce and moving to Queensland together. But when Heath suspected the affair and confronted his wife on 31 August 1886, all the sordid details came out, and it ended up with Heath shooting McKinnon dead on their doorstep. Heath immediately took a Chinese sampan to Port Darwin and gave himself up to Inspector Foelsche.

Dr Wood had the unenviable task of carrying out an autopsy on McKinnon many days after he was killed. At the inquest he reported:

> ... his hair and beard was grey. He was clothed in a white coat, singlet, pair of trousers, and boots. The body was in an advanced stage of decomposition. I saw that the right side of

the head had been almost completely blown away, and the head was very empty of brain; what was left of the brain was very decomposed. After some trouble I found the four shots produced in a cavity of the brain. On further examining the body I found two ribs broken (third and fourth) in front and on the left side: and on the inner side of the left arm, on the same level, were shot wounds. I traced some of the shot wounds and removed the two shots produced from the back of the left arm. I then examined the broken ribs, and found they had been penetrated by shot, one of which I produce. I then removed the heart, and found two shots embedded in it … From what I saw I consider both the wounds would have proved fatal (*North Australian*, 17 September 1876).

Heath was sentenced to 10 years in prison for the manslaughter of Donald McKinnon* on 31 August 1886. He was a sympathetic figure, though, and 3,850 members of the community petitioned (nearly 50% of the non-Aboriginal population) the courts for a remission of his sentence in early 1887:

… Heath may have been guilty technically of manslaughter, his conducting shooting the seducer of his wife, when that scoundrel approached his house with revolver in his hand and defiance in his manner, amounted morally to nothing more than justifiable homicide… (*Express and Telegraph*, 13 January 1887).

and

… The *Register* today strongly supports the petition, and remarks that everything tends to show that Heath is not a criminal in the true sense of the word, and that his claim for release rests more on the grounds of his being justified, rather than on those of mercy (*NTTG*, 15 January 1887).

Heath was lucky. On 21 June 1887, the Government decided to release twelve long-sentence prisoners as a part of the jubilee celebration (50 years of both Queen Victoria's rule, and the State of South Australia), and there was an all-round reduction in the sentences of all the remaining prisoners (*North Australian*, 11 June 1887).

---

* McKinnon is buried in plot No. 15 in the Gardens Road Cemetery in Darwin. The burial cost £1 16 6 (NTRS 686/5).

The end of sugar

Brandt abandoned Shoal Bay in 1891. The soil and the climate in the Top End could not compete with Queensland's sugar regions, and there was never enough juice in the plants for a good harvest. Nevertheless, the optimistic farmer was willing to try again in the Daly River region:

Figure 73: A camp on the Daly River, 1887 (SLSA B7246).

... It is a fact to lie deeply regretted that Mr Brandt did not establish a plantation there years ago. With the thousands that have been wasted on Shoal Bay we feel sure that a most gratifying result would have been secured at the Daly. (*NTTG*, 27 March 1891).

185

During the 1890s, however, both the Daly River Sugar Plantation Company and Brandt's sugar venture were doomed to failure, because there was little suitable land in the area selected. Brandt was more successful growing tobacco but, in the end, it was another industry doomed to failure:

> ... The leaf grown was of the highest grade, and is said to have topped the market when sold, but quarrels between the general manager and sub-manager at Rum Jungle, and the neglect of the South Australian Government to take any notice of the letters written by Mr Brandt, regarding the acquisition of a new site, caused Mr Brandt, in a fit of temper, to abandon the whole enterprise, and ... the tobacco industry has lain dormant ever since, and opportunities which might have yielded hundreds of fortunes, and employed thousands of people, have been utterly neglected (*NTTG*, 8 February 1907).

Chapter 13
The South Australian
parliamentary visit of 1888

Figure 74: The 1888 Parliamentary Party: The Hon. Joseph Johnson, Government Resident Parsons, David Lindsay and John Knight and others, with people who are probably Larrakia (Foelsche, 1888, LANT PH0002/0052).

The visit of South Australian parliamentarians in 1888 highlights the changes that occurred during the 1880s. The new Minister of Education and the Northern Territory, the Honourable Joseph C.F. Johnson, arrived in Port Darwin on 2 March.

Johnson first spent a week examining sites around Palmerston, such as the botanical gardens run by Maurice Holtze; the gaol at Fannie Bay; and the quarantine station on Channel Island.

There were many questions the residents of Palmerston and the goldfields wanted to put to the minister, and he was happy to receive deputations from them. Some of the questions were listed in the *North Australian*:

His opinions of our mineral country …

His ideas about the employment of Chinese on Northern Territory mines of any kind whatever.

When a start will be made with the erection of our promised coast lighthouses.

If there is any chance of the Burrundie Hospital being "bedded" between now and the Day of Judgment.

When the people of the Territory are likely to have to pay as little for colonial telegrams as the people of South Australia …

When the Pine Creek to Katherine section of the big line is to be marked off …

Whether he has formed any settled views on the labour query, Whites vs. Chinese.

Whether Cingalese, Malays, Tamils or Chinamen make the best colonists.

If he believes in Chinese being allowed to tender for or work on Government contracts.

If he or any other member of the party saw in their travels any extensive areas of country that appeared to be suitable for the production of a particular description of bamboo of Eastern origin … (*North Australian*, 31 March 1888).

The minister catches a train

On 9 March, Johnson caught a train south to the goldfields as guests of the railway contractors, the Millar brothers. Government Resident Parsons, Inspector Foelsche, David Lindsay and John Knight travelled with him. To Parsons, the changes must have been stark. In 1882, he had been the Minister of Education who was shown around the

Figure 75: View of Burrundie township 1890 (SLSA B9044).

goldfields, but on horseback. He was now the Government Resident showing his parliamentary successor around, and he was travelling on the railway he instigated.

The railway line was only complete as far as the '72-Mile', about 116 kilometres, which meant they needed to catch buggies to reach Adelaide River and Burrundie, the new major town in the area. The Burrundie Hospital, Warden's Office and Police Station were in operation, and the telegraph station building from Southport was being transferred. It would soon be manned by staff from The Shackle*.

The minister was met by D'Arcy Uhr†, George Deane and others, who expressed the need for a proper road to be constructed to Katherine. There were, they said, many people wanting to travel south by coach, but it was not yet possible (*NTTG*, 31 March 1888).

The minister replied that the government would certainly investigate the problem, and the gold warden, Charles Nash, had

---

* Burrundie was abandoned by 1911 as the town of Pine Creek took over. Burrundie was established after a push from the Northern Territory Progress Association, after its first meeting at James Johnston's Store at Port Darwin Camp, on 24 March 1883. Today's visitors can tour the ruins on 'The Northern Goldfields Loop' off the Stuart Highway, although travellers beware—Burrundie is signposted like any other town, but little of it is left among the trees.

† D'Arcy Uhr (1845–1907) was primarily a bushman and drover. He spent several years mining gold in Pine Creek to finance his cattle droves.

already been instructed to report on what was needed. In any case, he was about to find out about the road himself, as the party took to horse-back. The tracks were rough but passable to horses, and a vast improvement on what they used to be. The party travelled on

Figure 76: Charles Brown Fisher's Steam launch *Victoria* at Beatrice Hill, 70 miles up Adelaide River (LANT ph1060-0068).

to Pine Creek via the Port Darwin Camp, the Union, and several other gold mines, then returned to Burrundie via the tin mines of Mount Wells and the tin lodes at Mount Shoobridge. The minister interviewed many of the locals en-route, heard their complaints

191

and recommendations, and developed a good impression of the north (Parsons, 1889). The sun was hot, but they were untroubled by the heavy rain and boggy roads that had dogged the previous Parliamentary Party in 1882.

The minister's opinion

The honourable minister was most impressed by the goldfields, which he

> ... considered to be good, kindly country, carrying the lodes in slates, and easily workable rocks. He had never before seen such a number of metalliferous lodes in the same extent of country (*NTTG*, 21 April 1888).

After his return, the parliamentary party rounded off their visit by a trip on the steamboat *Victoria*, up the Adelaide River, to the sugar plantations near Beatrice Hill, where Johnson was:

> ... very pleased ... It is indeed a glorious river, a splendid navigable stream with deep water from bank to bank. Grand plains of rich alluvial soil stretch back from each bank of the river, almost entirely destitute of timber and other obstructions to the plough. The only timber in sight seemed to be in belts, apparently skirting watercourses, which divided the plains into sections (*NTTG*, 21 April 1888).

Of agricultural land, he had seen:

> ... patches of land in the mining districts that ought to be capable of growing many tropical and sub-tropical products. In some places there are considerable tracts of rich land bordering the numerous watercourses, while between the Finniss and Rum Jungle, the railway works, by their trenches, have proved the character of the soil, and nature of the subsoil for miles (*NTTG*, 21 April 1888).

Johnson was told of the need for the construction of a lighthouse, a second telegraph line to accommodate more traffic (particularly news), and the Channel Island Quarantine Station. He was also advised of problems at the Palmerston Assay Office, and with the Palmerston water supply, difficulties in mineral exploration licencing, and the 'Chinese question'. On the latter, he was:

Figure 77: Mount Wells Tin Mine 1885 (Foelsche, LANT ph0111-0070)

... very decided in his opinion... and favours restriction generally. He would prevent them from engaging in mining anywhere, except as servants, and prevent them from holding freehold property, but to encourage those who are already here to develop the land, he would grant them cultivation leases for garden and agricultural purposes under special conditions (*NTTG*, 21 April 1888).

The Palmerston school disappointed Johnson. He was, after all, the Minister of Education:

> On Monday last the Minister of Education accompanied by the Government Resident and Mr Evans paid a visit of inspection to the State School where he was received by the master, Mr F. P. Kitchin. About 15 children were present, which Mr Kitchin stated was about the average attendance. The Minister examined some of the children's work, and the premises. He expressed himself as very disappointed with the attendance and intends to put the compulsory clause of the Act into operation at once (*NTTG*, 14 April 1888).

Overall, the minister was thoroughly satisfied with the result of his trip. He said his new knowledge would help him in legislating for the Territory in a 'much more satisfactory and intelligent manner than if he had never seen the place.'

193

He also declared himself to be an enthusiastic supporter of the Territory. After his visit, he now had 'such an interest in it, and in its welfare, that whether in the Ministry, or in his place as a private member, he should always be a representative of this portion of South Australia' (*NTTG*, 21 April 1888).

Chapter 14
The hanging of Wandy Wandy

Figure 78: Edward Osborne Robinson (LANT, PRG-280-1-5-374).

In 1879, Edward Osborne Robinson* and his partner, Thomas Howard Wingfield, took out a lease over the whole of Croker Island and built a homestead at a place named Walkey (or Wolgie). There, they collected trepang for the Chinese market and planned agricultural developments on the island. According to Robinson, the pair employed about 30 of the local Iwaidja people, and they were on good terms with them—until December 1879, when Robinson left Croker Island to take their catch to Port Darwin. While he was away, Wingfield was murdered.

---

*   E. O. Robinson arrived in the Territory in 1877. He was a 23-year-old Englishman seeking his fortune, and he turned his hand to any business that was going: He managed John Lewis's buffalo harvesting station in Port Essington, and bought a small ship named *Essington*. He used the ship to transport government officials and tourists to the port. He enjoyed success at buffalo hunting for the skin trade, trepang collection, and pearling. From 1881, he also worked as a customs officer in Port Essington and Bowen Straits (near Croker Island) on a salary of £20 p.a. (LANT A5167/1881). He spoke the Macassan language and traded with the praus who visited the coast annually. He also understood some of the Aboriginal languages along the coast and was known to be 'a hard citizen but he was cool, level-headed, and straight as a cue in all business dealings ... and a deadly shot with the rifle' (*NTTG*, 22 Nov 1917, p 23).

Wingfield's murder

In the storehouse, Wingfield kept flour, rice, tobacco, and rum—the wages for the native employees. Wingfield's initial trouble started with the rum.

An employee named Mayuna arrived early one morning, bringing jungle fowl eggs to Wingfield. Wingfield paid for them with five sticks of tobacco and enough rum to make Mayuna drunk.

Mayuna wanted more rum and returned to the homestead twice to demand it. Annoyed, Wingfield set the dogs on him and took out his revolver, possibly just as a threat. However, someone else threw a spear–later claimed to be at a pigeon–near the homestead, and Wingfield, startled, shot Mayuna dead on his veranda.

The Aborigines were incensed. All day they mulled over the events of the morning, and the call for revenge grew. A man named Wandy Wandy (aka Wandi Wandi), who was not an employee of the white men, was designated to act on their behalf. Whilst Wingfield slept on the veranda after dinner that evening, Wandy Wandy took a tomahawk and hit him three times over the head.

The story was followed closely by the *Northern Territory Times* and the transcript of the Police Courts published in full:

> … Wandi Wandi, an aboriginal, was charged with the wilful
> murder of Thomas Howard Wingfield, at Croker Island,
> on or about the 13th of December last. Edward Osborne
> Robinson, sworn, said… I was about a fortnight away from
> the island and arrived at the camp on the 17th of December
> last. When I returned, I found the camp deserted. I looked
> inside the hut; the door being shut but not fastened. I called
> out for Wingfield, at the same time looking about. I saw a
> straw mattress at the door covered with coagulated blood. One
> of the crew of the boat pointed out … where Wingfield was
> buried—it was about six yards on the south side of the hut.
> The hole would be about a foot deep. The body was partly
> covered with earth; it was Wingfield's. I recognised it by the
> head. He was buried in his coat. I uncovered his head and
> identified his features. The wound I saw on the head was from

the back to the front, about four inches long, and about two inches broad. He appeared to have had several blows. His left arm was broken, and his hand was sticking up. I then left the body without further examination and went to Port Essington. I went there for assistance, and I returned to Croker Island with Kite and Coppenborg and some natives, one of whom was Jack Davis[*]. I got back on the 20th of December last, about four o'clock in the afternoon.

We disinterred the body—it was too much decomposed to make a minute examination. I further examined the premises. There was a broken stretcher with blood on it near the grave, it had been removed from the hut alongside the grave. There was a piece of paper tacked on to it with the date of the 13th of December. It was usually kept nailed up on a box outside the door, under the veranda. I found a tomahawk [produced] covered with blood, standing close to the door, outside the house. Everything was gone—the place had been ransacked of six months' stores, excepting half a ton of rice and some tea …

… Prisoner was brought to Port Essington on Sunday, the 8th of August. He came to me in company with other natives— there were about 120 altogether. I called him inside the house. I was sitting on my seat with my revolver. A sheet of paper was on the writing desk. I said, 'What name another one darky kill Wingfield?' He said, 'No one, only myself'.

From my own knowledge of prisoner, I knew he understood. I did not give him any caution whatever. I never used threats or inducements to prisoner. I was sitting on the veranda.

After he made the statement, I took hold of his arm and covered him with my revolver and said, 'I will put you in chokey'. Kite put the handcuffs on him. Kite was sworn in as a special constable at the same time that I was. Kite said, 'I arrest you in the Queen's name, and anything you say will be used against you', or words to that effect. Prisoner said nothing … (*NTTG*, 28 August 1880).

---

[*] For a biography of Jack Davis (Mildun) see *Port Essington*, (Pugh, 2020).

Witnesses

Inspector Foelsche sailed to Port Essington to gather witnesses and bring them into Port Darwin for Wandy Wandy's trial. Many witnesses were keen to participate: several hundred people gathered 'to partake of flour and tobacco at government expense for a few weeks' and the inspector needed to make a judicious selection of the Aborigines and 'not bring the whole mob' (*NTTG*, 14 August 1880).

The witnesses he selected told the court of the deaths of both Mayuna and Wingfield in statements that were formatted by a literate lawman, most likely through an interpreter:

> … Allawal [aka Prince] said: I know prisoner Wandi Wandi. I know Robinson sit down at Croker Island, also a white fellow Wingfield, name of place Walkey. When trepang fishing, remember Mr Robinson go away boat, with Paddy and Harry … I, Wandi Wandi, and other blacks walked to Walkey and saw Mayuna dead. Blacks say they kill 'em Wingfield—all about plenty. Wingfield sleep on a bed outside the house, on veranda. I see him lying down. I was along a cookhouse. I could see him on bed when I was in cookhouse. Mangu and Maccaroni were in cookhouse, also Big Jack. Linda was there, and plenty more black fellows all about. Wandi Wandi sat down along cookhouse. He go up and get tomahawk, put 'em behind his back. He went up to where Wingfield sleep. A little bag that Wandi Wandi had hanging round his neck he put into his mouth. He cut 'em Wingfield along the head with the tomahawk. He cut 'em three times, then come out and put down tomahawk. The large one produced is the one. Saw plenty blood come from Wingfield. Him dead. I and others took him out and buried him. Wandi saw us do it. Wandi went inside house, brings out tobacco, handkerchiefs, knife, trousers, some rice flour. Some blackfellow take 'em bottle—plenty bottles of rum. We drink 'em all, then went back. When black fellow growl and be cross, he put 'em bag in mouth. Wandi Wandi went along Alligator. We belong to same country.

> Moyur, a native, said: I know Mr Robinson. I know Wingfield, he live Walkey. I know when Wingfield die. I sit

down along camp. Close to house, can see house from the camp. Saw Wandi Wandi kill Wingfield. He killed him with tomahawk. I saw him strike him with the tomahawk. Here is the one. He hit him three times. He walk away outside. I saw blood come from Wingfield's head. When I saw him, he dead. Helped to put him in ground. Wandi Wandi then went away. He took plenty tobacco, rum, rice from the house (*NTTG*, 28 August 1880).

Wandy Wandy sentenced

Wandi Wandi was initially remanded for sentencing. He was, thought the public, clearly guilty of murder, but the court at the time was not entitled to try a capital offence. The provocation of Mayuna's death was considered and Wandi Wandi was found guilty of manslaughter. He was sentenced to 10 years in prison with hard labour (*NTTG*, 14 May 1881). He almost immediately escaped, but was caught near the jetty, and punished by having to spend the first 12 months of his sentence in irons (*NTTG*, 21 August 1880).

After ten years, the *Times* was happy to report that Wandy Wandy served his time. Apart from now spelling his name differently, the paper was impressed that the man was now well-disciplined, could speak perfect English, was a Catholic, and was taking up residence at the Rapid Creek Mission with Father Donald MacKillop (*NTTG*, 23 March 1889).

Unfortunately, this was not the last the residents of Palmerston were to hear of this man. He worked well at the mission, and Father MacKillop was able to give him a character reference:

> … during the few weeks he remained there his conduct was all that could be desired. He tried hard to persuade us to return with him and establish a Mission among his countrymen. He said that should we do so his tribe on learning our true intentions from him, the son of their former King, would to a man become Christians (MacKillop, Letter to the Editor, 1892).

The *Evening Journal* reported that Wandy Wandy:

… was wont to say that 'the blacks did not know how to work, but he had learnt in gaol, and could show them'. On one occasion he said to Father MacKillop, 'Don't ever let me go into the bush, for if you do, I will become a bad black-fellow.' (22 July 1893).

Wandy Wandy kills again

But return to the bush he did and, as he predicted, soon got into trouble. In 1892, he and five other men were arrested for the slaughter of the entire crew of a Malay fishing prau, about six months earlier:

> … Six aboriginal natives named respectively: Wandy Wandy, Capoondur, Ingeewaraky, Dooramite, Mintaedge, and Angareeda were charged with the wilful murder of six Malays at Mandool, near Bowen Straits (*NTTG*, 18 November 1892)

> … Before giving notice of commitment, prisoners were asked if they wished to say anything. Wandy Wandy, who was the first one interrogated, made the following statement, which we render as near as possible in his own pidgin-English:- I sit down at Wanmook: all about blackfellow go along Mandool; Capoondur first time go: him go first along beach and find 'em proa; other blackfellows come up behind; Capoondur then said he been find 'em Malay him been break 'em proa; then all blackfellow say 'Come on, we go down and see 'em'; all blackfellows go and see them and I come up behind; the Malays made signs to take the parcels and we all went a little way and got dinner; after we have dinner we take 'em everything away and walk; Malay and me go easy; two fellow, Goolardno and Marakite, go first time and him run away; then me hear Mangerippy sing out 'What for you run away;' then all about blackfellow run away; then we go back where make 'em camp before; me sit down; Goolardno yabber me first time 'You and me kill 'em all about' and all blackfellow say 'All right, kill 'em;' then me sit down little while and Goolardno yabber longa me; he say 'You take away that revolver and knife and I kill 'em'; then I sit down little bit and by and by get up and catch 'em that revolver and one knife; then me run away a little way; Dooramite catch 'em two fellow gun and bow and arrow and sit down longa me; then blackfellow kill 'em all about Malays; Goolardno kill 'em two

fellow first and Capoondur kill one fellow; then Mintaedge
kill another one; Angareeda and Marakite kill one fellow; then
we take 'em all about clothes and go along Mandool; then
next day me go down along Wark and sit down there; Jack,
Lark, and Prince come up along Wark; me sit down there long
time.

None of the other prisoners ventured any statement and they
were all then committed for trial (*NTTG*, 13 November 1892).

At the trial, the accused and other witnesses all gave similar
testimonies. The police reported on their forensic studies of the Malays'
camp and digging up the skeletons, and Doctor L. S. O'Flaherty was
able to report at length on the six skulls the prosecution had collected
as evidence—still with Asian hair and scraps of desiccated brain
attached to them.

The court found that the well-known murderer, Wandy
Wandy, was the ringleader of the group. He had killed none of them
personally but had disarmed the Malays before they were attacked.
He was sentenced to death, and told his execution was to take place
in his own country, in front of his clan, as a warning to the tribe.

It took almost a year to organise, and many were the letters
to newspapers about the justice of killing a black man, when white
men were receiving less harsh punishment*. Father MacKillop agreed
that Wandy Wandy 'would be the arch-plotter' and that it was 'only
natural, for he was born head of his tribe'. But MacKillop did not

---

* The white man most compared to Wandy Wandy worked in Port Essington for
E.O. Robinson as a buffalo catcher. Rodney Claude Spencer was charged with
shooting an Aborigine named Manulocum, at Port Essington, during 1889.
Aboriginal witnesses told how Spencer 'caught hold of Manulocum by the hair
of the head with one hand and shot him in the forehead with the revolver;
Manulocum then fell down on his face; [Spencer] then shot him in the back as he
was lying on the ground' Manulocum had stolen some rice from Spencer. (*NTTG*,
14 March 1890). Spencer was found guilty of crime as 'one of the most wanton and
cowardly ever perpetrated in the colony'. He was sentenced to death, though this
was later commuted to imprisonment, and he was released in 1901. Four years after
that, Spencer was murdered near Cadell Straits. 'He was speared whilst asleep on
shore, and when attempting to reach [his] revolver, was brained with the blow of a
tomahawk' (*NTTG*, 27 January 1905). Perhaps justice had been served.

sympathize with murder, and believed, 'that Wandi Wandi [sic] should die' (MacKillop, Letter to the Editor, 1892).

Wandy Wandy hangs

As luck would have it, John Little, who by then was 'deputy sherriff' of the Northern Territory, as well as the chief of the Overland Telegraph, was available to accompany Inspector Foelsche and Wandy Wandy to Malay Bay for his execution. He was then pleased to be able to report the event to the *Times*:

> ... The Deputy Sheriff, Inspector of Police, Guard Loydon, and the executioner, with the condemned aboriginal prisoner, Wandy Wandy, left Port Darwin per steamship Darwin early on Sunday, July 23rd, and arrived at Malay Bay on Monday morning. The gallows for the execution was landed and erected at a most suitable spot, the place being a camp much frequented every year by natives, Malays, and others for the purpose of obtaining trepang and preparing it for export. The prisoner was executed on the evening of Tuesday, July 25th. The drop was 6ft 6in, and death was instantaneous, not even a tremor or movement of the body of any kind occurring after the drop fell.
>
> Mr Foelsche had collected about thirty natives who witnessed the execution. Three of these natives spoke English fluently, and had been witnesses at the trial of Wandy Wandy.
>
> The body was left hanging for twenty minutes and was then cut down and buried at the place of execution. The gallows was left standing as a warning to natives, Malays, and others (Little, 11 August 1993).

Wandy Wandy was the second man executed legally in the Northern Territory. Just ten days earlier, on 15 July 1893, Charles Flannagan was hanged at Fannie Bay Gaol for the murder of Samuel Croker at Auvergne Station*. John Little was present then also.

---

* Only three other legal executions occurred in the Northern Territory during the 19th century. An Aborigine named Moolooloorun was sentenced to death by Justice Dashwood and executed on 17 January 1895 for the murder of an unnamed Chinese man near the Roper River. He was hanged on gallows specially constructed at Crescent Lagoon in the presence of 50 members of his community, and the deputy sheriff, John Little. (*Adelaide Observer*, 2 February 1895). Later, on

According to the *Advertiser*, Flannagan:

> … freely acknowledged his guilt and manifested no fear. He walked to the scaffold with a firm step, saying he was going 'to die hard'. The execution, which was the first that has taken place in the Northern Territory, was carried out without a hitch, death being instantaneous. (*Advertiser*, 17 July 1893).

10 August 1899, Chung Yeung and Lem Kai were hanged in a double execution at Fannie Bay Gaol, for the murder (and cooking) of Chee Hang at Yam Creek (*Sunday Times*, 13 August 1899).

Figure 79: Larrakia people in Palmerston (Foelsche, SLSA, B11948).

Chapter 15
Larrakia

The writer, William Sowden, was naturally interested in the Larrakia people he met in Palmerston in 1882. One generalisation he made echoed an observation of members of the First Northern Territory Expedition in 1864—Aboriginal people seemed to be natural mimics. The settlers at Escape Cliffs watched Wulna people march up and down with sticks on their shoulders in imitation of the drills enforced on the settlers by Colonel Finniss (Pugh, 2018a). In Port Essington, about 1910, Jack Davis would perform a parade ground pantomime that mimicked the Royal Marines he had seen in the settlement 70 years earlier (Pugh, 2020).

Of the Larrakia, Sowden said that:

> … they imitate anything which strikes them as peculiar in a stranger. Such as one, strutting pompously down the street, for example, may find at least a couple of exact copyists of his movements shuffling up close behind him, and a squatting audience laughing and clapping their hands in appreciation of the joke. There interviewed me one night a black named 'Billee', dressed in white, with a pith helmet crowning all. The way in which he imitated the Government resident would have done the heart of Maccabe good… (Sowden 1882).

Many Larrakia lived in a camp on the beach below the town. They had built 'huts compounded of bits of kerosene tins and driftwood, of bark and old bagging, and one with an old insurance plate stuck upside down over its portals …' Some huts were more temporary, being sheets of paperbark that acted as a windbreak. In general, Sowden was unimpressed with their standard of living and lamented the loss of the Wesleyan Church leaders, Reverends J. A. Bogle and W. Hanton, who had worked hard in the 1870s to help the Larrakia. They had been, as historian Matthew Stephen observed, mostly relegated 'to an underclass of fringe dwellers in their own country and a 'problem' to be solved, as had occurred throughout Australia' (Stephen, 2010).

Inspector Paul Foelsche was one of the few Europeans to undertake anything like an anthropological study, which he based on his 11 years of experience living in the Top End. In 1882, he read a paper to the Royal Society of South Australia, titled *Notes on the Aborigines of North Australia*. Foelsche commented on everything from law and language to marriage, funeral rites, and medical procedures. His description of cannibalistic practices is graphic and disturbing but was not backed up by evidence. Foelsche's information came from 'friendly natives', but he did not claim to see the practice himself, and few believe these days that cannibalism was ever widely practised in Australia. 'Cannibalism', Foelsche wrote:

> ... 'is practised by all natives on the north coast... with the exception of the... Port Essington [tribe]. The eating of grown-up people—that is, of natives—is, as far as I can ascertain, not practised. Only children of a tender age—up to about two years old—are considered fit subjects for food, and if they fall ill are often strangled by the old men, cooked, and eaten, and all parts except the head, which is skinned and buried, are considered a delicacy. Parents eat their own children, and all, young and old, partake of it' (1882)*.

Rapid Creek Mission

In 1882, many of the Larrakia were enticed away from Palmerston by the Jesuit missionaries who were setting up their mission at Rapid

---

* For the senior policeman of the Northern Territory to declare this without evidence is quite extraordinary. Such comments fuelled the justification the whites had for the excess of racism that characterised nineteenth century Australia, and the resultant massacres that occurred across the continent.

Creek. They were given small gifts of food and promised employment in clearing land and planting bananas and pineapples. This lasted for nine weeks, when most returned to Palmerston to live 'by begging and sin' (Reid, 1990). Some soon moved back to the mission, camping on Rapid Creek nearby. They continued to work for the Jesuits, and a school was started for their children—with lessons given in the Larrakia language (see Chapter 16).

Holiday sports days had been organised for the Aboriginal population by the settlers since the earliest days of colonisation, and this continued in the early 1880s. It was one way that the Europeans could encourage Aborigines to wear clothes, and an opportunity to provide food and other items of use to them. For example, on New Year's Day in Southport:

> ... our native population came in for their share of the good things of the season. The stores provided many with new suits of clothing, and the townspeople got up some sports for their benefit. The sum of £3 15s. was subscribed in cash and Messrs Adcock Bros. and Allen and Co. each added a bag of flour and a pound of tobacco. The sports consisted of the usual programme of flat races for men, lubras, and youngsters, and a hand-cart race which was the best event of the whole, wound up by a general scramble for lollies. Our sable friends retired to camp at the usual hour with untold wealth in shillings, flour, and tobacco; and our correspondent even goes so far as to say that one native has placed money to his credit with one of the firms mentioned (*North Australian*, 9 January 1885).

In 1885, Dr Percy Moore Wood, the Protector of Aborigines, became concerned about potential violence breaking out between the Larrakia and Malay pearlers. Pearl shell had been discovered in Darwin Harbour during 1884, and the Malay pearling fleet was welcomed—it was the dawn of a new industry. Several Larrakia women went to live with them and occasionally were taken to sea in their boats (Reid, 1990). Mary Ann, an Aboriginal girl who had chosen to live with a Malay, took her brother Charley to court in 1884, after he had forcefully tried to remove her. 'What for Malay keep 'em that girl?' he said, 'that not right.'

However, some men thought it their right to sell their women and children as prostitutes. A group of people from the Adelaide and Alligator Rivers areas visited the town annually:

> ... The morals of our young men have been sorely tried this
> week, and it would scarcely surprise us to find that some
> had fallen from the pathway of virtue and moral rectitude.
> On Monday, the 20th inst, the day kept as a public holiday,
> the blacks from the Adelaide and Alligator rivers, hungering
> after tobacco and money, arrived on the outskirts of the
> township. The following morning, they were all about
> anxious to vend their merchandise, and to obtain the highest
> market prices. They were free traders certainly, but of a
> questionable type; they recognise the Bright principle of
> buying in the cheapest market and selling in the dearest. And
> what do 'southern Christians,' who spend so much money
> on missionary enterprise, think of their wares, when we tell
> them that women and children were freely offered (not in the
> marketplace for sale) but for the purposes of prostitution in
> the city.
>
> The order of doing business was peculiar. They were about
> in lots of twenty and thirty of mixed sexes, and no sooner
> did a European stay to look at their uncouth figures than the
> salesman of the party stepped forward pointing to the sorted
> lot. The old women were offered at sixpence, whilst others
> ranged in value to one and two shillings, the latter figure
> being demanded for quite young children under ten years of
> age. Towards dusk their value had depreciated, lower prices
> obtained, and choice specimens were submitted at a sacrifice
> (*NTTG* 24 June 1881).

The *Times* then suggested—in one of the earliest calls for reserves—that the best way to stop this behaviour was to keep people in their own country:

> ... As the country is being rapidly taken up for settlement,
> and their chances of living becomes less, we ask, have any
> portions of the Northern Territory been set apart as aboriginal
> reserves? The colonial surgeon, their protector, should see to
> this (*NTTG* 24 June 1883).

Rules for protection

Dr Wood was keen to protect Aborigines against abuses, and he agreed that the only way was to keep them out of town. He recommended that no Aborigine be allowed in town between sunset and sunrise, and only those employed as servants, with a permit issued by himself, should be allowed in the town during the day. None should be allowed to join boats on coastal trips. In the remote areas, taking women and children into stock camps would be outlawed. He also favoured flogging over incarceration for thieves, because 'it was no disgrace to them to be living in the same conditions as Europeans' (Reid, 1990). Anyone wishing to employ Aborigines would need permission from the protector, and large fines would be issued to anyone who broke the rules.

Government Resident Parsons considered Wood's recommendations and asked Inspector Foelsche for his opinion. Foelsche replied that legislation specifically for Aborigines was difficult to achieve—they were, after all, British subjects and equal under British law. 'Class law' was against British principles, which meant laws that protected one race against the abuses arising from the advantages of another, did not fit within them. It would be another decade before the legal arguments ran their course and the first Aborigines protection legislation was passed by the Queensland Parliament in 1897 (Reid, 1990).

Scant habiliments

Many of the settlers were affronted by the dress of many Larrakia in town. The scant 'habiliments of these sable nymphs of the forest' challenged the sensibilities of the colonisers:

> … Aborigines were described 'prowling the street in a semi-nude state' and 'caricaturing the decencies of civilised citizens by an ostentatious display of semi cinctures almost as repulsive as nudity itself'.

Unable to tolerate this state of undress, Protector of Aborigines

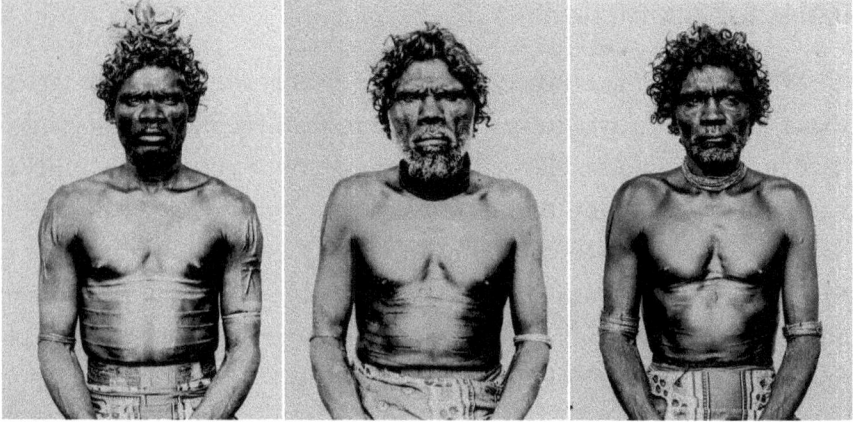

Figure 80: Larrakia men, Davey, Miranda, and Peter (Foelsche, 1888, LANT PH0560-0084, 89 and 91).

Wood requested in 1889 that Aboriginal women who were employed in the town, be given 'some form of gown, simply but strongly made' and after they had been given it 'not be allowed in the streets unless decently dressed'. Wood also recommended that men not be allowed in the town 'unless decently dressed' (Wells, 2003).

Unconcerned about their nudity, Inspector Foelsche made a photographic record of some of the Larrakia men and women who lived near Palmerston in 1888. He already knew some of them professionally. For example, he had arrested Davey and Miranda in 1879 after they had killed a notorious and unpopular Wulna man named Scotchman. They got away with murder, while the entire community, both black and white, breathed a sigh of relief at his demise:

> … It did not take long to find out who the killers were, with Inspector Foelsche on their trail. They appeared in court in February 1879 before the Government Resident, Mr Price:
>
> Davey, Sambo, Rowdy, Miranda, and Benham, aboriginals [sic], were charged with feloniously, wilfully, and with malice aforethought, killing and murdering one, 'Scotchman' an aboriginal native.
>
> Mr Foelsche, inspector of police, sworn, deposed: 'On the 23rd of January last, I obtained a warrant for the arrest of the prisoners charged with the murder of the aboriginal named

Scotchman. This morning they came and gave themselves up
… Sambo … stated that Scotchman went into camp in the
evening and that he (Sambo) told him that they did not want
him, and that he had better walk. Scotchman went a little
way out of camp into bush, then stopped and threw a spear
at Davey; Davey popped down his head and the spear missed
him, and after that they threw several spears at Scotchman.
They had no intention of killing him but wanted to drive him
away as they were afraid of him, stating that he had killed
Nosey and Black Douglas, and that he was only waiting to
bring back the Woolners here …

Mr Price, in his wisdom as magistrate, considered a warning
and a little Christian evangelism was all that was necessary.

… The magistrate here warned those indicted for this terrible
tragedy, that they must be more careful in future. We could
not quite catch all he said, but we know this much, that the
advice he gave them was taken to heart, as they left the court
more than ever persuaded to forsake their Mosaical notions
and become solid Christians (*NTTG*, 8 February 1879).

Miranda

The Miranda in Foelsche's photograph may be the same man first
met by Government Resident Douglas in 1870, although Miranda is
a Larrakia clan name. Douglas thought he was 'king' of his tribe, as
did his daughter, Harriet, who wrote of their meeting in her memoir
(Daly, 1887). He was well known in the 1870s and 1880s. He was
often called 'king' and was no stranger to the courts. In 1883, he was
called as a witness in a trial of a Malay man, named Damul, accused
of providing alcohol to Aborigines in exchange for women. 'I give you
grog if you bring me lubra', Damul had said. He was found guilty and
fined £2—or three weeks imprisonment (*NTTG*, 17 March 1883).

In 1887, Miranda was gaoled for a month for fighting with a
constable:

… King Miranda, of the Larrakeyahs, a powerfully
built aboriginal, was on Tuesday sentenced to a month's
imprisonment for 'going for' Constable Smith. The native's

Figure 81: Aboriginal people living near Port Darwin (c. 1887 Foelsche SLSA B-8315).

offence is singular, and it occurred thus: The constable, taking the dusky monarch to be one of the plebian black loafers that usually squat around town, commanded him to go to camp. Miranda replied that he had business in town, and declined to move, whereupon the doubting constable pushed him by way of giving him a start. This so riled his majesty that he immediately 'put up his props' and gave battle to Smith in true British fashion and with a certain degree of success; but finding in a few minutes that he was slightly overmatched, he wished to make things more even with the assistance of a womera but was stopped by his brother, the 'next in suit' for the crown. Miranda was then arrested and marched off to the lockup just as though he wasn't a king and didn't rule over the mighty tribe of Larrakeyahs. The S.M. [Stipendiary Magistrate] had a mind to imprison the royal offender for a quarter for introducing such a precedent, but Corporal Waters testified to his previous good character and so got him off with a month (*North Australian*, 11 June 1887).

Miranda was not the only Larrakia to get into trouble in the 1880s:

> … Manson, Sambo, and Davey, aboriginals, were charged with larceny from a warehouse, viz.: breaking into the store of P. R. Allen & Co and stealing liquor therefrom. Manson pleaded guilty; Davey and Sambo pleaded not guilty.
>
> Henry Alfred George Rundle, sworn: I am a storekeeper, and was formerly in the employ of P. R. Allen & Co; I remember the morning of the 21st December; heard a noise at 4 a.m. in P.R. Allen & Co.'s yard; after listening a few minutes I went out, and saw two natives crossing the yard from the centre store, going out of the yard; I was about ten yards from them; I called out 'Halloo'; they ran away, and I followed them; I caught Sambo opposite Hopewell's; I only saw two of the prisoners, Sambo and Davey; Davey escaped; when I caught Sambo he had a candle in his hand; he was drunk; I brought him back to the yard; he showed me where he got into the store; they had taken a sheet of iron from the corner of the centre store, leaving room enough for a man to get through; recognised Davey; did not see Manson at all; none of them had any right to be on the premises; there was rum in a cask in the store; I saw a tin which had recently had rum in it.
>
> To Sambo: I did not find any grog on you.
>
> Ernest Edward Smith, sworn; Am a mounted constable; remember arresting Sambo, Davey, and Manson on the morning of the 21st of December; I cautioned them; Sambo said, 'me no break 'em store'; Davey said, 'me not steal 'em, Jimmy steal 'em.'
>
> The jury, without retiring, found the prisoners guilty. Sentenced to two years imprisonment, with hard labor (*NTTG*, 26 May 1888).

Billiamuk

Back in 1869, when the *Moonta* dropped anchor in Darwin Harbour, Goyder and his men were astonished when two young men paddled out from the shore, climbed confidently on board, and began to sing *Ole Virginny* and *Old John Brown*, in English. They were Billiamuk

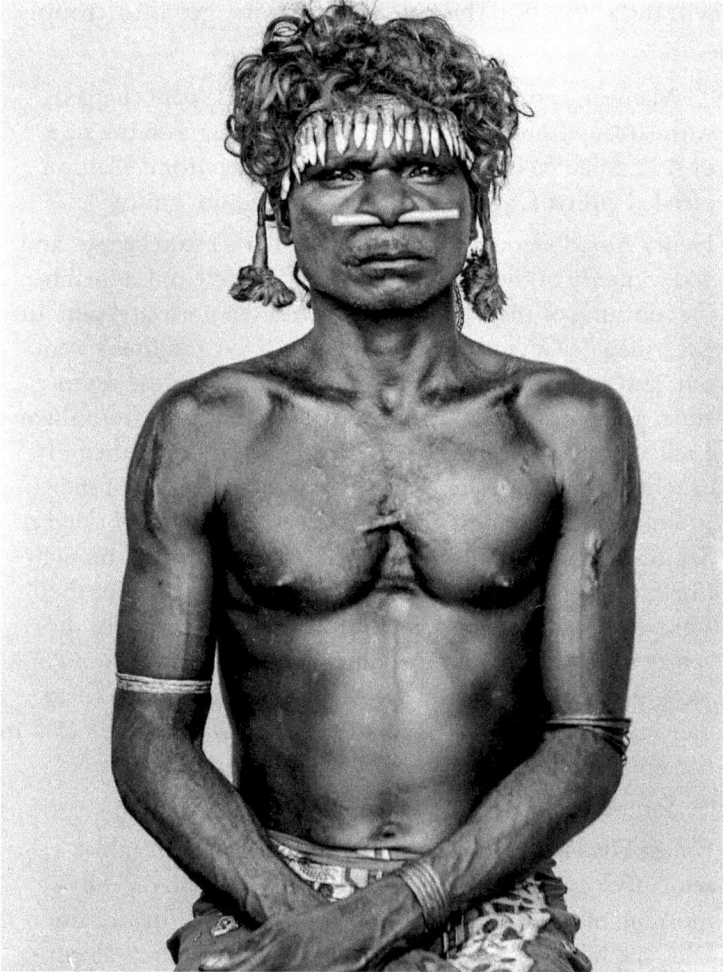

Figure 82: Billiamuk welcomed the South Australians to Port Darwin in 1869. The Darwin suburb of Bellamack is named after him (Foelsche, SA Museum, AA96).

and Umballa, and they had learned the songs by hanging around the Escape Cliffs settlement nearly three years earlier. Both became useful guides as the settlement grew, and Billiamuk—called Billy Muck by the whites—was a translator, guide, and informant for decades.

On occasion, Billiamuk worked for Inspector Foelsche, and in the courts as a translator. He lived in the community almost continuously after Goyder arrived in 1869 and was of great use to the original settlers. For example, he saved the life of Goyder's botanical collector, Schultze, when some tribesmen threatened to spear him after an argument about some emu meat. Goyder said he was 'a handsome, well-built Aboriginal whose intelligence was outstanding among his tribe and was well-liked by all the members of the expedition who encountered him.'

Billiamuk, and his mates, Lillawer and Umballa, travelled to Adelaide in 1870, with John McKinlay and Dan Daly, and returned in triumph, wearing the uniform of the Adelaide Volunteers. He spoke English well—and may also have learned to write, or at least dictate letters, as several appeared in the newspapers (Pugh 2018). Wildey described him as 'a fluent speaker of English and one of the finest to demonstrate a remarkable ability to adapt to the European culture whilst retaining his responsibilities as a Larrakia' (Wildey, 1876). He also sided with the Europeans against the Chinese miners on the occasion of a small riot at the Margaret River diggings in 1880. The riot was bravely quelled by Constable Lucanus but, the *Times* reported, Billiamuk entered the fray to lend a hand as well:

> ... Billy Muck came up at the end with a tomahawk, and there was no mistake as to which side of the ranks he intended to fight on, but at the same time he was anxious to know 'What for Chinaman growl?' (*NTTG*, 28 August 1880).

He was a personable and intelligent man who garnered respect from many Palmerston residents—although his notoriety came from occasional troubles stemming from alcohol. Several settlers found themselves in court on the charge of providing Aborigines with alcohol, and Billiamuk was repeatedly called in as a witness, as he was often its recipient. Once, in 1883, Billiamuk and a woman named Elsy had been given two bottles of Auldana* wine by Joseph Webb

---

* Patrick Auld was a member of the wine-producing family in South Australia, Auldana Wines. He was also a member of Stuart's 1862 successful crossing of the continent and it was he who guided Stuart back to Adelaide as his sight failed. Auld was then a member of the First Northern Territory Expedition to Escape Cliffs (see Pugh 2018).

and they became very drunk. Webb was found guilty of supplying the wine and fined £3 and sentenced to two weeks hard labour for stealing it. Later, in July 1887, Fou Ah Hop was fined £1 for selling Billiamuk a bottle of gin.

Billiamuk was not always cooperative:

… Three aboriginals, including, the incorrigible 'Billy Muck', gave the police 'leg-bail' on Monday when their attendance was desired at the Police Court, as witness against a defendant who had supplied them with grog. The case was adjourned to Wednesday, but as the runaways were not brought in when the case was called, the offender escaped scot free. Since one or two natives were imprisoned for aiding and abetting in similar offence the niggers have learnt the enchantment of a safe distance between the police and themselves (*North Australian*, 31 December 1886).

In 1885, he was in trouble again because of alcohol, and foolishly, he resisted arrest:

… The redoubtable 'Billy Muck,' an aboriginal who has gained for himself a reputation for being the greatest scoundrel among our semi-civilised blacks, came before Mr Pater on Monday on two separate charges. The first, was for assaulting his dearly beloved Mary, for which ungentlemanly offence he was sent to the 'salubrious' for one month. The second count charged him with assaulting the Police who wished to take him to the lockup for beating his 'fairer half.'

According to Corporal Waters, Billy made a most determined resistance with stick and teeth, at one time going so far as to attempt to make a feed off the Corporal's leg. It took three of the police to land him at the lockup. We may here remark that the playful native had a considerable quantity of grog under his hide at the time of the occurrence. We might also state that Billy Muck is the same nigger who caused (quite inadvertently) a certain member of the Force to give him leg bail a short time back. He will now wear the prison badge for two months, and likewise assist in Her Majesty's hard labour for that period (*North Australian*, 4 December 1885).

It was while he was in prison that Billiamuk came to the notice of the gaol's Superintendent, John Knight. Knight took his

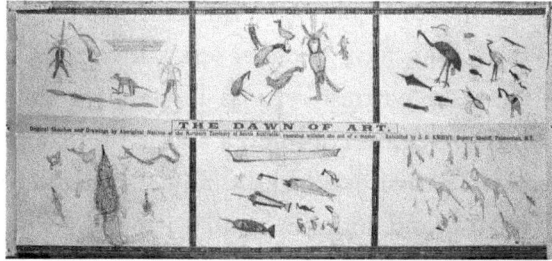

Figure 83: *The Dawn
of Art*, Aboriginal
artworks from Fannie
Bay Gaol 1888.

role seriously and cared for the inmates as best he could. At some point he offered them art materials. The results so impressed Knight that he had the artworks framed and exhibited at the Centennial International Exhibition in Melbourne in 1888, to great acclaim. The display was called the *The Dawn of Art*. It made Billiamuk, Wandy Wandy, Davey, Mindilpildil, and several others from Fannie Bay Gaol, the first Aborigines to exhibit works of art[*]—a fact that is proudly remembered by Larrakia artists today. Knight was thrilled:

> … As I predicted, the drawings made by Billy Muck, Davey, Jimmy Miller, Paddy, Wandy, and other native artists attract almost undue attention, especially from real artists. The other evening Mr Folingsby, a painter of some renown, after a careful inspection of these original works, declared that the executants were all worthy of being made honorary members of the Australian Academy of Arts. I have had the sketches mounted and put into six frames, each 6ft by 2ft 6in, with six pictures in a frame (Knight, 1886).

Billiamuk lived well into the twentieth century—a letter signed by him (as 'Billy Muck) appeared in the *Times* in February 1912, complaining that Aborigines were being forced to move to a new camp (Wells, 2003). His historic welcome of the South Australians to Port Darwin in 1869, his contribution to their successful settlement, and his ongoing participation in the town, is remembered in the modern suburb of Darwin named after him: Bellamack.

Billiamuk, despite his occasional troubles, trod the line between his culture and the new arrivals well. Many other Aborigines

---

[*] Until then, artworks by 'natives' from across the world were exhibited in ethnographic collections, and were not considered art.

probably did too, and the cultural clashes so keenly felt by the whites may have been of less concern to them. What comes down to us—in written records left almost exclusively by white men—are disparaging comments about the Aborigines. They are variously called 'natives', 'blacks', 'niggers', 'sable brethren', 'savages', and similar—and sometimes all within the same paragraph. The editors of the two Palmerston newspapers did nothing to hold back the misunderstandings and racial generalisations. The *Times*, for example, complained of 'crowds of loafing, lazy, opium-smoking and grog-drinking natives' who formed 'camps as near to the town as possible', with their 'infernal everlasting singsong... dismal chants... warlike whoops' and their 'incessant din'.

Bright suggestions

Not all the whites agreed with the editors. Some saw another side of the Aborigines. George Bright, for instance, a saddler and businessman in Southport, felt their plight keenly, as his letter to the editor on 16 March 1886 shows:

> Sir,—The question of outrages by blacks is supposed by most people to be worn thread-bare, but it is my intention in this letter to look at it from a new point of view, and at the same time in as few words as possible. We will try and find the very root and first cause of these outrages, and perhaps it may be found to rest with ourselves in a great measure, and the unjust way in which we as a stronger, more civilised, and enlightened race have treated the aboriginals of this vast continent. In former times we came to these shores and found a country which we saw was desirable as a possession, suitable as a home for our race, and rich in commercial prospects, so we occupied it. In course of time settlement spreads, and the grass is used to support countless herds of cattle, horses, and sheep, and as the occupation extends, the domain of the aboriginal becomes so much less, and the situation begins to dawn upon his mind. He is driven from his favourite haunts and hunted from the waterholes which slaked his thirst, because the white man wants them for his stock, and they must not be disturbed.

Whichever way he turns his face he is a trespasser on the very land which the Almighty gave him as a birthright from time immemorial, and as a set off against this loss what have we given him in exchange?

Nothing! If he were to ask such a thing he would only be laughed at.

The black is fast losing his waterholes, hunting grounds, and the wildfowl; he visits our camps, and his eyes see provisions heaped up galore, which measured by his standard is the common property of all, yet when he asks for some, he is told to go and hunt for it; "clear out, don't come loafing here," is often his answer.

… we English boast we are the most just, upright, fair dealing nation under the sun. Our law looks upon the aboriginal as a British subject, and when he commits a crime according to our law, he is tried for life or liberty with all the pomp and circumstance of an English tribunal, has sentence passed on him, and marched off to his fate with as much coolness as if we had been educating him up to our standard all his life…

I am Sir, etc.,

George H. Bright (*NTTG*, 16 March 1886).

Aboriginal reserves

Bright suggested there were just three possible courses of action to take on behalf of the Aborigines. The first was to 'abandon the country', which, of course, was impossible. Another was to set aside large reserves of land where Aborigines could 'follow their natural instincts in hunting and fishing for a living'. The third course, said Bright, was that the government should provide a 'sufficient portion of the revenue to feed them… Having taken by force the aboriginal's land, his game, his fish, his very birthright', it was 'simply an act of justice to keep him free from care for the rest of his days, in return for the wealth we make at his expense'.

There was another way, and that was to 'wipe the whole race from off the earth'. Many people thought that this was already happening 'under the present system of mismanagement' and that 'no power [could] save them'. Bright thought that action must be taken to extend the Aborigines' 'lease of life' through the provision of food (*NTTG*, 16 March 1886).

Even Charles Kirkland, the editor of the *North Australian*, believed that 'the Aborigines would be extinct … before many years'. His concern was that the whites would carry the stain of the Aborigines' annihilation with them through history. He advocated that the South Australian government provide 'reserves whereupon the remnants of a once-powerful race may end their days', so that 'history should [not] have to record that they were downtrodden by a more intelligent race' (*North Australian*, 8 November 1889).

Government Resident Parsons thought hard about what to do about the Aborigines. He recognised their rights to their land for sustenance and tribal life, and agreed that these rights were interfered with by turning huge areas of the Territory into cattle stations (*Observer*, 12 May 1888).

> … Reserves, no doubt, should be dedicated. These reserves should include permanent waters and river frontages. The rights of the aborigines to as much of the land—the best of the land—as may be necessary for their sustenance and tribal life are indisputable. But these rights, as a matter of fact, are treated rather in a poetic than a practical sense…
>
> But what is the usual course of procedure? A capitalist or a syndicate applies for or buys at auction the leases for a certain number of hundreds or thousands of square miles of country, carefully following the permanent watercourses, and including the permanent lagoons and waterholes. The aborigines who have the vested interests of hoary antiquity are only considered by the State to the extent of the above-recited clause in the pastoral lease. Afterwards the squatter or his manager comes on to the country with his overland herds, and usually tries to cultivate friendly relations with the natives. How often these kindly-meant attempts are frustrated is only known by those who have attempted them. In nearly all cases the early results of the white man's intrusion is a permanent feud between the blacks and whites. The blacks frighten and spear the cattle

and hold themselves in readiness to attack boundary-rider and stockman, or to make a raid upon out-stations or the storeroom.

The whites look well to their Winchesters and revolvers, and usually proceed on the principle of being on the safe side. It is an affectation of ignorance to pretend not to know that this is the condition of things throughout the 'back blocks' and the 'new country' of Australia. The problem is plain enough, but its solution is not. If the inland tribes could only be induced to emigrate to Melville Island that would be a solution* (Parsons J. L., 1887).

Parsons recommends

Parsons made five recommendations to the South Australian Parliament:

(1) that an aboriginal reserve should be laid out in each tribe's country of sufficient size, with sufficient water, for the tribe's use.

(2) That tribes should be warned, where the country is occupied by pastoralists, that they must keep to their reserves; when they wish to visit other tribes, they must give notice of their intention, and proceed by a route and on a date to be fixed.

(3) That where practicable labor engagements with blacks should be made in writing, full details of nature of service,

---

*   The idea that Aborigines from across the Territory could be packed up and sent to Melville Island seems farcical, but in 1941 the government did just that. The Garden Point Mission was established on the island for children of mixed race by the Catholic Church. In 1910, the *Northern Territory Aboriginals Act No. 1024* of 1910 ('An Act to make provision for the better Protection and Control of the Aboriginal Inhabitants of the Northern Territory, and for other purposes') was the first legislative provision for Aboriginal people in the NT. It was repealed by the *Aboriginals Ordinance* in 1918, and the 'Northern Territory Aboriginals Department' and a 'chief protector' was then responsible for the control and welfare of Aboriginal people in the Territory. The chief protector was the 'legal guardian of every Aboriginal and every half-caste child up to the ('apparent') age of 18 years' and had the power to confine children to an Aboriginal reserve or institution. The children became known as the 'stolen generation' (*Aboriginals Ordinance No. 9 of 1918*, Museum of Australian Democracy, retrieved 28 October2020).

wages, and rations to be given, before the Protector of Aborigines or a Justice of the Peace.

(4) That, except in the case of those in European employment, the carrying of firearms should be absolutely prohibited.

(5) That an Act should be passed for the better government of aborigines, and for taking the evidence, and for the punishment of their crimes (Parsons J. L., 1887)

Nothing came of Parsons' recommendations for years, but the stage was set for setting aside large areas of land for Aborigines—such as the whole of Arnhem Land and parts of the interior in later decades—and for greater 'protectionist' policies, such as forced removal of children from their families.

Chapter 16
Jesuit missions

Father Strele

Saint Joseph's Mission was built about 11 kilometres outside the town of Palmerston, on the banks of Rapid Creek. Started on 10 October 1882 by Austrian Jesuits from Sevenhill (in the Clare Valley of South Australia), Father Anton Strele (1825–97) and his colleagues, Father O'Brian, Father Conrad, and Brother Kramar, initially pitched tents in the bush.

Strele had successfully raised £1,200 to establish the mission. They brought carpentry tools, clothing, tinned meat, farming implements and seeds to plant in the soil from South Australia. A few Larrakia and Wulna people were soon attracted to the settlement:

> … The site selected for the station is on Rapid Creek, about seven miles north-east of Palmerston, and comprises an area of 320 acres, or a block of land one mile in length by half a mile in breadth. At the time of my visit, there were about twelve natives employed on the station, all of whom received a regular allowance of rations and tobacco, but the whole camp contained some fifty, including a large number of children (*NTTG*, 18 August 1883, p. 3).

The fathers suffered an initial setback: the survey pegs left by Goyder's team in 1869 were gone. As a result, the boundaries of their land were uncertain and when they were properly defined, Father Strele and his assistants were told that they had erected their buildings outside their allotted area, and they had to be moved.

Three years later the mission was a hive of industry—a cluster of buildings were complete and many different plant species were being trialled in the farms. The *North Australian* visited in a quiet news week, to observe the progress:

> ... We found the rev. fathers at home and received the usual
> hearty welcome they accord to all visitors. After some little
> conversation, Father Strele kindly volunteered to show us
> around the premises. The buildings consist of a schoolhouse,
> in which a number of the younger natives are tutored; a
> dwelling-house for the blacks, a luxury of which those sable
> gentry seldom avail themselves, usually preferring to live in
> the open air after the manner of their fathers; a neat little
> chapel; and the dwelling-house occupied by the fathers, with
> storeroom and kitchen (*North Australian*, 26 February 1886).

Education

The schoolhouse provided hope to the fathers in the success of their mission:

> ... the teachers are sanguine of success, as they consider the
> natives of the Northern Territory very bright and intelligent,
> and on the whole superior to the aborigines of South Australia
> (*NTTG*, 21 January 1888).

A century before Northern Territory educators would lead the world in bilingual education, Father Conrad was already attempting it:

> ... On our return to the house, Father Strele showed us a
> small printing plant they have just imported, with which they
> propose printing small elementary works in the Larrakyan [sic]
> language (the difficulties of its acquisition Father Conrad having
> successfully overcome) and teaching the younger natives to read
> and write (*North Australian*, 26 February 1886).

The difficulties in teaching Aboriginal children were exacerbated by the cultural acceptance of children's behaviour and lack of punishment. The Jesuits found that they could not discipline Aboriginal children as they would others. As researchers for Griffith University noted:

> ... If school children were punished for offences such as theft,
> causing a fracas, making noises at night, or going to the camp at

night, they would almost invariably abscond from the mission, usually supported by a small group accompanying them …

30 April 1888: Fr. Kristen slapped the boy, Andrew, who had been making immoderate complaints about the food—he went away and took with him four other of the children: Peter, Anthony, August and Thekla … (GU, 2020).

In the diaries written by the Jesuits, the disciplinary terms used were 'scolding', 'slapping', 'light punishment', and 'punishment', although the latter disappeared from the diaries entirely after 1892—either the children learned not to run away, or the Jesuits learned not to strike them.

Some children took advantage of their education in the streets of Palmerston:

… a number of native children, who, having received a certain amount of musical training at the Rapid Creek Mission Station, turn their, not by any means unmusical, childish voices into account, as a means of obtaining the eleemosynary* contributions of their hearers (*NTTG*, 21 January 1888).

Strele visited the United States on a fundraising mission in 1886. He had already found little charity in Europe—too many groups were seeking support, and there were too few willing to donate. In San Francisco he went from house to house among the German and Polish migrant communities, begging for funds. Eventually, a Tyrolean family donated $1,000, on the condition it pay for a church that would be dedicated to the Holy Rosary.

Father Donald MacKillop

About the same time, in 1886, the priest who became most well-known among the 19 Jesuits who worked in the Northern Territory Mission arrived. He was Father Donald MacKillop, the 33-year-old younger brother of Sister Mary MacKillop†. Father Stele asked MacKillop to study the Mulluk-Mulluk (Malak) language of the Daly River area near Serpentine Lagoon—which had recently been scouted

---

* Eleemosynary: charitable.

† Mary MacKillop was beatified on 19 January 1995 by Pope John Paul II. She is Australia's only saint.

out by Father O'Brian—and was deemed to be 'grand country' (*North Australian*, 14 August 1885). McKillop was selected to start the new mission station there and work with the Madngella and other people who had never seen whites. The Church of the Holy Rosary was soon built, and the donations quickly used up.

At the end of 1890, Strele returned south, and Father MacKillop was promoted to be the superior. He was then responsible for the whole Jesuit mission in the Northern Territory, and funding was getting harder to come by. He had little government support, and overseas donations ceased. Worse, finance promised him by the bishops never appeared. The Rapid Creek Mission also failed as a place of Christion conversion:

> ... The Larrakeeyahs [sic], the Port Darwin tribe, appear to be utterly unaffected by the efforts for their evangelisation by self-denying fathers and brothers; the missionaries themselves say that this tribe has been too long and too closely associated with the white settlers to give any hope of being affected by Christianising influence... it is said on excellent authority that recently a corroboree of the old men took place... in which the attitude of the Larrakeyahs to Christianity was discussed. Whatever may have been the aspects in which it was viewed, whether it was too much work and too little tobacco, too much morality and too few shillings or not, the decision arrived at was—'Religion along Rapid Creek no good'. I fear this may be said to apply to nearly all the other forms of the faith. For months, none of the Larrakeeyahs have gone near the mission station (Parsons J. L., 1887).

The Rapid Creek Mission Station was a continuing drain on his resources and MacKillop closed it* in 1891. The eleven Jesuits

---

* Millner resident, Ian Passmore, lives on the site of the old mission. He has dug up several items in his garden left behind by them: a metal hook used to pull down shutters and a brass biscuit cutter (shaped like a wheelbarrow) of the type used to make confirmation biscuits. The latter is marked with the word 'Paris' and had the numbers 174 stamped on it, with the 4 reversed. Passmore's research led him to believe that a reverse 4 was a symbol from the plague days, although it may also be a merchant's mark (Scottish Masons also used reversed numbers).

then focused their work on the people of the Daly River, who were unsullied by 'the vices' and the 'diseases of the whites':

> … The proximity of the township and the corrupting influence of intercourse with the Europeans has militated seriously against the success of the Rapid Creek Station, while on the other hand, the absence of European influence on natives at the Daly Mission Station has left the Fathers with almost virgin soil to work upon, and they are very hopeful of good results, the natives submitting very cheerfully to the light discipline necessary, and very readily performing the work set them on the plantation (Parsons J. L., 1887).

Darwin: Growth of a City

Chapter 17
Top End explorers of the 1880s

By any measure, the Northern Territory is a vast tract of land. Much of it was still unknown to Europeans in the 1880s, and explorations outside the known districts were critical. Some of it was explored by serendipity—as drovers crossed the land, they recorded what they found. Others were expeditions that required substantial funding and resources. The South Australian Government was keen to see its northern parts explored. The unknown and unlocked pastoral potential of the land was most enticing, but not everyone was successful:

> … Induced by the favourable terms offered by the South Australian Government to pastoral lessees in the Northern Territory, two brothers named Prout, started out with one man, looking for country across the Queensland border. They never returned, and it was not until they had been given up for months that some of their horses, and finally the bones of one of the brothers, were discovered by Mr W. J. H. Carr Boyd.

> It was evident, from the fragments of a diary recovered, that they had extended their researches far into South Australian territory and met their death by thirst on their homeward way, probably from some of the waters they depended upon for their return having failed them (Favenc, 1888).

Explorations had two main purposes: opening pastoral properties and discovering minerals. In 1883 alone, four different expeditions were sent out—two by pastoral companies and two by the government. The explorers concurred: 'no better pastoral lands are to be found in Australia than in immense areas of the Northern Territory. And also … there are still vast mineral deposits which only await the advent of the prospector for development' (*NTTG*, 5 January 1884).

The geographical societies of Australia were mostly satisfied with the level of exploration in the Northern Territory by 1886, so the focus of explorations was then placed on Western Australia. Luckily, several expeditions needed to travel through the Northern Territory to get there, and new parts of the Territory were then explored by default. Ernest Favenc, addressing the Sydney Geographical Society in 1886, exemplified the thoughts of the time:

> … Australia is almost fairly bisected by the overland telegraph line, which follows closely the track of Macdouall [sic] Stuart, the explorer. This line may be considered a line of demarcation between the explored and the unexplored portions. To the westward is still supposed to exist a huge desert, unfit to sustain human life, and impracticable for settlement. This is vouched for on the authorities of the different men who have crossed it—Giles, Forrest, and Warburton. And… in spite of the undeviating testimony of these three men, strong hopes may still be entertained that good habitable country and enormous areas of well-watered pastureland may still be found (Favenc, 1888).

The explorer most well-known to Palmerston residents of the 1880s was David Lindsay, a man who first arrived as a government surveyor in 1878.

David Lindsay

David Lindsay was born in 1856 in Goolwa, South Australia. His first employment in Palmerston was as a junior surveyor and clerk in the land office of the Department of the Northern Territory. After four years, he resigned and started his own business as a surveyor, draftsman, and land, stock, and station agent in Palmerston.

On 4 July 1883, Lindsay took a government contract to lead an exploration party into Eastern and Central Arnhem Land. It

Figure 84: David Lindsay (c 1890, SLSA B495).

was a five-month overland expedition from the Overland Telegraph Line near Katherine. It was a remarkable journey that took Lindsay and five others with 23 horses east to the Roper River, north to Blue Mud Bay, and west over to Castlereagh Bay. The party was harassed continually by Aborigines as they passed through their country and was attacked by about 300 warriors near the Goyder River. Some of their horses were speared, and local people set fire to the country around them*. When Lindsay returned to Katherine Telegraph Station, he immediately sent a telegram to the Minister of Education, John Parsons, summarising his journey:

> … Arrived last night. Party all well. Left telegraph fifty miles from here. Travelled east crossing Waterhouse, Chambers. Excellent country. First day one horse knocked up. Country all recently burned. No feed, long stage, without water, forced me on to Roper. Another horse knocked up. Continued easterly, north of Roper, horse drowned. Lost three weeks' rations. Traced Wilton to its source, grand country, excellent soil, and grass along Roper. Twenty miles from coast on large lagoons. Natives gathered in large force to attack us at night but were prevented. They speared four horses, three fatally. Passed north through miserable scrub; thirty-six hours without water.
>
> Discovered fine river, traced it from source to mouth, and named it the Parsons, very fair country. Followed coast to Blue Mud Bay; Thirty-eight hours without water. Discovered

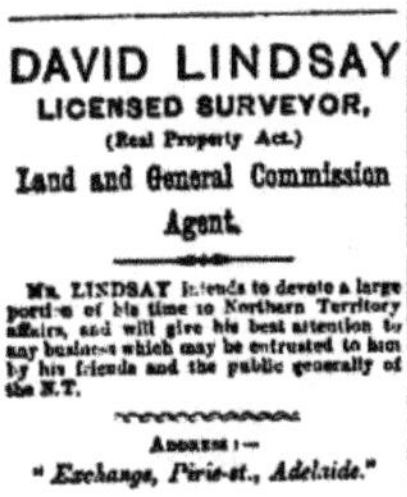

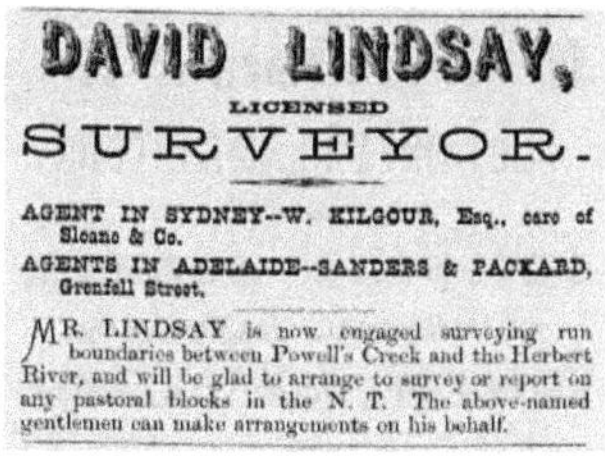

Figure 85: Examples of David Lindsay's advertisements in 1884 (left) and 1886 (NTTG).

---

* Lindsay may not have felt welcome then, but he was thick-skinned enough to return in a second survey to eastern Arnhem Land in 1917, albeit after 37 years.

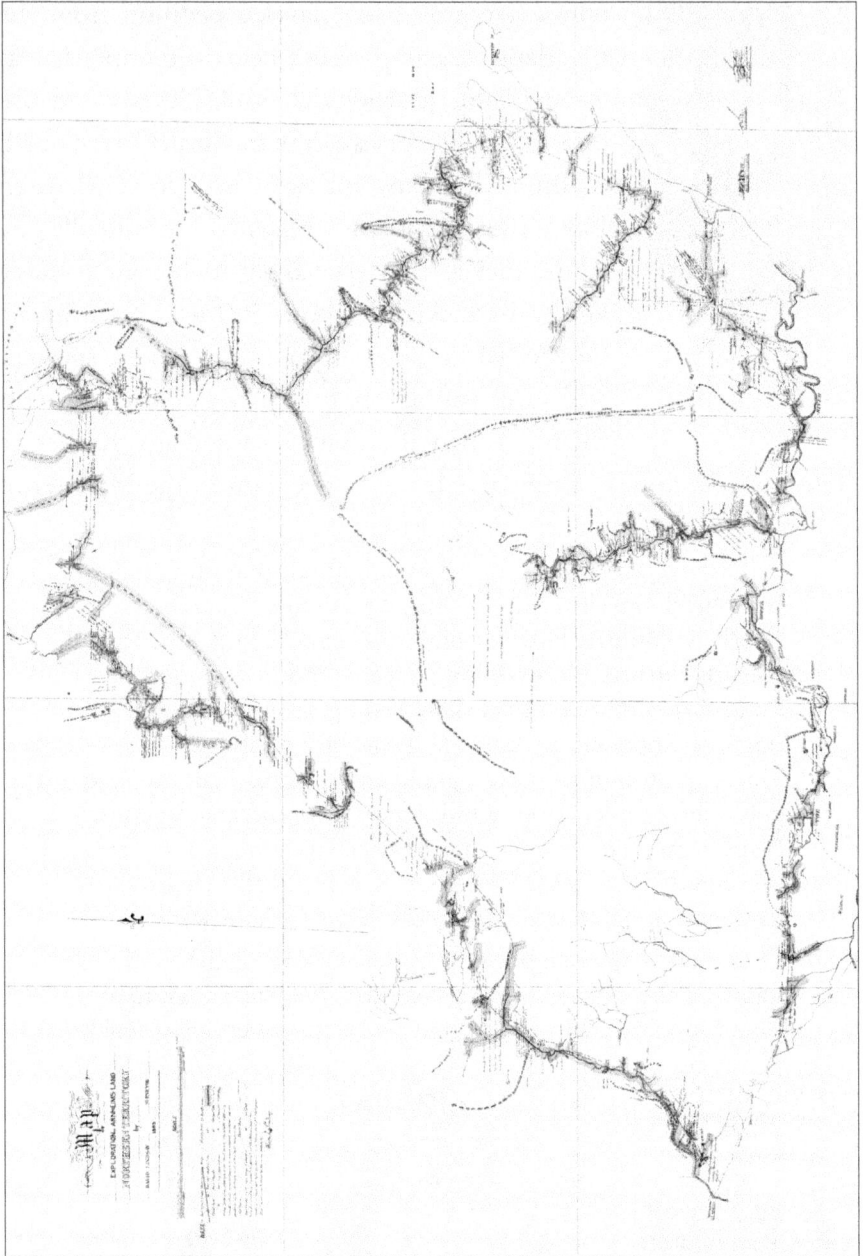

Map 7: David Lindsay's 1883 exploration of Arnhem Land (nla.obj-231441249).

another fine river; natives friendly; followed it to its source. Two more horses knocked up.

Decided that it was impossible to attempt north-eastern corner. Followed grand river into Castlereagh Bay; magnificent pastoral and agricultural country; good sugar lands; extensive plains. Natives numerous and hostile. From coast went west. Lost seven horses in tableland.

For five days natives surrounded us and attempted to prevent our traveling; compelling us to fire at them, which prevented any further trouble. Discovered two more good rivers before striking the Liverpool, which is a poor river above head navigation, followed it up through terribly broken sandstone until found it impossible to travel either south or west. For eight days only made ten miles. Knocked our horses about, and before we got out to the south-east had left six horses; one of which we ate. Then got into good country.

Our horses were very weak owing to the scarcity of feed, the whole country being burnt just previous to our passing over. During the next week left four more horses. We had abandoned every possible thing*. Salted another knocked-up horse. Descended tableland into magnificent and extensive valley … Here was the first auriferous-looking country we saw.

Followed the Katherine into the Station. Good country to thirty miles from station, then rough to eighteen miles; remainder very good. Two more horses knocked up yesterday but will be able to get them again. Reached here with only thirteen horses. Scarcity of feed and some long stages without water caused our horses to knock up. We had no good feed on which we could spell them. We had but thirty pounds of dried horse in our packages. Nothing else. We were two days and nights without water except what we could get from the trees. With exception of a few patches, the whole of the country is excellent for grazing. I leave to-morrow by the mail. Reach Palmerston on 15th. One week on goldfields, and then leave by Tannadice… (*Adelaide Observer*, November 1883).

---

* Of the abandoned equipment—one of Lindsay's pack saddles appeared in a rock painting in a shelter in what is now the south of Kakadu National Park.

Lindsay took another commission in 1885–86 and took seven men and twelve camels to explore the Gulf of Carpentaria, surveying the country between the Overland Telegraph Line and the Queensland border. He then explored the MacDonnell Ranges, the Simpson Desert, and the country between Lake Nash and Powell's Creek. In 1887, he spent five weeks riding 2,253 kilometres from Darwin to the southern coast. He was afterwards made a fellow of the Royal Geographical Society, London. He spent 1888 exploring the MacDonnell Ranges for rubies and other precious stones, and he discovered a deposit of payable mica. He became a broker on the Adelaide Stock Exchange in 1889 and later led the Elder Scientific Exploring Expedition to Western Australia. He then spent decades in Western Australia, and in Sydney, but returned to Darwin for his final years, surveying for the Commonwealth government. On 17 December 1922, he fell ill and died in Darwin of a heart attack, aged 66 (Carment, Maynard, & Powell, 1990).

Despite Lindsay's warnings of the troubles with the 'blacks', his report on Arnhem Land inspired the establishment of a cattle station.

When Lindsay crossed the country in 1883, he described a section that became known as Florida, as 'magnificent, either for grazing or agriculture, and unsurpassed in the Northern Territory, these magnificent plains extend for 40 miles.'

As a result of Lindsay's description, Florida Station was established on a lease by a Mr J.A. McCartney. His manager, Mr Randall, drove a mob of cattle in from Waverley Station, and he employed Chinese 'coolie' labour to build a cypress pine homestead on the beautiful Horseshoe Billabong. Station staff included an English stockman named Epworth, and a French cook named Louis Fayre, whose speciality was *bouillabaisse de barramundi*! One man in the 'coolie' labour gang was not Chinese at all, but African[*].

---

[*] This was Charley Araby, an African ex-slave, who died in Darwin in the 1950s as one of the Territory's great characters (Pugh, 2014).

Everything started well at the station. A journalist who visited soon after the station was established, waxed lyrically about the beauty of the country. 'Florida Station', he said, 'might without exaggeration be styled as A Squatter's Paradise,' and that there was, 'nothing finer than Florida' (*South Australian Register*, 22 February 1888).

But he also gave some forewarning as to what was to come when he wrote:

> … The pioneers of Arnhem Land may at first experience some little trouble with the natives, but that will be easily overcome. A few well applied judicious lessons may be necessary, after which I think it will be found that the natives will prove of considerable value in working the stations (*South Australian Register*, 22 February 1888.

He did not linger on what a 'judicious lesson' might be but one of them was a cartload of poisoned horse meat presented to the tribe by McCartney and Randall. The meat was eaten by men, women, and children alike. Many died slow and painful deaths.

The settlers were quickly at war with the traditional landowners. The local tribesmen saw Randall and his staff as invaders of their land and, of course, they speared cattle for food and as part of their resistance. Two Malay workers who arrived at Florida in 1888, Ali and Salim, both disappeared—their bodies were never found but their clothing was discovered spread around a campsite. This led to punitive expeditions with elephant guns—the famous Martini-Henry rifles. The white men in their cypress pine, tin-roofed homestead then lived in such fear that they slept every night with their 'nine-inch colts.'

E.O. Robinson ran a supply boat out from Darwin for them about every six months. He said that he would never approach the homestead without firing a shot first—and then waiting for a shot in reply. He always expected the men would be dead or insane by the time he returned.

In 1892, McCartney gave up. He dismantled his house and sent anything valuable back to Darwin on the steamer Adelaide. He then employed a party of stockmen, led by Jack Watson*, to round up what was left of his cattle and quit Florida. They drove them west to Auvergne Station near the Western Australian border, and never returned. Watson was a 'wild and reckless fellow' who would 'charge hell with a bucket of water'. He was also, according to contemporary accounts, a merciless slayer of Aborigines. He thought 'the blacks of Blue Mud and Caledon Bays good hombres, but he had to wipe out a lot to make them so'. Watson, 'threw the lead at them, and threw it to kill' (Gaunt, 6 July 1934). Watson was manager of Lorne Hill Station in Queensland in 1883. When the Creaghes visited, Emily Creaghe noted without any hint of surprise or emotion, that Mr Watson had:

> ... 40 pairs of black's ears nailed around the walls collected during raiding parties after the loss of many cattle, speared by the blacks' (Creaghe 1883).

Ernest Favenc

Ernest Favenc, (1845–1908), was an explorer, journalist, poet, and historian, who made at least two expeditions through parts of the Northern Territory, from the Overland Telegraph Line to the Queensland border. Favenc immigrated from England to Sydney in 1864, at the age of 19, after being educated in Germany. In 1865, he moved to Bowen, Queensland, and spent the next decade working on stations in North Queensland, learning and honing bush survival skills that he would later become famous for. He wrote occasional stories for the *Queenslander*, and in 1878, was selected by the editors to lead an expedition to prove the practicability of a transcontinental railway to Port Darwin:

> ... The leader of the expedition is Mr Ernest Favenc, a gentleman who has high claims for the arduous work before him. He is a first-class bushman; a journalist of tried ability,

---

* Jack Watson was the son of George Watson, who was the starter of the Melbourne Cup for many years. He was the manager of Victoria River Downs when he drowned in the Katherine River in 1896.

having been for many years a valued contributor to these pages
... (*Queenslander*, 22 June 1878, p368).

His bush skills were extraordinary, as this correspondent attested,
after spending seven weeks with Favenc in the Territory in 1884:

> ... this I must say that Mr Favenc is the best bushman and
> explorer that I have ever had the pleasure of being in the bush
> with, and I have now been knocking about the colonies for
> the last 30 years ... I have been out on several occasions with
> men who were considered first-class bushmen, prospecting
> about both in Victoria and South Australia; but I was with
> none equal to Mr Favenc. He is a thorough bushman and
> gentleman to travel with. All the country we have been over
> seemed like one big run that he had been living on for years,
> and as if he knew every hole and corner of it. He travels
> all day, and when it is near time to pull up, he turns into
> camp as though going into one of his stockman's huts in
> the neighbourhood of which he knew there was good grass
> and water; and, sure enough, there would be plenty of both.
> We never were one night without good feed and water for
> ourselves and horses (A 'Correspondent', *North Australian*, 7
> November 1884).

Favenc's optimistic views on the country played an important
part in his success. 'There must be permanent supplies of water
throughout' he wrote to the Sydney Geographic Society:

> ... or generations of blacks could not have existed; and
> although heavy falls of rain cannot be expected, the grasses
> and herbage are naturally of a drought-resisting habit (Favenc,
> 1886).

The Transcontinental Railway Exploration Party departed
from Blackall in Queensland in July 1878 and arrived in Palmerston
in February 1879. Favenc wrote and published his diary in the
Queenslander, under his penname, 'Dramingo'. The diary was not,
it was made clear, an official report, but a 'way of amusement to
while away, now and then, an evening in camp' (*Queenslander*, 14
December 1878):

> ... we hunt as we go along. Galahs and corellas form the
> principal source of supply; they are in fact the only edible

birds visible; every other feathered fowl having left this inhospitable region. The parrots would not be here but for the bloodwood trees, which are laden with blossom on which they feed; and we feed on them—poetical justice. As for the water, in the course of a few more days I anticipate being able to give the horses a shovel and send them down to the creek to dig for themselves; it is quite laughable the way in which they wait about for a waterhole to be opened for them; what water we got, with one exception, we were lucky to get near enough the surface for the quadrupeds to drink when a hole had been made (*Queenslander*, 21 December 1878, p. 366).

Favenc later listed more of their travelling larder:

... We made up a list of game that had already been shot for ration purposes, nearly all by Hedley, who was our chief reliance as a hunter, and the following is the account up to 11th December: 50 parrots (corellas and galars [sic]), 350 ducks (black ducks, teal, whistling ducks, wood ducks and widgeons), 150 pigeons (principally flock), 11 geese, 4 turkeys, 8 spoonbills, 7 water hens, 2 shags, 1 emu, 1 native companion, making a total of 584 birds, and in addition we had consumed 100 fish. All of them were shot for actual food, nothing had been wantonly destroyed. We considerably added to this menu afterwards, including such choice delicacies as eagle hawk and frogs. Crows and hawks we carefully reserved to the last when all else should fail. The absence of kangaroos and other marsupials is a marked feature in this list, there being none on these wide-stretching downs (Favenc, 1888).

Favenc also wrote poems. Some were well known in Queensland at the time, such as *Daybreak in the Desert*:

No cheerful note of bird in leafy bower,
No glistening water dancing in the light,
No dewdrop trembling on some modest flower,
No early cock to crow farewell to night.

Only a greater stillness in the air,
Save for hot sighs of desert-heated breath,
Only the stars, ceasing their sleepless stare,
Only the east, rose-flushing, fresh from death.

All the wide plain, hid 'neath the waning round
Of a tired moon, grew dimly into view;
With a dull haze hung on its furthest bound,
Then sprang the sun into the steely blue (Ernest Favenc).

When he reached Port Darwin, Favenc was able to report good news back to the *Queenslander* by telegram:

> … Advices from Mr Favenc, the leader of the party, state that the expedition has been completely successful. The proposed route for a trans-continental railway is found to be easy for construction purposes, and it passes through available pastoral country over the whole distance. Mr Favenc further adds that Port Darwin is a fine harbor, and as a site for a town unequalled in Australia (*Queenslander*, 29 March 1879, p. 390).

Perhaps, unfortunately, the railway from Queensland into the Territory was never built.

Favenc's high profile as a journalist and writer, and his expert bushcraft and knowledge of Queensland and the eastern part of the Northern Territory, attracted pastoral investors. He was the perfect leader for expeditions to scout for new pastoral country. In 1881, he was recruited by the De Salis brothers, Queensland pastoralists who wished to extend their interests into the Northern Territory. This led to Favenc establishing Creswell Creek Station late in that year. Then, in 1882, he organised an expedition to explore parts of the Northern Territory bounded by the Nicholson River, Powell's Creek, and the McArthur River. In his *History of Australian Exploration, 1778–1888*, Favenc wrote that he travelled with G. Hedley, S.G. Briggs, 'and a black boy'. He left out the fact that his wife, Emma, initially joined the expedition, and so too did Harry Creaghe, and his wife, Emily. Two European women on an exploration trip were remarkable in 1882, to say the least. Unfortunately, Emma fell ill in Normanton before the overland trip had started, and Favenc accompanied her back to Brisbane—delaying the expedition by 10 weeks. The expedition finally consisted of Favenc, Lindsay Crawford, and Harry and Emily Creaghe.

Whilst waiting for Favenc to return from Sydney, Harry—and Emily Creaghe—did some exploring on their own. Emily thus became North Australia's first female explorer (see the next section)*.

Favenc and his party then explored the area between Creswell Creek and the Overland Telegraph Line, reaching Powell's Creek after long dry stages, on 14 May 1883. He then successfully explored the country watered by the McArthur River, leaving Powell's Creek on 28 May with Lindsay Crawford, who had worked as a telegraph officer at Powell's Creek two years earlier †. By following the river, Favenc‡ and Crawford found the only practical road to the gulf, and then returned to the telegraph line, reaching Daly Waters on 15 July. The Creaghes separated from Favenc at Powell's Creek to drove the weaker horses north to Katherine.

Favenc made several recommendations to the South Australian government about the country around the McArthur River. A widely published telegram in October 1883 implored the government to continue exploring the gulf country, particularly in the region of the Sir Edward Pellew group of islands, but also:

> … he represents … very strongly the necessity of steps immediately being taken for a survey to definitely fix the boundary line between South Australia and Queensland. The disputed territory is represented to be 1,520 miles in width. The uncertainty regarding the ownership of this tract of country exercises a prejudicial influence upon its settlement. Mr Favenc waxes very enthusiastic over the discovery of 60,000 miles of grand sheep country and magnificent downs below the McArthur country. He emphasises the necessity

---

* Earlier female explorers had travelled with Charles Sturt on the Murray River: Eliza Davies, Julia Gawler, and Mrs Sturt (Monteath, 2004).

† Lindsay Crawford came to the Territory in 1873 and joined the Overland Telegraph as a Station Master at Powell Creek. From 1885 he was the Manager of the Victoria River Downs Station for at least 5 years. Later, in 1897, he re-joined the Overland Telegraph. He died in 1901, on the Sturt Plains, from dysentery and exposure. Cape Crawford, in the Roper Shire, was named after Lindsay Crawford by Favenc.

‡ There is a Favenc Range and Mount Favenc in the Roper River region. It is thought that David Lindsay named them after Favenc in 1883.

of establishing a port at the mouth of the McArthur River, whence a good road to the interior could be made. The locality indicated has been declared a port for about two years, but there is no Customs officer or office there, and nothing to prevent a shipload of goods being landed there without duty being paid.

It is pointed out, further, that as this sheep country is 700 miles from Port Darwin, and only 150 from the mouth of the McArthur, it is absurd to expect settlers to import goods from Palmerston thither if the road is possible for cartage, and exceedingly expensive (*Sydney Morning Herald*, 14 October 1883).

In 1885, the town of Borroloola was established on the banks of the McArthur River. Gilbert McMinn was sent as its first stipendiary magistrate.

Favenc return to Sydney and settled down for a while to write. Published on the centenary of settlement, his book, *The History of Australian Exploration, 1788–1888*, was a great success and is still useful as a reference (Favenc, 1888).

Favenc later undertook several explorations in Western Australia before joining the *Evening News* in Sydney, as a journalist. Between 1893 and 1905, he published five novels and a book of verse, which were reviewed as 'competent, uninspired and often melodramatic', but it was 'his faithful portrayals of inland Australia [that] secured him a place in Australian literature' (Gibbney, 1972).

Emily Creaghe

Women were few and far between in the remote areas of the Northern Territory in the 1880s. One extraordinary woman, however, became famous as the first, and probably only, female explorer of the Top End of Australia in the 1880s. Emily Creaghe (with her husband, Harry) was part of the expedition led by Ernest Favenc in 1883.

Emily Caroline Robinson was born on board a ship in the Bay of Bengal, in 1860. Her father was a captain in the Royal Artillery, based in India. She grew up mostly in Somerset, England and migrated

241

Figure 86: Emily Creaghe, 1883.

to Australia as a 16-year-old, in 1876, and married Harry Creaghe, a station manager, in Ipswich, in 1881.

When Ernest Favenc, and his wife Emma, were contracted to explore parts of the Northern Territory to the east of the Overland Telegraph Line, the Creaghes were keen to join them. It meant that there would be two European women on an exploration of remote areas for the first time in Australia's history. The expedition met up on Thursday Island in December 1882 and transferred to Normanton, in the Gulf of Carpentaria, by ship. Unfortunately, Emma fell ill, and Favenc delayed the expedition for 10 weeks, by escorting her to Sydney.

While waiting for Favenc, the Creaghes and four others made a 320-kilometre journey to Carl Creek Station and then backtracked to Gregory Downs Station, where they reunited with Favenc and prepared to travel into the Territory. Their journey was tough. A young man named Warner died of sunstroke after three days of suffering— 'his groans were something terrible ...' wrote Emily Creaghe (1883). It was a tragedy, but at least the Creaghes were travel-hardened and ready for the expedition—which finally began when Favenc returned from escorting his wife to Sydney, on 14 April 1883.

There were only four in the expedition: Earnest Favenc, Lindsay Crawford, and Harry and Emily Creaghe. It was no picnic. Long days in the saddle, and trouble crossing creeks and gullies with bogged horses became the norm; before they entered dry country where thirst drove them westwards for day after day, looking for water.

And the 'flies were frightful!' One day, Crawford shot two ducks for dinner and Emily curried them to eat for breakfast the next day.

... We had the curry for breakfast this morning and I accused Mr Crawford of leaving the quills in the ducks instead of plucking them clean. Later, however, when it was broad

daylight, when I went to empty the remains of the curry out
of the billy, I discovered the supposed quills to be thousands of
flies ... (Creaghe, 1883).

The travellers were constantly in fear of attack by Aborigines:

... We sleep every night now with 2 revolvers in bed with us,
& a double-barrelled breech-loader. Outside, at the tent door
a loaded carbine Schneider stands already for use (Creaghe,
1883).

Every day Emily recorded what they saw of Aborigines. Usually,
it was tracks, old campfires, or smoke in the distance. However, it was
very different on 3 May. The party were despairing of finding water,
and after a dry camp, had travelled all day without finding any at
all. Campfire smoke about three miles north of them made Favenc
change course—Aborigines camping might mean water. After passing
quietly through the bush, suddenly Favenc and Crawford galloped
ahead, and when Emily caught up with them, she found that they
had captured two Aborigines. They assumed the Aborigines had never
seen white men before, because they showed no fear of their revolvers:

... we ... saw Mr Favenc holding a man with one hand & in
the other pointing his revolver at him, & Crawford holding a
gin ... When Mr Favenc came upon them, they climbed up a
small tree and when he made signs for them to come down the
nigger threw his gin down thinking that might satisfy them...
We were not going to do them any harm we merely wanted
them to take us to water ...

Favenc explained what they wanted with sign language, and the
couple agreed to lead them to water. It was three miles away, and there
was a larger camp of Aborigines there—seven men, nine women and
several children:

... the gins bolted at our appearance & we saw nothing of
them. One poor little baby was left by the mother in her fright,
& it was toddling about crying. The poor things were quiet and
frightened. Not having been molested by white men, they did
not attempt to do us any harm (Creaghe, 1883).

They left the Aborigines alone after they watered their horses
and filled their water bags and then travelled four hours into the night

before camping. It was two days before they next found water—
the Aborigines had saved their lives. Then it was another 59 hours,
travelling the last 80 miles to Powell's Creek Telegraph Station, also
without water. Their horses were nearly driven 'mad' by thirst, but
only one became so 'knocked up' they needed to shoot it.

The party reached Powell's Creek Station on 14 May, and there
split up; the Creaghes took the weaker horses north to Katherine,
whilst Favenc and Crawford (joined by a third man, Rogers) explored
the McArthur River area. It was much easier travelling for the Creaghes
because they rode along a track next to the Overland Telegraph Line.
They were also accompanied by a dray as far as Daly Waters Telegraph
Station. It carried three tanks of water, so the 80-mile dry stage was
easy to cross. This easy travel was a boon to Emily, because by this
time she was pregnant, and not feeling well on most days.

Daly Waters Telegraph Station, wrote Creaghe, was not as grand
as the Powell's Creek complex. The house was made of slabs, and
beams of light streamed through the cracks. It was manned by Mr
Johns and Mr Kemp, who had not seen a white woman for three
years.

The next stop was Elsey Telegraph Station. Elsey was manned
only in the wet season, so was a simple affair, consisting of little
more than a log hut. The operator, Mr Tuckfield, kept the telegraph
equipment in his bedroom.

In Katherine, the Creaghes stayed a few nights at the Katherine
Telegraph Station with Mr and Mrs Murray, who ran the station, and
lived there with their three children. Their house was a 'very poor
affair', soon to be replaced. They were invited to stay at Springvale
Station by Alfred Giles, who managed the station with his wife Mary
Sprigg, who had 'only been married about 3 years, but [was] over 33
years of age' (Creaghe 1883).

The Creaghes travelled with the Giles to Port Darwin, via
Pine Creek, The Shackle and Southport. They arrived on 14 August
1883, and Acting Government Resident McMinn hosted them at the

Residency. He proved to be a pleasant host indeed. He drove Emily around to visit the government gardens and the new gaol (which was still under construction), while Harry played tennis at the B.A.T. Afterwards they shared a musical evening, with McMinn playing the violin, and Emily an American organ. The next day, McMinn took Emily sailing with Paul Foelsche's two daughters, Rosie and Mary Jane, John Little, and a few other gentlemen. She found time to visit the newly completed town hall and borrow books from Mr Baines, the librarian for the Palmerston Institute. She also ran into Favenc, who had been joined by his wife. They were staying with John Little.

After several days in a whirlwind of social life, the Creaghes and Mrs Giles boarded the *Feilung* and departed for Sydney on 22 August.

Emily's diary of the overland journey is a valuable document. Her observations of the country and the lives of the Aborigines and frontier cattlemen and their relations offer a unique view—and differ occasionally to those in Favenc's record.

Harry Creaghe was killed in an accident with a horse in 1886, whilst Emily was again pregnant. In 1889, she married Joseph Jupp Smallman Barnett, a friend of Harry's, in Rockhampton, Queensland. Together they had six children, one of whom was killed in action in France during World War 1.

In 1909, Emily took five of the children and a nurse on board the *Perthshire*, intending to visit her sister in New Zealand. Instead, the ship drifted for seven weeks in the Tasman Sea with a broken propeller shaft, before they were rescued.

Joseph and Emily Barnett lived for 20 years in Marlborough, then moved to Rockhampton in Queensland, where Emily ran a boarding house after Barnett's death in 1921. She later moved to Sydney, and died there on Armistice Day in November 1944, aged 84 (Monteath, 2004).

J.P. Hingston, H.W.H. Stevens, and R.J.S. Buckland

John McDouall Stuart, one of Australia's greatest explorers, crossed the continent in 1861–62, and on 24 July reached the beach at Chambers Bay. 'I dipped my feet, and washed my face and hands in the sea, as I promised the late Governor Sir Richard McDonnell I would,' wrote Stuart in 1862. In Palmerston 20 years later, no one had yet found exactly where he did this, and there were mounting rumours that Stuart's party had never actually arrived at the coast at all.

Three of Stuart's party (Fred W. Thring, W. Patrick Auld, and Stephen King) returned to the north coast to the settlement of Escape Cliffs, just three years after their long expedition across the continent (Pugh 2018). Their integrity was in question, so they must have been angered by the rumours. In October 1866, the acting government resident of Escape Cliffs, James Manton, took Fred Thring and sailed east along the coast in the *Julia*, looking for Stuart's tracks. Even with Thring's help and experience, the searchers had no luck*. The coast was just too similar: there was a 'sameness about it,' Manton wrote, 'which defies identification, almost all being low-lying and fringed with mangroves …'

In 1862, Stuart had marked his presence on a large tree:

> … After all the party had some time on the beach, at which they were much pleased and gratified, they collected a few shells; I returned to the valley, where I had my initials (J.M-D.S.) cut on a large tree, as I did not intend to put up my flag until I arrived at the mouth of the Adelaide. Proceeded, on a course of 302°, along the valley; at one mile and a half, coming upon a small creek, with running water, and the valley being covered with beautiful green grass, I have camped to give the horses the benefit of it. Thus have, through the instrumentality of Divine Providence, been led to accomplish the great object of the expedition and take the whole party safely as witnesses to the fact, and through one of the finest countries man could wish to behold to the coast, and with a stream of running

---

* Fred Thring had recently arrived at Escape Cliffs with another great explorer, John McKinlay

water within half a mile of the sea (Stuart, 1862).

Gilbert McMinn, the acting government resident in 1883, had faith in Stuart's reports. McMinn could not believe that Stuart would lie about the culmination of his journey, because he had:

> ... touched upon the track of this indefatigable and renowned explorer, whose name will be a household world in Australia for generations to come, for more than a thousand miles in Central Australia, and have always found his descriptions of country most truthful (*NTTG*, 13 December 1883).

In 1882, McMinn made a short expedition to the Mary River Region himself, to no avail, but he offered local Aborigines rewards if they could tell him where the tree was. And then he received:

> ... information from them which led him to suppose that they had found it; but not being able to leave his official duties in Palmerston he had to depute the work of verifying the information to others. For this duty, Mr H.W.H. Stevens, manager for Messrs. Fisher and Lyons, volunteered, and kindly placed himself and cutter at Mr McMinn's disposal for the purpose. He was accompanied by Mr J.P. Hingston, of the Survey Department, and Mr R.G.S. Buckland, of the E.E. and A. Telegraph Company, starting on the 3rd inst., they were towed as far as the Vernons by the steamship *Tannadice* ...

They then went ashore with their horses and made a careful exploration of the coast, using bearings Stuart had recorded of the headlands and creeks. They found:

> ... the place where Stuart reached the Indian Ocean in Van Dieman's Gulf [and] also the tree marked by him with his initials J. M-D. S. in block letters ... The letters are described as being two feet in length, deeply sunk in the wood, and as distinct, though of course partly grown over, as the day they were cut, over twenty years ago ... (*NTTG*, 13 December 1883).

Hingston, Stevens, and Buckland, therefore, join the list of explorers of the Northern Territory, despite their trip lasting only five days, because the 'result of this expedition will forever set at rest the question of the great explorer's integrity' (*NTTG*, 13 December 1883).

Figure 87: Stuart's Tree (*Terminalia microcarpa*) in Chambers Bay (Foelsche, 1885, LANT, PH1002-0108).

In 1885, Inspector Paul Foelsche visited the site and photographed the tree, and it was re-discovered by Government Resident Justice Dashwood and Alfred Searcy in 1893. Searcy said the tree was hard to see from the sea because the letters were on its landward side (Searcy, 1909). Dashwood is said to have:

> … forwarded to the Treasurer two pieces of the memorable tree marked by the great explorer Stuart on reaching the shores of the Indian Ocean. They are portions of a limb which showed signs of decay, and which Mr Dashwood had lopped off. He had engraved on them the letters and figures which appeared on the trunk of the tree, viz.—'J. McD. S., 1862'. One of the pieces of wood will be sent by the Treasurer to the Museum (*Adelaide Observer*, 23 October 1893).

A large piece of timber with painted (not carved) lettering is now a part of the collection in the Northern Territory Museum in Darwin. It may be one of the same pieces Dashwood collected. The Museum's history curator says it was delivered to the museum after it was stored for decades, wrapped in a blanket, in a disused chimney in

South Australia. It was originally collected, it is believed, by Samuel Brown, the captain and owner of the steam launch named *Maggie*, used by Dashwood's expedition (Archibald, 2021).

W.J. O'Donnell

William J. (Billy) O'Donnell was an experienced explorer who learned the business as a member of the Victorian Exploring Party that brought back the remains of Burke and Wills, in 1864. He was later a well-known explorer of Western Australia, particularly the East Kimberley. He is worth mentioning in the list of Northern Territory explorers because he crossed large parts of the Territory in February 1883. His ambitious expedition left Palmerston and travelled to the Victoria River Region and then the Kimberley to examine land taken up by the Cambridge Downs Pastoral Association (Lewis, 2004). His party included Messrs. Carr-Boyd, O'Malley, Linacre, and Wells. The expedition was professionally managed, and after eight months in the bush, the men were 'in as good health and spirits as when last at Palmerston'. Carr-Boyd said that they crossed 'some of the finest pastoral country, splendidly watered, that he [had] ever travelled over'.

O'Donnell wrote to the *Times* while he was still in Katherine:

> … I am sorry that I cannot send you full particulars of trip through Western Australia. Must give first report to Syndicate in whose interest we were sent out but will give you brief outline of travels through your Territory. Making a final start from Dr Browne's cattle station, Delamere, and steering on a general South by West course, and parallel to the Victoria, we reached the latter river in 125 miles. After running the Victoria up for three days we struck a large tributary, which we followed for 20 miles. This creek I have called Giles' Creek, after Mr A. Giles, of Springvale, who was very kind to us. After running up Giles' Creek for one day we crossed over and came on some splendidly grassed downs and plains, until we struck the course of another large tributary of the Victoria … (*NTTG*, 13 October 1883).

Henry Stockdale

Henry Vane Stockdale was an Englishman whose 1919 obituary describes him as a 'well-known figure in Sydney racing circles' (*Barrier Miner* 4 February). He was a great friend of the poet Adam Lindsay Gordon, and was inspired by his bush poetry, and, like many bushmen of the nineteenth century, would recite verse around the campfire.

In 1884, 43-year-old Stockdale led an expedition from Port Darwin to Western Australia's Kimberley region by ship and returned overland through the Territory. Stockdale was employed by the Leopold Downs Pastoral Company, the Victorian Squatting Company, and others, to look at land that each already owned in the Kimberley and evaluate it for its grazing potential. He departed Port Darwin on the S.S. *Whampoa* and was dropped off in the Cambridge Gulf. His team of explorers included Henry Ricketson, John McIlree (surveyor), Patrick Mulcahy (assistant surveyor), George Ashton, Carl Battmer (aka Paul, blacksmith), and Richard Pitt. They used horses and drays, and had plenty of provisions, but things started to go wrong when the country proved rough. They took months to travel short distances and eventually had to abandon their drays.

> … One of our best pack mares fell down and injured herself, and unfortunately died during the night. The fearful places we have had to go up and down have been very trying to our pack horses, and as we have made nearly a straight line to here, we have had to face some great difficulties, more or less of mountains for 100 miles, and gullies and ravines that I never thought a horse could cross, but in many places we have had to make roads for them, and now they are so clever that they would literally climb a ladder … (Stockdale 1885).

One of Stockdale's main issues was time—he had signed an agreement to have a report to his employers by 14 January 1885, and the delays through the rough country frustrated him. A late report would cost him money:

> … It will now give me great trouble and put me to much extra expense to try and get my report in within the specified time,

the 14th. Jan. It was very foolish on my part signing such an
agreement, as no one can possibly form any idea of some of
the country without seeing It. Through some of the country
we have crossed, has been so stony, and the unforeseen delays
that occur on a trip like this, had I not been bound by time,
I could have saved all my horses, and had much easier times
now. I am up early and late and harassed out of my life, but I
am going to get the report through at all hazards if my health
is spared me, and I can reach Panton & Osman's station
and get 3 or 4 fresh horses and push on to the telegraph line
(Stockdale 1885).

Then two of the men, Mulcahy (who was regularly using opium)
and Ashton, weakened by a 'bad disorder' he had brought from
Sydney, resigned from the party, and remained behind. Stockdale
wrote that Mulcahy:

> … eats very heartily, and so does Ashton, and both have
> strong, lusty voices, but seem to have lost all heart, and the rest
> of the party are getting discouraged at the many and serious
> delays they are causing us. I have used every means to induce
> them to rally and pluck up heart, but it seems all to be totally
> lost upon them. It is a very trying situation for me, and I trust
> God will guide me, and help me to do what is right and just to
> all I have in my charge. Mulcahy acknowledged riding horses
> in depot out kangarooing, also to taking apples, biscuits,
> jam, flour, and peas, and to be unworthy of forgiveness or to
> remain one of the party. We all forgave him the wrong he had
> done us freely and truly.

> December 17 (Wednesday). Fine morning after very cool
> night. Thermometer at daylight, 60 deg. Mulcahy and Ashton
> both looking better, but both came to me and said if I would
> allow them, they would take three weeks' rations and camp
> for a spell on the river, and perhaps I would send help after
> them. I tried all in my power to induce them to struggle on
> a little further, if only as far as the Wilson River, but could
> not alter their determination. Called the rest of the party
> together, and as they one and all thought it was best under
> the circumstances, I had to consent, so, with Mr Ricketson's
> assistance, measured out to them twenty pannikins of flour,
> ten of white sugar, ten of peas, fifteen of dried apples, four

pounds of tea, and a tin of preserved meat. Left them two double-barrel guns, etc., with about one hundred and fifty cartridges, fishhooks, and lines, and camped on the Laurence River. We then packed up the remainder, and with sad hearts bade them good-bye, and firmly advised them to get either fish or game, as game is fairly plentiful around them. Ashton and Mulcahy both expressed a desire to write a few lines in my diary, and, in the presence of all hands, I allowed them.

Ashton also forwarded by me a note to his aunt in England, but Mulcahy, although I earnestly desired him to, would not write to either wife or parents, all he would say being, 'They will see you at no loss, old man.'

It is a dreadful state of affairs, the two biggest and strongest of our party collapsing like this, and has had a very depressing effect on me, though I must not show it, for fear of causing a despondent feeling in the others. I do hope we shall now have fair travelling and reach Panton and Osman's [Ord River] station and send back horses and relief to those left behind. They have had any amount of provisions, meat excepted, sometimes five meals a day, and never less than three (Stockdale, 1885).

Stockdale claimed he discovered and named five rivers, but when they unexpectedly arrived at Victoria River Downs Station, his navigation came into question (and this became a Territory, rather than a Kimberley, story).

Stockdale thought he was on the Ord River in Western Australia. Running short of supplies, he had set up camp on the river and ordered three of the men, Battmer, McIlree and Pitt, to remain there, with three week's provisions, and wait for him for nine days. Then he, and Henry Ricketson, set off for Osmand and Panton's station on the Ord River for fresh supplies. Stockdale told the others that if they did not hear from him, they should consider that some fatality had occurred, and should travel east to Katherine (Lewis, 2004).

Stockdale and Ricketson then wandered about in the neighbourhood of the Victoria River without knowing where they were. Finally, 'I had a parley with one old gin', he recorded, 'and imitating on all fours the bellow of a bullock, she seemed to understand I had evidently seen cattle, and she said what we took for white fellow sit down (pointing down the creek)'. With renewed vigour, they travelled on, and they reached Fisher and Lyons' Victoria River Downs Station on New Year's morning, 1885:

> ... Found the acting manager, Mr T.F. Armstrong all to be desired, doing everything in his power to make us at home and comfortably so. Arrived there about 6, and got a grand breakfast, beef, eggs, bread, jam rice and tea—what lucky dogs we are to fall into the hands of such a good Samaritan (Stockdale, 1885).

Finding out that they were lost and so far out of their way came as a shock: 'we must have unwittingly crossed the Ord and left it many miles behind according to the distance and course we have travelled' (Stockdale 1885). They knew the rest of their party was, as a result, in dire straits, but hoped they would be aware enough to strike out for Katherine as planned—McIlree had skills in navigation.

Stockdale and Ricketson reached Springvale Station and the Overland Telegraph Line on January 11, within plenty of time to telegraph a report to his employers. They then went safely back to Palmerston, arriving there at the beginning of February.

Stockdale paid two bushmen, Samuel Croker, and Kelly, £125, to head west to search for the lost members of his party, but he could not wait for them to be found. He immediately sailed to Melbourne on the *Ellerton* to report to his employers that he had found much country that was suited to pastoralism, particularly of sheep.

Battmer, McIlree, and Pitt waited the agreed nine days and then started east. Croker and Kelly found two of them—Pitt and Battmer—but McIlree was dead, and no trace of Mulcahy and Ashton was ever found. Kelly escorted the survivors to Springvale Station, where they were met by Alfred and Mary Giles:

> ... at last, there arrived at Springvale Station, Katherine River, two members of Stockdale's party, named Pitt and Carl, the latter a German not long in Australia. They were accompanied by S. Kelly and Ross from the Victoria River. Our information

is that Pitt and Carl were met by Croker, who had, it was stated, been sent out by Mr Stockdale to look for McKay [sic. Mulcahy] and his mate, the men reported as having stayed behind to prospect.

Pitt is insane, but from what can be gleaned from Carl it appears that Mr McIlree, the surveyor of the party, died from exhaustion, though he could not give the exact locality.

They had very rough times although they were never short of provisions. Croker is still looking for McKay [sic. Mulcahy] and mate.

The men are still at the station, where they are being cared for. Pitt has to be watched. We trust the Government will at once institute searching enquiries with reference to this suspicious looking matter (*North Australian*, 7 March 1885).

By the end of March, Pitt was safely in Palmerston Hospital, suffering severely from dysentery, but he was 'gradually working off the insanity.'

McIlree's death was inexplicable—he repeatedly mentioned his 'continued weakness and wasting away' in a diary that was given to Alfred Giles, 'for which he could not account'. Pitt and Carl said that he had died some days before they met Croker, but they did not know how to get back to the place:

> … McIlree used to eat well but seemed to waste away every day and had to be lifted on to his horse for several days before he died. On the morning of his death, he stated that he felt better, and would take some observations and got out his instruments for that purpose. He then said that he felt unwell and sat down by the fire. Mr Pitt took him in his arms to support him, when McIlree almost immediately died (*North Australian*, 6 May 1885).

Croker* continued and explored the country between the Victoria and Ord Rivers, looking for the missing men, Mulcahy and Ashton, but returned at the beginning of May without finding them. They were never heard of again.

---

* Samuel Croker was killed in a gunfight over a card game at Auvergne Station in 1893.

By late 1885, Harry Stockdale was back, with Linacre and Wells (who had explored with O'Donnell), overnighting in Port Darwin on the steamer *Taiwan*, with 1500 sheep. They were bound for Cambridge Gulf to start carving a sheep station from the bush.

Harry Stockdale's career was full of odd twists and turns. He was back in Palmerston in 1889, collecting curios for the Coogee Aquarium. He wanted 'some full-sized alligators' and several 'intelligent' Aborigines he could put on show in Sydney after, 'of course, first giving a bond to the Protector of Aborigines, for their good treatment and safe return' (*NTTG*, 16 February 1889).

During the 1890s, he was back again, dabbling in the buffalo and tourism industries, taking a lease over the Cobourg Peninsula, and collecting more curios. He claimed that it was 'no trouble at all to get a skull or two' from the Port Essington district-caves he discovered. They were full of 'Aboriginal drawings and hieroglyphics, and heaps of skeletons … No trouble at all' (*NTTG*, 2 October 1891).

Philip Saunders and J.P. Hingston

In October 1887, Government Resident Parsons wanted an exploration of the larger of the two Tiwi Islands. Melville Island had been the site of the first British attempt at settlement in the north (1824–29). It was called Fort Dundas, but it lasted under five years, with 33 of its members left behind in lonely graves. It was a settlement of soldiers, convicts, and Royal Marines, built on the eastern shore of Apsley Strait, which runs between Melville and Bathurst Islands. The Tiwi people had not welcomed the settlers, and several of the 33 deaths were caused by Tiwi spears. The rest died of diseases such as scurvy, and malaria (and one in childbirth) (Pugh, 2017).

In the 1880s, the Tiwi were still unwelcoming, and few white men had ventured there in the 58 years since the British abandoned the fort. One group of adventurers, whom the *Times* failed to name, had gone across over the Easter holidays of 1887 for some buffalo hunting:

… A party of sportsmen spent their Easter holidays pleasantly
by taking a cruise to Melville Island in the S.S. *Victoria*.
Arriving at the island on Friday morning, two days were
devoted to shooting and rambling over the country, and as
buffaloes were plentiful, there was plenty of exercise for those
who carried rifles. The country is described in glowing terms
by every member of the party, as quite different to the coast
land near Port Darwin. The natives were rather shy at first,
but afterwards got over their timidity, and presented the party
with some spears, which kindness was reciprocated by some
of the sportsmen presenting the natives with a few choice
specimens of Martini-Henry bullets and No 3 shot. The
natives then retired to make another collection of weapons for
the Jubilee Exhibition, which will probably be waiting for the
next visitors to the island. One of the members of the party,
who has travelled over a considerable portion of the Territory,
states that the land on Melville Island is superior to any he has
seen elsewhere, either for pastoral or agricultural pursuits, but
there is no sign of mineral bearing country. It is quite time
this valuable island was properly explored, and as the natives
are fond of sport, a strong party will be needed for the work
(*NTTG*, 16 April 1887).

Buffalo skins were worth money, and the island had resources
that could be taken advantage of by the South Australians, so Parsons
was keen to find out what was there. To lead an expedition, he
employed the miner, Philip Saunders, the same man who led the
civilian reprisal party against the Woolwonga in 1884. To map their
discoveries, he recruited the surveyor J.P. Hingston.

The expedition was the talk of the town for weeks. Everyone
had an opinion:

… One of the chief topics of conversation during the week
has been the proposed exploring trip to Melville Island. People
seem to have formed the opinion at once that no good will
result from the expedition, believing that the aborigines in that
part of the world will show their feelings towards their white
brothers by surprising the party before their labours are at an
end. Our consoling advice is that each and every member of
the party should take the precaution to make their last will

and testament before leaving Palmerston, or have it executed by Mr Solicitor Stow before setting foot on the island (*North Australian*, 8 October 1887).

Saunders decided against taking horses because of the difficulty of landing them on the island and reloading them after they had crossed it. Instead, he employed Coolie labour—five Chinese workers willing to carry 50 pounds of gear on their backs—for a few pounds in cash (unfortunately, they were never named in the records of the expedition). He also press-ganged a small band of six Larrakia men into accompanying the expedition:

> ... It was with great difficulty that a few town blacks were pressed into service, for, knowing the combative disposition of the islanders, they do not anticipate any real enjoyment from the trip, and they are loud in their praises of the martial spirit of the inhabitants of the land to be examined. They relate many striking instances of how the natives of Melville Island played the deuce with the mainland blacks in bygone days, all of which, in their opinion, goes to show that to attempt to travel through their country is nothing short of hanging life on a very slender thread. But then they overlook the difference between Martini-Henry rifles and the adopted weapon of the darkie. It occurs to us that twelve white men of average pluck with rifles of perfect construction, will, if occasion demands it, establish a funk on the island, and make it more admissible to civilised settlers. Still, there is more than an ordinary degree of danger in the expedition, and it will be no surprise to us to find that some of the novelty seekers are made to suffer from that process of perforation peculiar to the spear (*North Australian*, 8 October 1887).

The Aborigines—who also remain unnamed in the records—were made to accompany the expedition because their fear meant that they would be wary of attacks by the Tiwi: 'The aboriginals were taken to assist the Europeans in night watching, and it is doubtful if they enjoyed a good sleep during the journey' (Saunders P., 20 October 1887).

Eleven white men were willing to take the five-day walk across Melville Island. Apart from Saunders and Hingston, Parsons, and four of his mates from the Port Darwin Rifle Club, E.H. Whitelaw, N. Waters, K. Stevens, and Charles W. Hughes, decided to go along as well. All carried their pistols and Martini-Henri rifles. Others to tag along were R.M. Stow (the Crown Prosecutor), G.W. Martin, Maurice Holtze the botanist, and renowned bushman E.O. Robinson. Charles Millar, the railway man, would have liked to go but, instead, he lent them his steamship, *Active*, at no cost. The plan was to be dropped off on the south part of the island and picked up on the north side. The *Active* would wait for them near some 'bright red cliffs'.

They set off on 5 September. An article summarising Saunders' report[*] appeared in the *North Australian* on 15 October 1887:

> ... A camp was formed on the south side of the Island about four miles inland, where everything was got in readiness for a start on the morrow. Shortly after getting into camp an incident happened that put the party on the QUI VIVE for niggers. A solitary savage stalked up towards the whites and began yelling, evidently to attract others of his sort, for some time afterwards a squad of blacks joined him and took stock of the visitors. There were several gins among this number.
>
> No inducement was sufficient to attract the mob to close quarters. Handkerchiefs and other presents were deposited on the track for them in hopes of inducing friendly relations, but all in vain. At 8 p.m. several of them moved up close to the camp, but on account of the lateness of the hour they were ordered off, though it was only after great deal of gentle persuasion that they were prevailed on to withdraw; and the night went by without further incident.
>
> Next morning, at about 8 o'clock, after breakfasting, the expedition moved on a northerly course over very rough ironstone country, natives following the whole way, but showing no desire to openly molest the travellers. At midday, a buffalo was shot, the tongue and some steak meat were appropriated by the slayers, and the remainder of the carcase was left for the blacks.

---

[*] Saunders' report is lengthy and available online (Saunders P., 20 October 1887). Philip Saunders died in 1931, at the age of 93, in Kalgoorlie Hospital, 60 years after he discovered the first gold in the Kimberley.

Soon after this a halt was made for refreshment, and it was here that the leader had a spear thrown into him. He and Mr Hingston strolled from the camp down to a creek about 200 yards away to get some water. They were allowed sufficient time to get the water and were starting back to their mates when a number of spears dropped among them. Saunders was in the act of lighting his pipe at the time, and his revolver lay in front of him on the ground, and before he could bring the trusty weapon into play, he was struck by a spear which passed quite close to his comrade and went through the left arm near to the elbow. Two other spears just grazed the right arm, coming from right and left of where the two white men stood, there being six blacks on one side them and four on the other, and the spears were thrown from an ambush not more than fifteen yards away. Mr Saunders advised his companion to run for assistance, but the shots from the revolvers of the attacked ones had already carried the alarm, so that before Mr Hingston could signal the camp, help was on the way down, upon seeing which the natives retired to the scrub.

All then returned to camp, where the spear was carefully extracted from the arm of the leader, and the expedition moved on.

During the voyage across from this… until reaching the opposite side nothing of special importance happened. The travelling was through rough country, barren in some places, boggy in others, and intersected with numerous creeks which caused much detention. One of these threatened to prove a serious bar until Mr E. Robinson swam to the other side for a canoe in which the company were paddled to the opposite side. Another was crossed by means of a raft, and where others were met with, they were generally got over by felling trees to act as bridges.

On Tuesday evening the party struck Brenton Bay, reported to be a splendid harbour with hilly country bordering it. This being 10 miles from Lethbridge Bay, where the *Active* was anchored, it was necessary to walk round to that place, and this task was made easy by having a grand beach to tramp over the whole distance. Lethbridge Bay was reached by 3 o'clock on Wednesday afternoon. On arrival there, unmistakable

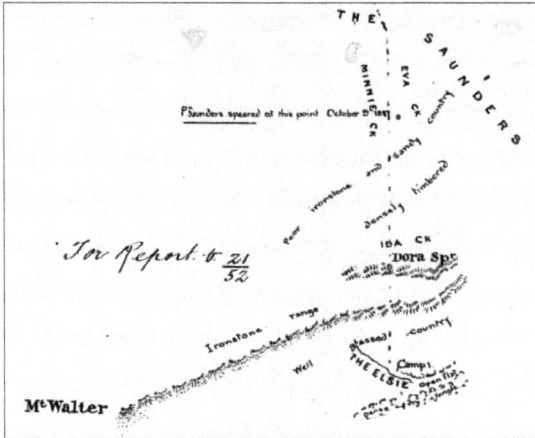

Map 8: Section of Hingston's map of the Melville Island crossing, 1887.

evidence of blacks being in the vicinity was supplied by the appearance of a dog which had previously been seen with some natives near the starting point.

A signal was given to the steamer to send off a boat, but while resting preparatory to going aboard, the party were surprised by the treacherous savages who, from a neighbouring cliff, delivered a shower of spears at the unsuspecting whites, some of whom had very narrow escapes. In return for this, a volley of bullets was directed at the spot from whence the spears came, but the result was not discovered. One native who was fired at from about 100 yards dropped as though killed outright, but very soon jumped up again and made all sorts of insulting gestures at the whites. The party then embarked, and the steamer was headed for Port Darwin. It is said that while waiting for the land party some of those in charge of the steamer pulled ashore at Lethbridge Bay to interview the aborigines and make an attempt to gain their friendship by presenting them with biscuits and other things, but this demonstration of kindness had no good effect whatever, as when the boat was shoving off to return to the steamer one darkie clung to it with such good will that he had to be forcibly dealt with before he would let go, his companions meantime flourishing spears and yelling and gesticulating with every appearance of hostility (*North Australian*, 15 October 1887).

This last action did not appear in the authorised report.

The whole expedition sounded more like a holiday adventure—despite the attacks and the worn-out boots—than an exploration. It did, however, have unforeseen consequences. Within a few years, E.O. Robinson had taken out a lease over the whole island, and Joe Cooper, a buffalo hunter, had started harvesting buffalo skins on the island. Life for the Tiwi would never be the same again.

Chapter 18
And now?

When I wrote *Darwin: Origin of a City*, my search for remnants of the city dating from the 1870s was dominated by the Administrator's residence, now known as Government House. This magnificent 7-gabled house was called *The Residency* back then, and though renovated and expanded and unrecognisable from the original building built by Bloomfield Douglas, sections of the original building remain—mainly stone walls. It was rebuilt in the 1880s by Parsons, who ensured those structures remained, and subsequent renovations have followed the same basic design. However, for this book on the 1880s, I resisted the temptation to bother Her Honour once again to poke about her house.

As I wrote then, Darwin's ability to maintain her heritage sites has been poor for four reasons:

First, very few of Darwin's early buildings were constructed of anything other than wood—even corrugated iron houses had wooden frames, and these usually fell to the ravages of termites.

Second, the violent weather that regularly bears down on the city took the weakened houses to all points of the compass: Darwin was thrice destroyed by cyclones: in 1897, 1937 and 1974—the last of which, Cyclone Tracy, turned the stone-walled Town Hall into rubble.

Third, many buildings that were still standing in the 1940s were destroyed by Japanese bombs. They came in more than 100 raids, starting

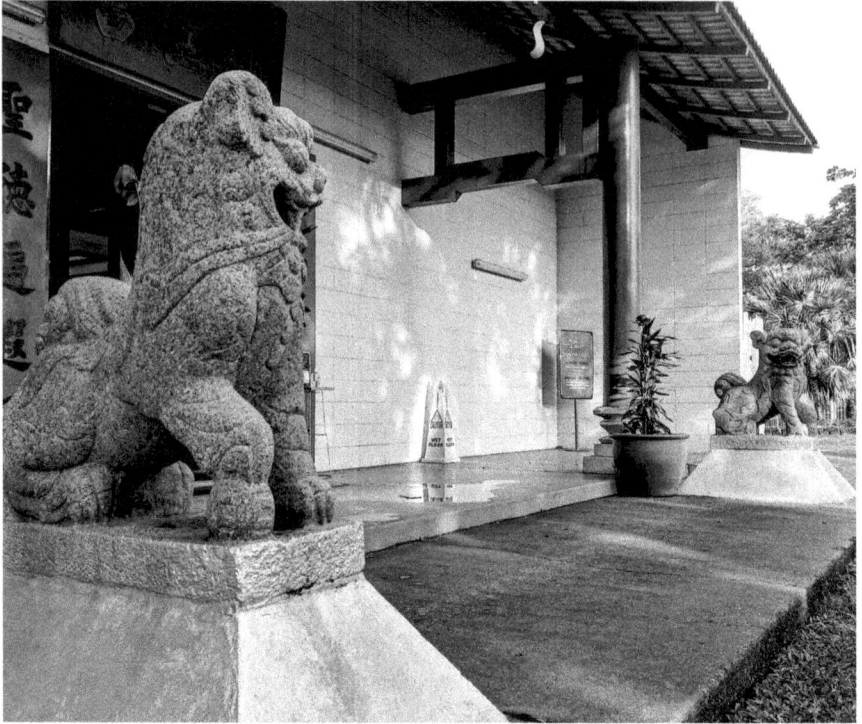

Figure 88: The original lions from the Brock's Creek Chinese Temple, now guard the temple in Darwin.

on 19 February 1942, and destroyed the Darwin Post Office, Telegraph Office, Cable Office and the postmaster's residence, and others.

Darwin's last heritage issue has been due to short-sighted politicians with agendas more aligned to progress than heritage. With luck, and a growing awareness of the loss of our heritage by the population, this is changing.

Chung Wah

To start my search for the remains of the 1880s in today's Darwin, I arranged to visit the Chung Wah Society's Chinese History Museum, which stands beside the temple in Woods Street. The temple, in various incarnations, has stood on the same site since 1887. The current temple replaces what was left after the 1937 cyclone and

World War Two. It is guarded by the lions that originally guarded Brock's Creek Temple, as discussed in Chapter 4.

The museum was opened for me on request by Neville Jones, who, despite his Welsh name, has an encyclopaedic knowledge of Chinese history in the Top End. The museum tells the story of the Chinese in Darwin through a number of themes, such as families, mining, agriculture, religion, and Chinatown, and is well worth a visit for anyone interested in history.

It was not hard to find relics of the 1880s, although they are hardly spectacular: a dozen or more carved porcellanite gutter blocks lay on the floor. They were removed from the Smith Street Mall area during the renovations of the 1980s and were most likely carved between 1878 and 1880. In the dry seasons, when there was no water for alluvial mining, the government resident employed destitute Chinese miners to install gutters along Smith and Cavenagh Streets. Neville said that some of the blocks have Chinese characters carved on them, though we could not find any.

There are some old farming tools on display. They are not dated, and probably much younger than 140 years, but they include handmade hoes, and small picks and similar tools. You can still buy tools like this in rural areas of China today—some things change slowly.

One interesting display is of a Chinese pig oven—or at least a fibreglass cast of it. The original sits in the bush near Pine Creek. It was used by Chinese miners for decades. It is a circle of rocks about a metre high and a metre wide, within which entire pigs were roasted. I made a mental note to keep an eye out for the original the next time I visit Pine Creek.

The only other major remnant of Darwin's Chinatown is the Sue Wah Chin Building in Cavenagh Street. It was often called the 'Stone House' and it was built in 1888 by Kwong Sue Duk, whose descendants can still be found in Darwin. Its originally had a hipped roof that was taken by Cyclone Tracy, and its replacement is flat. It is a single storey building that contains five commercial premises. Kwong Sue Duk (also known as Sun Mow Loong) was, among other things, an opium dealer in the premises now used by the modern Stone House Wine Bar. This is why the windows are barred—they used to protect the opium held there. There is a famous film of Chinatown from 1926. It shows smiling children and busy men walking along the Stone House veranda, or seated on small benches, smoking pipes and watching the day go by (NFSA, 1926).

Territory changes

Things are changing in the Northern Territory. Just as I prepared to wander the streets of Darwin looking for evidence of the 1880s, two events occurred that should be celebrated by all Australians. The first was a surprise—because they should have known better. Some well-meaning National Park managers were opening up an area of Litchfield National Park for day visitors and camping that had, until then, only been accessible by foot—but there was a problem:

> … The NT Government has been heralding the 'game-changing' $17.5 million opening of Litchfield Central Valley in mid-2021, which will give tourists access to new camping and swimming spots. But Indigenous leaders from around Litchfield say they're 'angry and disappointed' they were not consulted on the recent naming of those sites, like Red Rock Gorge and Cycad Springs.
>
> 'It's about genocide of a language,' said Koongurrukun academic Helen Bishop.
>
> Prior to her death, Ms Bishop's mother Ida mapped the Koongurrukun names for much of Litchfield*—or Purlugutj, in her language—including some of the soon-to-be accessible spots. 'It isn't about inclusion—it's about a vision government has," Ms Bishop said. 'It's almost like making us invisible.' (Matt Garrick, ABC News, 24 January 2021).

---

* Litchfield National Park is named after Fred Litchfield, who explored the area in 1865, when he was a member of the First Northern Territory Expedition at Escape Cliffs.

The park managers were out of step with the community, but it was not long before they were pulled into line. The Minister for Parks and Rangers, an Indigenous woman herself*, reacted immediately and directed them to 'renegotiate the naming of these sites with all traditional owner groups associated with the area'. These special sites, which have had perfectly good names for thousands of years, will now be allowed to keep them.

The other event was when a 70-year-old, retired school principal from St. Francis Xavier Catholic School on the Daly River, was awarded the title of Senior Australian of the Year for 2021. Dr Miriam-Rose Ungunmerr-Baumann AM (1950–) is a well-known activist, educator and artist of the Ngan'gityemerri language group. Her life has been a series of firsts: first Indigenous teacher and principal to work in the Northern Territory; first Indigenous woman to visit Antarctica; and founder of Merrepen Arts Centre. Dr Ungunmerr-Baumann, like many other extraordinary Aboriginal leaders, bears no malice for the way her people were treated in the past. She does, however, believe it is time for the wider Australian population to begin to understand what it means to be Aboriginal, and to develop an appreciation of Aboriginal culture. To do that, we all need to understand our history, come to terms with it, and build a shared future based on knowledge. As another Indigenous Australian, Hayden Bromley recalled in his acceptance speech as South Australia's Citizen of the Year:

> … We all know the saying … Those who don't know history are doomed to repeat it … (Haze Blak, 26 January 2021).

Searching the city

The monsoon rains of 2021 were a consistent dampener of the city in the last week of January 2021. When at last there was a break in the weather, I picked up my regular 'fieldwork' companion, Peter

---

* In 2021, the Honourable Selena Uibo is Attorney-General and Minister for Justice, Minister for Treaty and Local Decision Making, Minister for Aboriginal Affairs, and Minister for Parks and Rangers.

Whelan, and headed into the city. Peter has been a resident of Darwin since 1956. He grew up in the streets surveyed by Goyder's men on the peninsula, and knows the nooks and crannies of the old city as well as anybody. A keen golfer, he told me of some ruins on the edge of Gardens Golf Course he thought may be remnants of the dwellings of Chinese market gardeners. They were worth checking out, so we headed there first ...

The Gardens Golf Course was originally mostly a swamp, with a tidal creek running almost to the base of the low hills that surround it. Some of it was good agricultural land, and before Holtze took it over as part of the Botanic Gardens, the alluvial flats were farmed by Chinese market gardeners such as Soo Hoo Yoke. There were many huts where the workers lived, and the site we examined was certainly a building site at one time. There is a stone retaining wall on the hill above the 3rd fairway and a flat area that has the remnants

Figure 89: Gold nuggets found by 'Prospector 1' near Yam Creek in recent times.

of a concrete slab. The slab is old—it used local gravel rather than the more modern 'blue metal', but there was no way we could date the ruin. Because of the earthworks required to flatten the site, the building that was here clearly had a lot of effort put into it, but there is almost nothing left of it now.

Gold

The exciting find at the golf club was an old prospector who has spent 50 years looking for gold in the Territory and Queensland. He was a mine of knowledge on the goldfields south of Darwin, and still holds claims there. He talked of nuggets as big as ox tongues and assured me there is plenty more to be found. He showed me some of his nuggets. They weighed about 40 ounces, and he was happy for me to photograph them.

'Call me Prospector 1', he said.

The Botanic Gardens

We moved on, across to the Botanic Gardens, where Holtze had his house. There used to be an old house on the site named 'Holtze Cottage', but it was blown away by Cyclone Tracy, in 1974*. It was not the original building lived in by the Holtze family— that was destroyed by the 1897 cyclone, but it did have old parts. There was also a restaurant there for a

Figure 90: Holtze's brick stairs in the Botanic Gardens, hidden in the undergrowth.

---

* The Northern Territory Historical Society stored many papers, artefacts, and old papers in the building. They were all lost in the cyclone.

Figure 91: Holtze's stone stairs—renovated and on display, in the
Botanic Gardens.

while, names 'Holtze Cottage', but that too is long gone. Today, a
plant display house sits on the site, and Peter and I spent some time
rummaging around the gardens near it, looking for old bricks or other
tell-tale signs of a residence. We easily found the original concrete
and brick stairs hidden in the undergrowth. Remnants go all the way
down the hill. The bricks in them were, no doubt, fired in Fannie Bay,
a short way along the coast. A renovated stone section of the stairs
stands alone near the bottom of the hill, with a sign announcing they
were Holtze's stairs. Perhaps they are authentic, but we were happier
to find the ruined brick stairs further up the hill.

The Pioneer Cemetery

From the Botanic Gardens, it is a short drive to the Pioneer Cemetery
in Goyder Road. A signboard at its entrance lists the known occupants
of the graves. Many names will be familiar to readers of my books:
Tuckwell, Ryan, Little, Foelsche, McMinn, V.V. Brown, Solomon,

Figure 92: Edith Pater's gravestone, Pioneer Cemetery, Darwin.

and others, but I was keen to visit graves I had not paid much attention to on previous visits. The first was that of Edith Mary Pater, the judge's daughter who died of consumption at the age of 19, on 22 December 1886.

Edith's marble gravestone lies flat on the ground, and it looks younger than its 130 years. It is clear of lichen and the marks of time, and its gold letters must have been renovated in recent years, as they are clear and fresh looking. At the foot of the stone, the makers' names— Fraser and Draysey—were carved and painted in smaller letters.

Later, a quick search of the internet found that Hugh Fraser and Frederick Draysey were well-known monumental stonemasons located in Waymouth Street, Adelaide. They carved the marble base and pedestal for the large statue of Queen Victoria in Adelaide's Victoria Square, the granite base for the Robbie Burns statue in Kapunda, and numerous other stone constructions throughout the early city.

After a little more research, I discovered that the marble was imported from Italy. 'Carrara' marble has been exported directly from the quarries in Tuscany in large amounts across the world for several centuries. It is the same stone from which Michelangelo carved his statue of David.

Edith's marble gravestone was an expensive memorial, made from Italian marble, imported by an Adelaide company. Looking around the cemetery in 2021, I saw that Edith's was not the only gravestone carved from marble—and the others still look good too. Marble is harder wearing than many of the other types of stone used, so the judge's decision was sound.

Fraser and Draysey did not advertise themselves in the newspapers in the Territory, but I found their names in their agent's ads in the Adelaide newspapers. I also found an 1889 manifest for the S.S. *Airlie*, heading from Adelaide to Hong Kong, via Port Darwin, listing items to be unloaded. The *Airlie*'s cargo included 9 packages of marble sent by Fraser and Draysey to Palmerston (*Register*, 26 April 1889). Edith's gravestone was probably in one of those packages. If so, it took just over two years to install after her death.

Another marble grave belongs to John Archibald Graham Little. He died in 1906, at the age of 63, after 35 years as Station Master and Senior Inspecting Officer on the Overland Telegraph Line. His gravestone also lies horizontally and is embellished by a large marble cross, perhaps 10 centimetres thick. The marble has black stains on it in places, where algae has grown during the wet.

Near John Little, lie Paul and Charlotte Foelsche. They have a metal fence around them and splendidly carved marble crosses as headstones. Paul lived for 15 years after Charlotte died in 1899. He finally passed away at the age of 83, in 1914.

Foelsche arrived in Port Darwin on the first ship of settlers in 1870, so he was, indeed, an old Territorian. His legacy is an incredible collection of photographs, taken almost from the first day after he arrived.

Figure 93: The graves of Paul and Charlotte Foelsche.

A headstone with a poignant tale is that of Gilbert McMinn's first wife and their son. Anna Gore died on Christmas day in December 1880, aged 27. Her baby son, Willie, died nearly two years earlier, in March 1878*.

Anna was the daughter of Alfred Dewhirst Gore, who ran businesses in Palmerston and Pine Creek. Alfred Gore's father (also Alfred) brought the first church to Palmerston in 1872. It was sent by the Congregational Union in Adelaide 'in frame' and flat-packed, at the request of Pine Creek miners. It was to be put together in Pine Creek by Alfred Gore (senior), who had already conducted 'worships' on behalf of the Congregational Church. Unfortunately, he contracted malaria and returned south before he could do anything. Eighteen months later, the church was still lying, unpacked, on the beach near

---

* Gilbert McMinn remarried in 1884. His long career led him to return to Victoria, so he is not in the Goyder Road Cemetery. He died in St Kilda in 1824, aged 83, of heart failure.

the Fort Hill Camp. It was discovered by Reverend Bogle, bought by the Methodist Missionary Society of Adelaide, and constructed in Mitchell Street in 1874 (see Pugh, 2019). That first tin church building was destroyed by the 1897 cyclone, but its replacement was built almost immediately. That building still exists—it was moved to the Botanic Gardens and now holds Eva's Café. We stopped for a coffee there, on the way to the cemetery.

Figure 94: The grave of Mrs Anna McMinn (nee Gore), and William McMinn.

Railway to the jetty

Peter and I moved on to the Daly Street Bridge, which once crossed the original railway line. A bike path now eases through the cutting. The path rises a little as it heads south—no wonder the runaway iron ore train, that crashed near here in 1972, gathered so much speed as it ran downhill.

There was another bridge closer to Harvey Street we visited as well. The lines that crossed it are gone but, hidden among the trees are the concrete remnants of the bridge supports. Frogs Hollow Creek flows between them still. Nearby, protruding from the walls of a ditch

Figure 95: This seawall may be a part of the original stonework for the 1885 railway jetty.

is the last remaining rail. All the rest of the rails in this area were taken for recycling, although some were left in place further down the Stuart Highway, perhaps as a reminder of the past. Others were used as electricity pylons—there is one still standing in front of my house, although as the power supply is now underground, it has no current function.

The 1885 railway embankment and seawall on the approach to the Darwin jetty still serves well. The neatly laid porcellanite stones are reminiscent of the wall that can be seen in Figure 59. The original wall was straight, but it now curves near the end. Nevertheless, it is possible that many of the stones were those laid by the Chinese workers in 1885, and others may also have been reused during renovations.

The jetty is new, of course. Most of it needed replacing after World War Two. None of the original boards, where *Sandfly* was put together in 1886, exists anymore. However, *Sandfly* certainly still exists. The little engine was retired to Port Augusta in 1950, but

Figure 96: *Sandfly* was retired to a Port Augusta museum until 2005, when it was returned to Darwin. It is now on display in the QANTAS hangar in Fannie Bay, Darwin.

it was returned to Darwin in 1972. It spent some time rusting, on show on the wharf, but its home in recent years is the old QANTAS hangar in Fannie Bay. The hangar is not exactly a museum, but it is open to visitors and holds hundreds of privately owned treasures from Northern Territory history. *Sandfly* stands just inside the door, beautifully renovated*.

Travellers' Walk

Across from the jetty is a set of stairs known as 'Travellers' Walk'. For many decades newcomers to Darwin climbed these steps for their first look at the remote northern town. The steps are now renovated, but original concrete is still visible in places.

The OTL

We drove a few hundred metres from the jetty to Jervois Street, near the Deckchair Cinema. Here, on the beach, we could easily

---

* According to Leo Izod, the *Sandfly* was rusted through to its last rivet. Its renovation is extraordinary.

Figure 97: A section of a telegraph line that stretched from Port Darwin to Banyuwangi in Java. It is visible at low tide off Jervois Park, and is now heritage listed.

see the remnants of an undersea telegraph cable as it headed off to Banyuwangi in Java. There were several cables laid over the years as telegraphic traffic increased, but the cables are not always as visible as they were this day—recent monsoonal weather had washed away the top layers of mud and sand. The cables were recently heritage listed, and are a curiosity, if not yet a major tourist site.

The Mud Hut

Our last visit of the day was to the site of John Knight's 'Mud Hut', on the hill below Government House. A few years ago, Julie Maston, a student of archaeology, carried out a professional dig there, looking for artefacts and remnants of the house that had burned down in 1933. The site is complicated by a later house that existed there in the 1940s until 1963, and much of their detritus filled the collection boxes— beer bottles, navy buttons, 1940s coins, bullets, and hundreds of nails. However, Maston also found two opium bottles and a 19th Century bullet on the site from an earlier time. Definitive signs of the presence of Knight's house are a pillar, still visible in the wall supporting the

Figure 98: The site of the Mud Hut is now a rainforest, with this huge scrub-
fowl's nest covering much of the area.

road above, and a flight of steps, which Julie successfully excavated. When she was there, the hillside was lightly wooded. A few shade trees cooled the site, and it was a pleasant place to be, overlooking the bay. The hill had been cleared of a nasty weed known as 'coffee bush' (Leucaena leucocephala) by Brian Delaney of the Conservation Commission in the 1980s. The Commission had run sprinklers right across the hillside and planted more trees.

The trees have grown into a thick rainforest, but Peter and I were hoping, at least, to find the stairs the archaeologist uncovered. We were disappointed. Nothing is visible at the site except the pillar next to the road. Most of the rest is buried under a huge scrub-fowl's nest and the detritus of the forest.

Figure 99: Curator of Territory History at the Museum and Art Gallery of the Northern Territory, Jared Archibald, holds a piece of the Terminalia tree that was marked by John McDouall Stuart in 1862. It is a remnant piece, taken after the tree was rediscovered in the 1880s, and then found dead or dying, burned by fire, in the 1890s, by Samuel Brown.

Stuart's Tree

The next day, I had arranged to meet Curator of Territory History, Jared Archibald, at the museum. I was keen to see the piece of the Terminalia tree held by the museum, with the painted initials of John McDouall Stuart. It is kept in a large white cardboard box somewhere in the bowels of the museum, but Jared had it sitting ready on his desk when I arrived. It was an exciting moment—I held my breath as he donned rubber gloves and opened the box. Inside was a rough-cut branch about a metre long, with letters neatly painted on a flat side. At some time, the timber had been oiled, and the letters were originally bright orange or gold, but they had now faded to brown. The link to Stuart was palpable—it is part of the tree that he, or his men, had spent time blazing with his initials. Although it was salvaged from the tree decades after Stuart's time, Jared was convinced of the providence

279

of the item—it was donated by Lennie Brown, a descendent of Captain Samuel Brown whose steam launch had carried Dashwood's expedition to the site. Lennie knew the branch was stored in a disused chimney wrapped in a blanket for decades and, for just as long, in an old sleeping bag on top of a wardrobe in the family home.

The timber is almost certainly *Terminalia*, the dates fit, and the story rang true. It is authentic, and the keepers of the museum are glad to have it (Archibald, 2021).

City remnants

Our search for the remnants of the 1880s in the modern city of Darwin was successful. It concluded with a quick look at the ruins of the 1883 Town Hall, destroyed by Cyclone Tracy, and the beautiful 1885 Brown's Mart, which was thought worthy of repair after the cyclone, and now functions as a theatre. Across the road from them, the façade of the 1885 Commercial Bank building still exists, dwarfed by the modern Paspaley Tower. A little further down Smith Street Mall, the Victoria Hotel, which was built in 1889—and first opened in 1890 as the North Australian Hotel—also still stands, although it has been closed and 'boarded up' for some years now. As the last remnants of the early-1880s boom, they are treasures to be guarded by modern populations.

As we drove home, we passed the Fannie Bay Gaol. This complex, originally designed by John George Knight in 1883 but much altered since, operated as the Darwin gaol for nearly 100 years. It closed in 1979 and is now a museum. Visitors can tour the old cells and enter a small building which was the infirmary in 1887, but later became the gallows room. It was used twice as a gallows—to execute two murderers in 1952. During the wet season, the museum only opens for visitors on Saturday mornings, so we drove on by.

Gallery

Figure 100: Browns Mart, constructed in 1885, was restored after Cyclone Tracy. It is now a theatre, after a varied career housing auctioneers, shipping agents, real estate agents, importers, and Lloyds Insurance Agents. It was also a torpedo workshop during World War 2, Crown Law Offices, Police Headquarters, and reputedly, a brothel.

Figure 101: The Palmerston Town Hall and Institute was built in 1883.
It was destroyed in 1974 by Cyclone Tracy.

Figure 102: The facade of the Commercial Bank at the corner of
Smith Street Mall and Bennett Street.

Figure 103: The Victoria Hotel opened in 1890 as the
North Australian Hotel.

Darwin: Growth of a City

Chapter 19
Towards the 'nineties

The furious growth of the Northern Territory in the early 1880s did not last through to the 1890s. The construction of the wharf and the railway targeted two important industries—mining and pastoralism—but the first was already declining. Between 1886 and 1888, gold production more than halved. A sudden spike in gold production in 1889 gave hope, but the old problems of the high costs of isolation, shortage of labour, lack of capital, and poor local knowledge, continued to plague the industry (Powell, 1982). The mining industry was partly supported by other metals—copper, tin, and silver—but they suffered the same problems.

Throughout the 1880s, the mines and the railway construction continued to bring Chinese workers. In 1888, there were more than 6,000 Chinese in the Territory, but with the demise of the mines and completion of the railway, they started to leave—3000 went home in 1889.

Not all of them could afford the fares: 50 Chinese passengers departed Darwin on the *Taiyuan* on 19 October 1989 for Hong Kong, but 20 others attempted to stow themselves away on board. Unfortunately for them, 'Captain Nelson frustrated their little designs by having the ship carefully searched' (*NANTGG*, 25 October 1889).

The Territory had so far been built by Chinese workers: their efforts had completed the railway, they had dominated the goldfields, and they had grown fresh vegetables for the Palmerston and goldfields markets. For all that, they suffered extraordinary racism. The white residents lived in fear that 'by and by, all China come, even the Emperor', as John Knight's Chinese cook put it.

The pastoralists had their issues of isolation, but the cattle tick—*Boophilus microplus*—nearly destroyed their industry before it had begun. The parasite carries red-water fever, and cattle herds across the Top End were decimated by it for years. In 1889, 30 per cent of land held under pastoral leases in the Northern Territory was rescinded as stations collapsed. C.B. Fisher's losses were the largest—up to £250,000—but most other speculators in the industry also suffered. The stations in the Barkly and the Victoria River regions mostly survived, but many in the Top End did not (Powell, 1982).

The big thinkers in the Southern states still dreamed of a transcontinental railway. At the beginning of the 1880s, South Australia built a 'development' line north from Port Augusta to a desolate bore named Government Gums. Then, building the northern section—from Palmerston to Pine Creek—made it look like the transcontinental would come to fruition, but about the same time, the South Australian Government's bonded debt swelled to £21.5 million. The South Australians began to view their Northern Territory as a 'white elephant'. As they struggled with financial problems, the Top End became increasingly ignored.

Readers who consider this as a plug for the next book in this series—containing stories of the 1890s—would be correct ...*

---

* In 2022, see *Darwin: Survival of a City. The 1890s.*

Table of images

Abbreviations

ADB	*Australian Dictionary of Biography* (http://adb.anu.edu.au/biography).
GU	Griffith University.
HSNT	Historical Society of the Northern Territory.
LANT	Library and Archives of the Northern Territory.
NLA	National Library of Australia.
NTG	Northern Territory Government
NTTG	*Northern Territory Times and Gazette* (*NTTG*): Editors Joseph Skelton 1876–84, and
	Vaiben L. Solomon 1885–90. (https://trove.nla.gov.au/newspaper).
North Australian	Editors George Mayhew and Charles Kirkland 1883–90.
NANTGG	*North Australian and Northern Territory Government Gazette* (from 1 June 1889).
RBGV	Royal Botanic Gardens of Victoria.
SLSA	State Library of South Australia.

Selected L.A.N.T. records / N.T.R.S 790

A4797   Minister of Education reports erection of new police station at Yam Creek cost £690.

A5167   J.A.G. Little writes to Govt. that E.O. Robinson should be appointed Customs Officer at Port Essington, salary £20.

A5180   Letter from David Lindsay complaining Gilbert McMinn appointed as acting G.R. rather than himself.

A5243   Letter saying that David Lindsay, John Knight, and Paul Foelsche will accompany the 1882 Parliamentary Party on tour.

A5280   Joseph Lorence applies for the bonus for discovering a goldfield.

A5342   John Little, annual report for 1881.

A5464   John Little, report.

A5549   R.R. Cruikshank reports a 'Chinaman' has smallpox.

A5650   Minister for Education approves 'reserves for natives.'

A5693   The government cannot approve special measures for 'native outrages.'

A5793   Roman Catholic mission land approved.

A6295   G. Altman complains about Gold Warden Nash.

A6296   G. Altman complains about Gold Warden Nash.

A6429   Alfred Searcy.

A6439   Father A. Strele re boundaries for Rapid Creek property.

A5840	Letter asking why McMinn's report on his exploration had not arrived at the Minister but was already published in the *N.T. Times*.
A6458	Giles re death of police party.
A6613	Dr R.J. Morice reports on lepers.
A6664	Dr Wood reports leprosy at the 12-Mile.
A6748	James Bath arranges two rooms for Pater at Hopewell's hotel.
A6944	J.G. Knight re residence (the 'mud-hut').
A7031	J.G. Knight re residence (the 'mud-hut').
A7149	Daly River Murders, W.K. Griffiths offering a 'party of bushmen to help the police re 'outrages.'
A7151	Daly River Murders: permission to 'seize any numbers of the tribe'.
A7161	2 telegrams (from Montagu and Hillson), reporting the Daly River Murders (see Figure 53).
A7164	Daly River Murders.
A7178	Daly River Murders, Griffiths, Masson and Lucanas are leaders of the search parties that left today.
A7192	From Minister of Justice: Daly River Murders: 'Do not relax and punish offenders' and go ahead and build Burrundie Railway Station.
A7318	Daly River Murders, W.K. Griffiths re extra expenses because search parties are larger than expected.
A7212	Dr Percy M. Wood re Burrundie Hospital, wooden floors less expensive than concrete.
A7267	Daly River Murders and prosecutor's fees.
A7515	Names of streets in Burrundie.
A7549	Mounted Constable Summers reports on the destitute condition of natives camped near Southport and requests rations.
A7538	E.F. Sanders write to G.R. asking if it was his brother murdered by natives (but it was Landers who was killed, not Sanders).
A7528	Gallows for Fannie Bay Gaol shipped on Guthrie.

A7506   Senior surveyor to survey Burrundie.

A6439   Strele requests to be told the boundaries of the mission land at Rapid Creek.

A7644   Deputy sheriff reporting death-row prisoners immediately 'heavily ironed' on arrival.

Bibliography

ADB. (1967). *Australian Dictionary of Biography*. Retrieved December 3, 2016, from National Centre of Biography, Australian National University.: http://adb.anu.edu.au/biography/nicholson-sir-charles-2508

—— (1993). Emily Caroline Bartlett. *Australian Dictionary of Biography*, http://adb.anu.edu.au/biography/barnett-emily-caroline-9439.

Advertiser. (26 April 1870). Northern Territory.

Anon. (1886, February 26). The Mission Station at Rapid Creek. *North Australian*, p. 3.

Archibald, J. (2021, February 2). *Stuart's Tree*. Darwin: History Curator, MAGNT, Personal communication.

Bartlett, M. (1990). *Port of Darwin 150 years: History of Port Darwin 1839–90*. Darwin: Darwin Port Authority.

Bathgate, J. (2004). *Replenished: Sources of meaning, sources of history in the Pine Creek area, Northern Territory, Australia*. Darwin: Thesis submitted for the Degree of Doctor of Philosophy, CDU, 2004. Retrieved from https://territorystories.nt.gov.au/10070/458159/0/0

Bisa, D. (2016). *Remember Me Kindly: A history of the Holtze Family in the Northern Territory*. Darwin: Historical Society of the Northern Territory.

Boland, J. (2016). *Know Where You Stand: Fannie Bay and Surrounds; Darwin's Industrial Heartland 1870–1950*. Darwin: Fannie Bay Historical Society.

Bridge, C. (1990). *Sir William John Sowden (1858–1943)*. Melbourne: Australian Dictionary of Biography, Vol 12, MUP.

Buscall, J. (28 December 1929). A Holiday trip in North Australia. *The Melbourne Weekly Times*, p. 12.

Carment, D. (1990). *John George Knight (1826–92)*. Darwin: Northern Territory Dictionary of Biography, Vol 1: to 1945.

Carment, D., James, B., & O'Brien, V. (1992). *Northern Territory Dictionary of Biography*. Darwin: NTU Press.

Carment, D., Maynard, R., & Powell, A. (1990). *Northern Territory Dictionary of Biography Vol 1: to 1945*. Darwin: NTU Press.

Carment, D., Wilson, H., & James, B. (1993). *Territorian: the life and work of John George Knight*. Darwin: The Historical Society of the Northern Territory.

Chronicle. (23 Feb 1884). The Giles Relief Party. *South Australian Weekly Chronicle*, p. 12.

—— (24 Jan 1885). The Daly River Murders. *South Australian Weekly Chronicle*.

Conor, L. (2016). *Skin Deep: Settler Impressions of Aboriginal Women*. Perth: UWA Publishing.

Creaghe, E. C. (1883). *The Diary of Emily Caroline Creaghe: Explorer*. Edited with Introduction by Peter Monteath: Corkwood Press, 2004.

Cross, J. (2011). *Great Central State: the Foundation of the Northern Territory*. Adelaide: Wakefield Press.

Daly, H. (1887). *Digging, Squatting and Pioneering Life in the Northern Territory of South Australia by Mrs Dominic D. Daly* (facsimile edition 1984 ed.). Hesperian Press .

Dispatch. (18 January 1886). The Daly River Revenge Party. *The Port Augusta Dispatch and Flinders Chronicle*, 3.

Donovan, P. (1981). *The Northern Territory: A history of South Australia's Northern Territory*. St. Lucia: University of Queensland.

Duminski, M. (2005). *Southport, Northern Territory 1869–2002*. Darwin: Historical Society of the Northern Territory.

Farram, S. (2017). *Charles James Kirkland: The Life and Times of a Pioneer Newspaperman in the Top End of Australia*. Darwin: CDU Press.

Favenc, E. (1886). Unexplored Australia. *Journal of the Sydney Geographical Society*, NTTG, 27 February 1886, p. 3.

—— (1888). *The History of Australian Exploration from 1788 to 1888*. Sydney: Turner and Henderson.

Fletcher, V. (2013). *The North/South Transcontinental Railway in Australia's Story*. Darwin: Historical Society of the Northern Territory.

Foelsche, P. (14/8/1880). *Report*. Adelaide: South Australian Parliamentary Papers. pp. 569–570.

—— (1882). Notes on the Aborigines of North Australia. *Transactions and Proceedings and Report of the Royal Society of South Australia*, Vol 5 pp. 1–18.

Gaunt, C. (6 July 1934). Old Time Memories: the Lepers of Arnhem Land and Sketches. *Northern Standard*, p. 4.

Gibson, E. (2011). *Beyond the Boundary: Fannie Bay 1869–2001*. Darwin: Historical Society of the Northern Territory.

Giles, A. (1926). *Exploring in the Seventies and the Construction of the Overland Telegraph Line.* Adelaide: W.K. Thomas and Co.

Goss, F. (1956). *Life in The Never Never Country of South Australia In The 70s To 90s (1956).* Retrieved from Telegraph Pole Appreciation Society: www.telegraphpoleappreciationsociety.org

Goyder, G. (1869, February 7). *Northern Territory Archives Service.* Retrieved from Transcript of the Journal of Goyder's Survey Party 1869: dtsc.nt.gov.au/__data/assets/pdf_file/0010/266779/NTRS-3733-Transcript-of-Goyders-Diary-250515.pdf

GU. (2020, October 23). *Griffith University: Jesuits in the Northern Territory.* Retrieved from German Missionaries in Australia: http://missionaries.griffith.edu.au/missionary-training/jesuits-northern-territory-1882-1902

James, B. (1989). *No Man's Land: Women of the Northern Territory.* Sydney: William Collins Pty Ltd.

—— (1990). *Darwin's Hotel Victoria—Its Life and Legends.* Darwin: Northtype Pty: for Tumminello Holdings.

—— (1995). *Occupation Citizen: The Story of Northern Territory Women and the Vote (1894–96).* Darwin: James.

Jones, T. (1987). *Pegging the Northern Territory: A history of mining in the Northern Territory, 1870-1946.* Darwin: N.T. Department of Mines and Energy.

—— (1990). *The Chinese in the Northern Territory.* Darwin: NTU Press.

—— (2003). Ping Que—Mining Magnate of the Northern Territory. *Journal of Australasian Mining History, Vol. 1, No. 1, September,* Article-13. Retrieved from Journal of Australasian Mining History: http://www.mininghistory.asn.au/wp-content/uploads/13.-Jones.Article-13.2003.pdf

Kelsey, D. E. (1975). *The Shackle.* Edited by Ira Nesdale. Lynton Publications.

Knight, J. (1888). The Northern Territory Court at The Melbourne Exhibition. *North Australian, October 20.*

—— (1890). *Government Resident's Report to the South Australian Parliament.* Palmerston: in Jones, 1990, pp. 141–2.

Lamond, G. A. (1986). *Tales of the Overland: Queensland to the Kimberley in 1885.* Perth: Hesperian Press.

Lewis, D. (2004). *A Wild History: life and death on the Victoria River frontier.* Melbourne: Monash University Press.

Ling, T. (2011). *Commonwealth Government Records about the Northern Territory.* National Archives of Australia.

Little, J. (11 August 1993). *The Hanging of Wandy Wandy.* Palmerston: Northern Territory

Times and Gazette.

MacKillop, D. (1892). *Letter to the Editor.* Palmerston: Northern Territory Times and Gazette.

——— (1893, March 20). Northern Territory Blacks. *The Barrier Miner*, p. 2.

Merlan, F. (1998). *Caging the Rainbow: place, politics, and Aborigines in a North Australian Town.* Honolulu: University of Hawaii.

Mildren, D. (2011). *Big Boss Fella All Same.* Darwin: Federation Press.

Monteath, P. (2004). *The Diary of Emily Caroline Creaghe: Explorer, 1883.* Adelaide: Corkwood Press.

Nesdale, I. (1975). *The Shackle, D.E. Kelsey.* Ira Nesdale, Editor. Adelaide: Griffin Press.

NFSA. (1926). *Darwin c 1926: National Film and Sound Archive.* Retrieved May 2019, from https://www.nfsa.gov.au/collection/curated/darwin-c1926

NTG. (2020, Nov 21). *The History of the NT Supreme Court.* Retrieved from Supreme Court of the Northern Territory: https://supremecourt.nt.gov.au/about/history

NTTG. (16 December 1876). Port Essington—supplied. *Northern Territory Times and Gazette*, 2.

——— (1873–1927). *Northern Territory Times and Gazette.* Darwin: https://trove.nla.gov.au/newspaper/article.

Obituary. (12 August 1892). The Late Mr T.K. Pater, S.M. *South Australian Register*, p. 6.

Observer. (12 May 1888). The Northern Territory Resident's Report. *Adelaide Observer*, pp. 33.

Parsons, J. (1882). Northern Territory. *Adelaide Observer.*

——— (1889). *South Australia Government Resident's Report on Northern Territory for the Year 1888.* Palmerston: Office of the Government Resident.

——— (23 September 1882). The Minister for Education. *Adelaide Observer*, p. 12.

——— (12 May 1888). The Northern Territory Government Resident's Report. *The Adelaide Observer*, p. 33.

——— (1887). *Northern Territory Government Resident's Report.* Digitised by AIATSIS Library 2007—www.aiatsis.gov.au/library 17, accessed 28 October 2020.

——— (8 Mar 1882). Telegraphed message. *South Australian Advertiser* , p. 3.

Pearce, H., & Alford, B. (2016). *A Wartime Journey: Stuart Highway Heritage Guide.* Darwin: Dept. Lands, Planning and the Environment.

Powell, A. (1982). *Far Country.* Melbourne University Press.

Price, E. (4 January 1882). Northern Territory Government Resident's Report. *South Australian Register, 4 February 1882.*

Pugh, D. (2014). *Turn Left at the Devil Tree*. Darwin: www.derekpugh.com.au.

—— (2017). *Fort Dundas: The British in North Australia, 1824–29*. Darwin.

—— (2018a). *Escape Cliffs: The First Northern Territory Expedition, 1864–66*. Darwin: www.derekpugh.com.au.

—— (2018b). *Darwin 1869: The Second Northern Territory Expedition*. Darwin: www. derekpugh.com.au.

—— (2019). *Darwin: Origin of a City*. Darwin: www.derekpugh.com.au.

—— (2020). *Port Essington: The British in North Australia 1838–49*. Darwin: www. derekpugh.com.au.

RBGV. (1982). *Atlas of Living Australia*. Retrieved from Royal Botanic Gardens, Victoria: https://biocache.ala.org.au/occurrences/059be56e-59c2-4fbf-b77c-fe6153cd1c58

Register. (13 Jan 1873). The Transcontinental Railway. *South Australian Register*, p. 6.

—— (18 July 1883). The Northern Territory. *Supplement to the South Australian Register 1883*, p. 1.

—— (19 June 1914). A Notorious Criminal Died in Parkside Asylum. *Adelaide Register*, p. 9.

—— (20 June 1893). Blacks vs Coolies. Interview with a Mission Father. *South Australian Register*, p. 7.

Reid, G. (1990). *A picnic with the Natives: Aboriginal-European Relations in the Northern Territory to 1910*. Melbourne: Melbourne University Press.

Rose, A. (1964). *Early Northern Territory Droving Epics*. Alice Springs: Australian Veterinary Journal, Vol 40, March 1964.

Rue, K. D. (2004). *The Evolution of Darwin 1869–1911*. Darwin: Charles Darwin University Press.

Ryan, L., & Pascoe, W. (2019). *Colonial Frontier Massacres*. Retrieved from University of Newcastle, Centre for 21st Century Humanities: https://c21ch.newcastle.edu.au/colonialmassacres/detail.php?r=704

Saunders, P. (20 October 1887). Official Report of the Exploration Trip to Melville Island. *Adelaide Observer*, pp. Land Office, Palmerston.

Saunders, S. (1989). *'A Suitable Island Site': Leprosy in the Northern Territory and the Channel Island Leprosarium 1880–1955*. Darwin: Historical Society of the Northern Territory.

Searcy, A. (1909). *In Australian Tropics*. London: George Robertson and Co.

—— (1912). *By Flood and Field: Adventures Ashore and Afloat in North Australia*. London: G. Bell and Sons, 1st Edition.

Smith, R. (2020). Water, Women, and Weapons: Northern Territory Frontier Massacres.

Northern Territory Historical Studies: A journal of history, heritage and architecture, Issue 31: pp. 15–35.

Smith, W. (17 November 1906). Report on the Diseases of the Northern Territory. *Adelaide Register*, p. 4.

Solomon, V. (1885). *NT Times Almanac for 1886*. Palmerston: Northern Territory Times and Gazette.

Sowden, W. (1882). *The Northern Territory as it is: a narrative of the South Australian Parliamentary party's trip and full description of the Northern Territory, its settlements and industries*. Adelaide: W.K. Thomas.

Stephen, M. (2010). *Contact Zones: Sport and Race in the Northern Territory 1869–1953*. Darwin: Charles Darwin University Press.

Stockdale, H. (1885). *Harry Stockdale journal of exploration in the far north west of Australia, 1884–85*. Retrieved from State Library of NSW: http://acms.sl.nsw.gov.au/_transcript/2013/D21617/a8202.pdf

Stuart, J. M. (1862). *Explorations in Australia: The Journals of John McDouall Stuart During the Years 1858, 1859, 1860, 1861, When he Fixed the Centre of the Continent and Successfully Crossed It from Sea to Sea*. http://www.gutenberg.org/ebooks/8911 accessed December 2020.

Tate, R. (May 13, 1882). *Professor Tate's Official Report*. Appendix in Sowden 1882: Thomas and Co.

Telegraph. (17 Sep 1891). Chinese Immigration Bill. *The Express and Telegraph*, p. 3.

Wells, S. (2003). *Negotiating Place in Colonial Darwin: Interactions between Aborigines and whites, 1869-1911*. Thesis submitted for the degree of Doctor of Philosophy, University of Technology, Sydney: https://opus.lib.uts.edu.au/.

Wildey, W. B. (1876). *Wildey's Australasia and the Oceanic Region*. Adelaide: George Robertson.

Wilson, H. (1994). *The Historic Heart of Darwin: the Tin Bank, Chinatown, the Terminus Hotel and the Civic Centre*. Helen J. Wilson, Darwin.

—— (2008). *Cox, Matthew Dillan (c1829–74) Northern Territory Dictionary of Biography*. Retrieved February 2019

Index

Further reading

DARWIN 1869
The Second Northern Territory Expedition

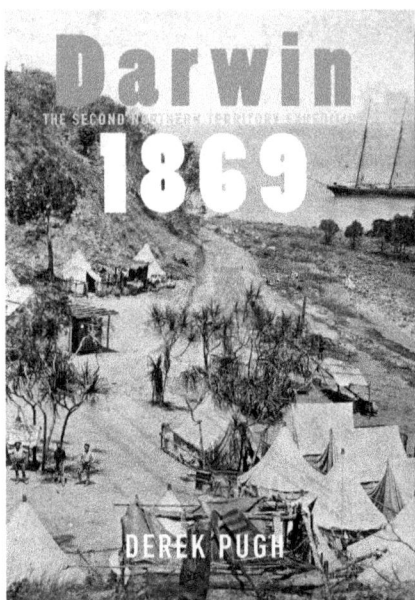

The Northern Territory had its beginnings under the governance of South Australia. Land was sold to investors, unseen and unsurveyed and in an unknown location. The sales raised the funds needed and The First Northern Territory Expedition was sent north to make it a reality, but it failed miserably, and the government faced huge losses with insufficient reserves to refund its investors.

To mitigate the loss, a new venture was envisaged—the Second Northern Territory Expedition, and there was only one man thought capable of ensuring a successful survey of the north: The Surveyor General, George Woodroffe Goyder.

Goyder was an extraordinary man, full of frenetic energy and with a phenomenal work ethic. The survey took him, and his expert teams of surveyors and bushmen, only eight months. It resulted in the laying out of the city of Palmerston (now called Darwin), three rural towns and hundreds of rural blocks, spreading over almost 270,000 hectares, all pegged out in the bush and Larrakia and Wulna lands—without permission or compensation—and conflict with the Aborigines was an ever-present danger. Two men were speared, one of them fatally.

Darwin grew from these somewhat humble but tumultuous beginnings. It was the only pre-Federation Australian capital established late enough to be photographed from its first settlement; and it is a survivor of challenges and privations unheard of in more temperate climes.

Darwin's story is written on its maps. Street names such as Knuckey, McLachlan, Daly, Wood, Bennett, Harvey and Smith Street recall the surveyors and their teams. Suburbs such as Millner, Larrakiyah, Bellamack and Stuart Park also remind us of the city's earliest days. It is the story of how the courage and diligence of a few led to the founding of the unique city of Darwin.

www.derekpugh.com.au

DARWIN: Origin of a City

A crocodile pulls a sleeping man into the river by one leg. Another breaks the neck of a swimming policeman. An out-of-luck miner drowns himself in the town's well.

Once called Palmerston, the City of Darwin was settled in the 1870s. It was a pioneer's paradise; sometimes as exciting as it was dull; full of potential but, too often, dangerous. Not everyone survived.

The first settlers arrived in January 1870, to find very little other than surveyed blocks of bushland sold to distant investors. It was a colony made from scratch, with little tangible reason for its existence until the Overland Telegraph Line came through from London and joined Australia to the rest of the world. Then gold was discovered, and hopeful miners rushed north from all over the country. Most went home disappointed; but only if they survived the privations of the bush and the distraction of the pubs. Then the government brought in Chinese 'Coolie' workers—and they kept coming, gold dust shining in their eyes, until, by the end of the decade, there were ten times as many Chinese as European settlers, and

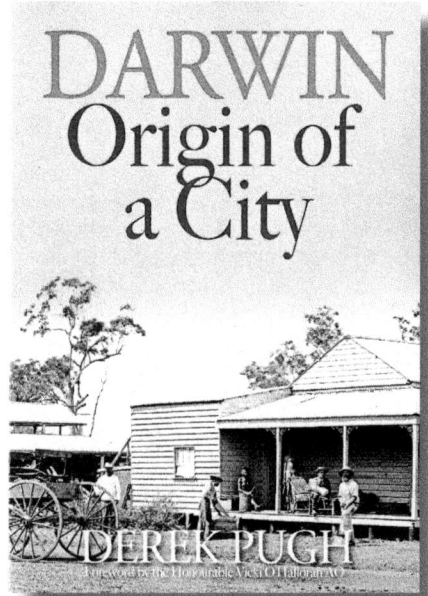

Chinatown was the most vibrant part of the settlement.

Known as Palmerston until it was renamed in 1911, Pugh brings the early colony to life once again, through this delightful and colourful account of Darwin's fascinating, unique early history, and the extraordinary characters who pioneered the settlement of the north.

Shortlisted:
Chief Minister's Northern Territory History Book Award, 2020

www.derekpugh.com.au

Lightning Source UK Ltd.
Milton Keynes UK
UKHW020758111122
412026UK00014B/677

9 780648 142188